David Wilson is Emeritus Professor of Criminology at Birmingham City University (BCU) and one of the country's leading criminologists. He was the founder and Director of the Centre for Applied Criminology at BCU and is a National Teaching Fellow. He has written several books and articles on the phenomenon of serial murder, including (with co-author Paul Harrison) *Hunting Evil: Inside the Ipswich Serial Murders*; *The Lost British Serial Killer: Closing the Case on Peter Tobin and Bible John; Mary Ann Cotton: Britain's First Female Serial Killer; Female Serial Killers in Social Context* (with Elizabeth Yardley); and *Serial Killers and the Phenomenon of Serial Murder* (with co-authors Elizabeth Yardley and Adam Lynes). His professional memoir, *My Life with Murderers*, was published in 2019.

Also by David Wilson

The Prison Governor: Theory and Practice
(with Shane Bryans)

What Everyone in Britain Should Know About Crime and Punishment
(with John Ashton)

What Everyone in Britain Should Know About the Police
(with John Ashton and Douglas Sharp)

The Longest Injustice: The Strange Story of Alex Alexandrovich
(with Alex Alexandrovich)

Prison(er) Education: Stories of Change and Transformation
(with Anne Reuss)

Innocence Betrayed: Paedophilia, the Media and Society
(with Jon Silverman)

Death at the Hands of the State

Serial Killers: Hunting Britons and Their Victims, 1960–2006

Hunting Evil: Inside the Ipswich Serial Murders
(with Paul Harrison)

The Lost British Serial Killer: Closing the Case

on Peter Tobin and Bible John
(with Paul Harrison)

Mary Ann Cotton: Britain's First Female Serial Killer

Pain and Retribution: A Short History of British Prisons, 1066 to the Present

Female Serial Killers in Social Context: Criminological

Institutionalism and the Case of Mary Ann Cotton
(with Elizabeth Yardley)

My Life With Murderers: Behind bars with the world's most violent men

Signs of Murder: A small town in Scotland, a miscarriage of justice and the search for the truth

DAVID WILSON

A HISTORY OF BRITISH SERIAL KILLING

sphere

SPHERE

First published in Great Britain in 2009 by Sphere
This revised edition published in 2020 by Sphere

1 3 5 7 9 10 8 6 4 2

A CIP catalogue record for this book is available from the British Library.

ISBN 978-0-7515-8107-2

Typeset in Caslon by M Rules
Printed and bound in Great Britain by Clays Ltd, Elcograf S.p.A.

Papers used by Sphere are from well-managed forests
and other responsible sources.

Sphere
An imprint of
Little, Brown Book Group
Carmelite House
50 Victoria Embankment
London EC4Y 0DZ

An Hachette UK Company
www.hachette.co.uk

www.littlebrown.co.uk

Preface to the Second Edition

The publication of this second edition of *A History of British Serial Killing* affords me an opportunity to accomplish two different but inter-related tasks. First, it allows me to look backwards to 2009, when the first edition was published, and to think again about the issues and ideas that at that time drove the narrative themes of the book. To what extent did these themes prove to be prophetic, so that they have become more pronounced and embedded in our culture over the last decade or, instead, which simply dissipated and then disappeared? An opportunity to look backwards also allows me a chance to correct some minor, factual inaccuracies and also to improve the text to take into account new research undertaken by others, such as Elizabeth Yardley and several of my other colleagues at Birmingham City University and Hallie Rubenhold. I have also incorporated some of my own more recent research about some of the issues which I originally discussed.

I can also update the text to now include those serial killers who were active at the time but who had not yet been apprehended, and those who at that point had only been convicted of a single (or double) murder, and who may have been in custody when the first edition was produced. In this latter category, for example, is the Scottish serial killer Angus Sinclair who had been convicted of the murder of eight-year-old Catherine Reehill in

1961 when he was sixteen, and was then given a Life sentence in 2001 for the 1978 murder of Mary Gallagher in Glasgow. When the first edition was published Sinclair did not fit the academic criteria of being a 'serial killer' – in other words, of having killed three or more victims in a period of greater than thirty days – as he had been controversially acquitted in 2007 of the murders of Christine Eadie and Helen Scott in October 1977 (which were known as the 'World's End' murders). He would only be found guilty of these crimes in November 2014, following the amendment of the law of 'double jeopardy' in Scotland. Sinclair died in 2019 and is widely suspected of having killed several more women than those for whom he has been convicted.

In England, Robin Ligus was convicted of the murder of seventy-five-year-old Robert Young in 1994. Robert had been killed during a burglary committed by Ligus, who was a heroin addict and appears to have been offending to fund his drug habit. In 2011 Ligus was put on trial at Birmingham Crown Court for three further murders committed in 1994 and eventually found guilty of killing two men: Trevor Bradley and Brian Coles. Like Sinclair, Ligus now fits the criteria to be labelled as a 'serial killer'.

My second inter-related task – as my mention of Ligus and Sinclair demonstrates and my description of them now being 'serial killers' indicates – I can look forwards, as well as backwards. In the past decade the number of British serial killers has grown (although not considerably) and our most recent serial killer, for example, is Stephen Port. Port is sometimes known as 'the Grindr Killer' by the media and between 2014 and 2015 he murdered four gay men in London. He was convicted of these crimes in 2016 and his story, and especially the story of his victims – Anthony Walgate, Gabriel Kovari, Daniel Whitworth and Jack Taylor – has made me consider again the themes I discuss in Chapter Six, where I considered the cases of Peter Moore, Colin Ireland and Dennis Nilsen, and the men that they killed. Indeed one of the themes that I had discussed in relation to these crimes was homophobia within police investigations and, on re-reading this chapter in preparation for this second edition, I was struck by how optimistic I had been about homophobia becoming less of an issue over time. Port's murders and the subsequent flawed investigation by the Metropolitan Police would suggest that my optimism was misplaced.

The first edition of the book opened by stating boldly that: *A History of British Serial Killing is not a history of British serial killers. I am simply not interested in any particular serial killer – his relationships with family and friends, what his schooldays might have been like, whether he prefers jam to marmalade.* This was and remains the dominant theme of my work. I am not interested in building up an ever more detailed clinical picture of an individual serial killer, but instead I'm much more concerned with trying to see patterns in who it is that serial killers are able to kill. I described how a focus on what might have *motivated* the serial killer emerged from a convention of writing about this phenomenon which is called the 'medical-psychological' tradition. It seeks to debate that age-old issue in Criminology of born or made, nature or nurture or, more popularly, whether individual serial killers are born 'evil'? These questions might be interesting, but answering them never seemed to me to help us reach a better understanding of what we could do as a society to reduce the incidence of serial murder.

On the other hand, discussing which groups of people are repeatedly targeted over time by serial killers might just allow us to understand why these groups are so vulnerable to attack and do something to overcome that vulnerability. The first edition pointed out that 'overwhelmingly' (and so it was tacitly acknowledged that there are exceptions) serial killers murder people from just five groups, and that women and girls are the dominant target within four of those five groups. Only one group of men – men who are gay – get targeted. The four groups of female victims are: women over the age of sixty; sex workers; 'runaways and throwaways'; and children and infants. Of course there can also be overlaps between these groups so that, for example, young women running away from home might also engage in sex work; some young gay men also sell sexual services. This victim focus, which I described within the first edition as having emerged from a 'structural tradition' of writing about the phenomenon of serial homicide, should also provide us with solutions to reducing the incidence of serial murder by eradicating the vulnerability that makes these groups attractive to serial killers. These solutions would therefore include: challenging misogyny and homophobia; having a serious debate about why we criminalise sex work; becoming more aware of the issues surrounding the numbers of young people who are homeless; and ending the isolation and invisibility of the elderly in our society. All of this seems to me to be just as important today as it was in 2009.

At the various lectures and public talks that I have given about serial murder since the book was first published, I am often asked if these same five groups are targeted in other countries – particularly in the USA. There are indeed overlaps with the pattern of serial murder in Britain, but I usually also draw attention to the disappearance and murder of the homeless in the USA and, of course, the issue of race. The confession of Samuel Little in 2019 that he had murdered over ninety women, for example, led to headlines about him being 'America's most prolific serial killer'. Little, who was already serving a life sentence, having been convicted of the murder of three women in

2014, stunned officials by confessing to further murders that he had committed over four decades in some nineteen states. He even drew pictures of the women that he had killed. What wasn't really considered in the media coverage of the case was why Little had been able to avoid detection for so long and why several of his victims – usually black women – had never been reported as missing. Or, if their bodies had been found and their deaths recorded, why this was sometimes wrongly attributed to 'natural causes'. These women were often described as 'marginalised'. It soon became clear that this was a euphemism for the fact that some of these women were homeless, many were drug addicts, a few were sex workers and that all of them were, as the media was keen to describe, 'on the fringes of society'. In other words, these women were already invisible to mainstream society, and that made them perfect targets for Little. Who would notice, or even care if they disappeared?

Could a serial killer like Little operate in Britain? Perhaps. There are some five thousand people recorded as rough-sleeping in England and Wales and it is surely obvious that this creates, or exacerbates, multiple mental and physical health issues, and other forms of vulnerability – such as a vulnerability to attack. How are we, for example, to make sense of the 726 deaths of homeless people recorded in 2018? 'Homeless' was defined in these figures as rough-sleeping and those who were living in emergency accommodation, shelters and hostels. This was the highest number of deaths which had ever been recorded. Some of these 726 deaths were attributed to drugs overdoses but, as with Little, could the vulnerability of this group be exploited in other ways too?

Another of the dominant narrative themes within the first edition was to try and separate fact from fiction; to discuss the reality of serial murder, as opposed to how it is presented on

TV or at the cinema. I note that I specifically mentioned the British TV series *Cracker* and *Wire in the Blood* and the US series *Dexter* and, of course, *The Silence of the Lambs* in the first edition. These programmes now seem hopelessly old-fashioned in a generation obsessed with Netflix. The use made of serial murder for entertainment shows no signs of abating since 2009 and, if anything, has become more pronounced. In the twelve months leading up to the publication of this second edition, for example, there have been movies such as *Extremely Wicked, Shockingly Evil and Vile* about the serial killer Ted Bundy, starring Zac Efron; *My Friend Dahmer*; and Quentin Tarantino's *Once Upon a Time in Hollywood* which used the backdrop of the Manson murders to prompt its narrative. On British TV *Killing Eve*, *Happy Valley*, *Marcella*, *The Fall*, and *Luther* (to name just a few) have all used serial killers to hook their audience, as well as a host of true crime documentaries – some of which, I should acknowledge, I have also presented – and which have become a staple of the entertainment industry. Even the main characters in the popular comedy series *Gavin & Stacey* are called 'Shipman', 'West' and 'Sutcliffe'. Ruth Jones, one of the co-creators of the series, commenting on her choice of surnames for these characters, suggested 'I suppose we were hoping that people wouldn't realise and then when it does come to light, it's even more delicious.'

In trying to make sense of this more academically I have suggested that serial killers are consumed by the audience through a 'protective veil' – in other words we know that what we are watching is 'not real', even if it is about actual events, or at least not going to harm us, and therefore it can be enjoyed in the same way that we take pleasure from the fictional monsters that populate horror movies. We scream in terror, but get pleasure nonetheless. More broadly, serial killers also seem to tap into a broader zeitgeist that has an 'attraction to repulsion'. In passing, I have also tried to understand why so many women, rather than men, want to consume true crime (and Criminology as an academic discipline), and have suggested that this might be one of the legacies of Clarice Starling.

My mention of Clarice Starling (*'You still wake up sometimes, don't you? You wake up in the dark and hear the screaming of the lambs')* in the first edition was meant to underscore the importance of the novels of Thomas Harris, given that he was given access to the FBI's Behavioral Science Unit (now called the Behavioral Analysis Unit), and the fictional serial killer that he created – Dr Hannibal Lecter. These novels, and the film adaptations which followed, created a number of serial killer tropes which still dominate a popular understanding of this phenomenon and, in particular, a belief that 'entering the mind of the serial killer' will deliver practical insights that can be used in subsequent policing investigations into a linked series of crimes. These insights are popularly known as 'offender profiling' and are, more often than not, associated with the work of FBI agents John Douglas and Robert Ressler.

I was not to know in 2009 that Douglas and Ressler would themselves become the templates for characters in the Netflix series *Mindhunter* – the first series, released in 2017, was based on Douglas's co-authored book *Mindhunter: Inside the FBI's Elite Serial Crime Unit* – and follows the exploits of 'Holden Ford' (Douglas) and 'Bill Tench' (Ressler) as they travelled around the country interviewing thirty-six convicted serial killers. These interviews were indeed the foundation of the FBI's approach to offender profiling, and their insight that crime scenes would be 'organised' or 'disorganised'. The idea that anything useful could be gained from interviewing such killers was one of the criticisms that I drew attention to in the first edition of the book, based on my own discussions with a number of British serial killers.

I had the pleasure of interviewing John Douglas on stage in 2019 at the London Apollo and, whilst I cannot claim that we had a meeting of minds on the subject, I was intrigued that over 1000 people had wanted to attend the event, and hear all about our different experiences of interviewing convicted murderers. There were some truly bizarre moments, such as when Douglas sat on my knee, put his arms around me and asked 'tell me about your mother'. To be honest, this was not even the most unusual thing that has happened to me since 2009, given my public association with this phenomenon. Perhaps the award for that would go to Peter Moore, the convicted serial killer who attempted to sue me for defamation of character, or to a well-known true crime author who incognito reviewed the first edition of the book on Amazon and gave it 1 star, only to be rumbled by an astute reader and then exposed by *Private Eye*.

In 2009, based on a simple statistical analysis of the numbers of British serial killers active since 1960 – and I stuck resolutely to the these murderers having to be 'British'; that they needed to meet the standard (at that time) academic definition of 'serial killer'; and counted only those victims that they had been convicted of killing at court – I suggested that, on average, there were two active serial killers operating in Britain in any given year and that between them they would kill, on average, seven people. I further suggested that the statistical high point of serial murder in this country was 1986, when four serial killers were active, as well as an Italian murderer who killed his victims in London. These killers were: John Duffy, who murdered three of his victims (and an accomplice would later also be convicted of these crimes); Kenneth Erskine, the 'Stockwell Strangler' who murdered seven elderly people; Robert Black, the Scottish serial killer, who murdered ten-year-old Sarah Harper; and, finally, Harold Shipman, who killed eight of his patients. Thankfully the rate of serial murder would seem to have slowed down over the last decade, and perhaps we therefore should consider why the 1980s was the decade when most serial killers were active both in this country and in North America.

There would seem to have been a number of inter-related reasons. First, there was a general increase in violent crime during the decade both here and in the USA; crime detection was poor (the first murderer to be convicted in Britain on the basis of DNA profiling wasn't until 1987); and a 'geographically transient' serial killer – someone who killed in different parts of the country, such as Robert Black and Peter Tobin – could exploit regional prejudices and different operational practices within the police and therefore, more than likely, escape detection. On the other hand those serial killers who were 'geographically stable' were invariably caught more quickly, having killed fewer victims. Indeed, more recent research by my former PhD student Adam Lynes has shown that driving jobs are favoured by many serial killers for this very reason.

Of course 1986 was also the high point of Thatcherism. This avowedly political observation was meant to underscore the relationship between serial murder and what I saw as the growing division between the 'haves and the have-nots'. Above all, for me, it was the have-nots who seemed to get targeted. It is therefore perfectly valid to query why the rate of serial murder has decreased of late – especially in the period since 2010, when Britain has been undergoing cuts to public services in the name of 'austerity' and, for example, when we know that more people than ever before are having to rely on food banks. Given all of this, why have we not had more serial killers if my original observations were accurate?

The first point to make is that many of the policing deficiencies that I drew attention to in the 1980s, and which undoubtedly contributed to the rise in the numbers of active serial killers, have significantly improved. These policing initiatives would include the development of HOLMES, which is an informational retrieval system that helps our police to link crimes that have been committed in different parts of the country, and the establishment of the national DNA database in 1995, which now stores some six million individual profiles. This is a tremendous benefit to law enforcement. Forensic science has similarly advanced since the 1980s to the extent that the 'Golden State Killer', who murdered at least thirteen people in California between 1974 and 1986, was finally arrested in 2018 through using DNA uploaded onto a genealogical website by people searching for parents or other relatives. This type of initiative, which is illustrative of the advances in forensic science more generally, raises a number of interesting jurisprudential questions, even if it did on this occasion help to catch a serial killer. Overall, especially in the last few years, whilst violent crime has risen, the picture, as far as murder is concerned, is not without hope. For example, Scotland reduced its murder rate by some sixty per cent between 2004 and 2014.

Bearing all of this in mind, my hypothesis would be that the numbers of offenders who would like to repeatedly kill has probably remained stable, but that they are now caught much more quickly than they were in the past, and are thus prevented from becoming a 'serial' killer. A recent example would be Ben Field who was convicted of the murder of Peter Farquhar in 2019. Field, a PhD student studying English Literature at the University of Buckingham, was described in court as a 'psychopath' and killed his elderly victim by repeatedly poisoning him in the house that they shared in Maids Moreton. After his arrest the police discovered that Field, who also volunteered at an old people's home, had a list of a hundred other mostly elderly people whom they suspect he may have wanted to target. Field was also going through the process of ordination within the Church of England, and it is hard to escape the conclusion that whilst Shipman used medicine to gain access to his victims and become a serial killer, Field was going to use religion.

Of course I may be being too optimistic. As my discussion of the 726 homeless people who died in 2018 was intended to draw attention to, there are multiple vulnerabilities in this group of people – vulnerabilities that a serial killer might want to exploit, or perhaps is already exploiting. Would we recognise a suspicious death within this group, or would we simply note that it was suicide, or death due to a drugs overdose? No one suggested that the ninety women killed by Samuel Little were murdered until he himself confessed to these crimes. His victims were 'marginalised' and those who are rough-sleeping in this country are marginalised too; they are on 'the fringes of society', just as much as the black women that Little targeted.

I ended the first edition by suggesting that serial murder *tells us something about our culture, our values and our civic society.* It still does. An understanding of the importance of this phenomenon does not come from entering the minds of serial killers, to discover why and when the light in their heads that connected them to the rest of society got switched off. Rather it emerges from accepting the fact that serial killers exploit fractured communities and prey on those whom we don't seem to care too much about, or those whom we view as a drain on our resources, time and attention. It is therefore no coincidence that serial killers target the poor and not the rich; the weak, rather than the powerful; women and not men; people who are gay, rather than straight; and those young people who, for one reason or another, are leaving or being thrown out of their homes. In this way serial murder as a phenomenon tells us something about ourselves, to the extent that it has become even clearer to me since 2009 that the serial killer is not so much a cultural aberration, but a perfect embodiment of those values which have come to dominate our lives in late modernity. That's why we should take the phenomenon of serial murder seriously; it should not be seen as entertainment, but a warped window through which to view Britain.

Contents

Introduction

A *History of British Serial Killing* is not a history of British serial killers. I am simply not interested in any particular serial killer – his background, his relationships with family and friends, what his schooldays might have been like, whether he prefers jam to marmalade. Rather, I want to understand *whom* he (it is almost always a 'he') was able to kill. This distinction provides this history with much of its narrative and focus. I want to tell the stories of the killers' victims, and shall attempt to uncover patterns of how, where and when they were killed. After all, pinpointing such patterns might help people to avoid falling victim to this type of murderer in the future.

Maintaining this focus has not always been straightforward. There is a vast industry related to serial killing, which generally takes as its starting-point – and usually its finishing-point, too – the serial killer, rather than his victims. As a result, it is often very easy to learn about the life and history of any particular serial killer. However, it is comparatively difficult to do the same for those whom he killed. This concentration on individual serial killers, rather than on their victims, can also be found in historical and contemporary theorising about the phenomenon of serial killing. So, there are interesting, lively, popular and more academic debates about what motivates serial killers to kill; and seemingly endless disagreement about whether they are evil, rational and calculating men who are exercising free will, or rather biologically, genetically, psychologically or socially 'programmed' to murder time after time. Such theorising is known as the 'medico-psychological' tradition in more academic circles. It attempts to explain everything from the perspective of the serial killer himself: how he was born and raised; whether he had good relationships with his parents and siblings; if he had 'brain trauma'; and how he responded to moments of crisis or difficulties in his life, such as when a parent, grandparent or partner died. I am not convinced that any of this gets us very far in understanding the phenomenon of serial killing.

The alternative method that I have used in this book might be described as a 'structural approach'. I investigate the phenomenon of serial killing by looking at victims, and try to make sense of why they were vulnerable to attack. By doing so, I hope, in a modest way, to reverse the trend that has prevailed in criminology, psychology, history and especially 'true crime', all of which have remained largely silent about the victims of serial killers.

My original interest in this subject stems in part from my practical experience of working with a large number of offenders, some of whom were serial killers, while I was employed as a prison governor at HMPs Grendon and Woodhill. I am frequently asked which serial killers I know or have met, what they were 'really like', whether I was scared by them, and – betraying the extent to which popular culture's interpretation of the serial killer now dominates any discussion of the phenomenon – if I attempted to 'enter their minds' to find out what they were thinking.

To me, questions about which serial killers I know are rather like being asked about a celebrity acquaintance, especially when they are followed by: 'And what are they *really* like?' I make the link with 'celebrity' because serial killers have indeed become celebrities in our culture, with their status created and maintained by numerous films and books. At times it seems that they are almost aspirational role models. As is the case with all celebrities, the less accessible they are, the more intriguing and glamorous they appear to a fascinated public. And what could be more inaccessible than a high-security prison?

This notion of 'entering the mind' of a serial killer can be traced to the FBI's Behavioral Support Unit (now known as the Investigative Support Unit), which was made famous by the novels of Thomas Harris – most notably *The Silence of the Lambs* – and to the British TV series *Cracker* and *Wire in the Blood.* Clever detectives and forensic psychologists stun the reader or viewer by always being one step ahead of the serial killer, able to predict how he will behave and where he will strike next. This is all very entertaining, but the truth is never quite as straightforward. Suffice to say that I have never felt it necessary to 'enter the mind' of a serial killer, and I would even go as far as to say that anyone who claims to do so probably cannot be trusted.

Do serial killers scare me? In all of my years of working in close proximity to offenders, I have sometimes been scared, but usually the prisoner in question was not famous, and often they had been convicted of a relatively trivial crime. I remember one man who would hide razor blades about his body – seemingly impervious to any pain that they might have caused (or perhaps enjoying it) – and later produce them during interviews in my office. Another frightening man could sit quite happily discussing his parole reports and then, with no warning, suddenly erupt in a torrent of threats and anger. Neither of these prisoners was a serial killer – each of them had been convicted of aggravated burglary – but both scared me. By contrast, when dealing with serial killers, my most common emotional responses are boredom and depression. Far from the charismatic, charming and cultured picture presented by Thomas Harris's Hannibal Lecter or Jeff Lindsay's Dexter, the serial killers I met were either wholly uncommunicative or so self-obsessed that they engaged in long, rambling, tedious monologues. They were fascinated by themselves, rather than by Bach, fine food, wine, architecture or blood-spatter analysis.

I do not deny that the serial killers I met were dangerous, and many of them had obviously psychopathic personalities: they could be manipulative, cunning or charming when the occasion demanded, and when they could gain some advantage from being so. One offender, on discovering from one of the prison officers that my son had just been born, made me a card, and for a long time wrote to me from prison asking about my son, commenting that he must be sitting his GCSEs, learning to drive and so on, even though I have scrupulously never given him any details about my family. Was this interest in someone he had never met charming or calculating? Was my suspicion of him fair or cynical? I felt more certain about the cunning of Dennis Nilsen who, when I had finished talking to him in an interview room, reached over the desk, put his hand on my arm, and asked, 'Do you have to go?' In all likelihood, Nilsen would have used exactly the same phrase with exactly the same gesture to convince his victims to stay the night with him.

Even so, it was what these prisoners lacked, rather than what they possessed, that was their most common feature. Theirs was a world of black and white – usually black – which left no room for grey. Each one of them lacked ambiguity or complexity in their lives, which seemed to have been stripped of all those confusing, messy, interesting, challenging, frustrating, funny, moving and inspiring elements that preoccupy the rest of us. They lived boring, depressing lives in the shadows. When the former Chief Constable of West Yorkshire and later the government's 'Drugs Tsar' Keith Hellawell went to interview Peter Sutcliffe – better known as the 'Yorkshire Ripper' – at HMP Parkhurst, he was asked how he had felt when face-to-face with a serial killer. Hellawell did not reply that it was 'exciting', 'scary', or any of the other emotions that might have been expected. He thought long and hard before answering simply: 'It's different.' That pretty much sums it up.

Most of what follows is based on my academic work that has been undertaken since leaving the prison service in 1997, but where it is helpful I have also incorporated my practical and applied experiences. My academic work has been largely concerned with two issues. First, I have explored whether we should see serial killing as a form of 'homicidal protest' by those from within a specific socio-economic group who feel that their position in society is under threat, and go on to murder those in the challenging group. This part of my research has led to an extended debate with the Canadian sociologist Elliott Leyton. Second, I have looked into whether serial killing has been facilitated by the widening of the gap between rich and poor over the last forty years, as well as other changes in British society that have made it primarily 'exclusive' rather than 'inclusive'. These two issues are woven into each chapter and provide the context for the conclusions that I reach.

Writing this book has been a fascinating and illuminating experience, and has allowed me to see a contemporary, cultural obsession in a much broader and more historical way. And the lessons are clear. If we really want to reduce – and perhaps even eliminate – serial killing, it is vital to explore the history of the phenomenon and attempt to understand which people become victims and under what circumstances. By adopting this historical approach it is possible to see patterns at work over time, and therefore learn lessons from the past that can be harnessed to predict which groups of people are likely to be killed in our own time and also in the future. In this way, *A History of British Serial Killing* offers the means for our society to tackle this most dreadful of crimes.

Chapter One

'Society's biggest plague'

> I am convinced that we have a degree of delight, and that no small one, in the real misfortunes and pain of others . . . there is no spectacle we so eagerly pursue, as that of some uncommon and grievous calamity; so that whether the misfortune is before our eyes, or whether they are turned back to it in history, it always touches with delight.
>
> Edmund Burke, *A Philosophical Enquiry into the Origin of our Ideas of the Sublime and the Beautiful* (1757)

Serial killing is neither a new phenomenon nor one that is peculiar to the Western world. We have stories from Britain's distant past of serial killers such as Sawney Bean, a notorious Scottish cannibal who was said to have preyed on travellers along the coast of Galloway. However, no records of Bean's activities emerged until the seventeenth century, some 300 years after he was supposedly executed, so he is probably fictitious. There is, though, more concrete evidence of the commercially driven murders of sixteen people in Edinburgh by William Burke and

William Hare in 1828; the activities of their English imitators John Bishop and Thomas Williams, who confessed to five killings in London in 1831; and Mary Ann Cotton, who disposed of perhaps fifteen unwanted children and several husbands in County Durham in the 1870s. More recently, there have been documented cases of serial killers all over the world. In Pakistan, Javed Iqbal Mughal is suspected of having killed about one hundred boys prior to his arrest in 1999. In Japan, which has one of the lowest murder rates in the world, Takahiro Shiraishi admitted to killing and dismembering nine young women, three of whom were still in high school, in 2017. In Mexico, Juana Barraza, a former female professional wrestler known as the 'Old Lady Killer', was arrested and convicted of murdering forty-eight elderly victims in 2006. In China, Yang Xinhai was executed in 2004 for having killed some sixty-five women between 1999 and 2003, and in 2016 Gao Chengyong, who had been dubbed 'China's Jack the Ripper', was finally arrested for the murder of ten women and an eight-year-old girl. He was sentenced to death in 2017. In Russia, Andrei Chikatilo was executed in 1994 for murdering fifty-two women and children, while Alexander Pichushkin – the 'Chessboard Killer' – was convicted in 2007 of murdering forty-eight people. In South Africa, Moses Sithole was sentenced to 2,410 years in 1997 for his part in the 'ABC' murders (named after three districts in Johannesburg), which saw thirty-eight people killed between 1994 and 1995. In the USA, perhaps the country we associate most with this type of killing, Jesse Matthew, Shawn Grate, Todd Kohlhepp and Michael Madison have all being convicted of serial murder in the last five years.

This book's timeframe, starting in 1888 and coming up to the present day, and specific geographical location, Britain, therefore does not encompass the whole phenomenon of serial killing. It does, though, allow for deeper examination of the data and help provide focus for the important questions that will be asked throughout the book. Which groups of people tend to fall victim to the activities of serial killers, and do these groups change over time? Why have there been periods when no serial killers were active in Britain, while at other times several emerged simultaneously?

The phenomenon now known as 'serial killing' – in Britain and elsewhere – formally begins on the night of 31 August 1888, when Mary Ann Nichols, known as Polly, was found by PC Neil 'lying on her back with her clothes a little above her knees, with her throat cut from ear to ear on a yard crossing at Bucks Row, Whitechapel'. Polly was the first of the so-called 'canonical five' victims, all of whom it has been alleged had at some stage of their lives sold sexual services, whose killer has never been identified, but who is universally known as 'Jack the Ripper'. On that night a seemingly new type of crime, and a new type of criminal, seeped into the public's consciousness, creating in almost equal measure a fear and a fascination that have continued to this day.

I will trace the history of serial killing in Britain from Jack the Ripper and his late Victorian and Edwardian counterparts George Smith, Thomas Cream and George Chapman to the murders committed by Stephen Port, our most recent serial killer, in London between 2014 and 2015. Port was given a life sentence in 2016. In between the stories of John Haigh, Reginald Christie, Ian Brady and Myra Hindley, Robert Black, Peter Sutcliffe, Dennis Nilsen, Fred and Rose West and Britain's most prolific serial killer, Dr Harold Shipman, will be told. These names are well known, but the book also discusses more obscure British serial killers, including Peter Manuel, who murdered eight (or possibly nine) people in Scotland and the North of England in 1956–7; Peter Moore, who blamed 'Jason' for the murders of the four men he killed; Colin Ireland, who set out to become 'famous' by killing victims picked up in London's S&M clubs; and Beverly Allitt, the only female British serial killer to have acted alone (rather than with a male accomplice) since the days of Mary Cotton.

By applying cutting-edge criminological research, along with my own experience, I hope to identify whom these people kill and under what circumstances they most easily achieve their purposes. Why, for example, were there no British serial killers in the 1920s and 1930s, while in the same period Germany produced twelve? After all, it is safe to presume that in all cultures – and at any given time – there will always be a small group of dangerous individuals who will want to kill repeatedly.

So what is it that allows them to start and then continue killing? And what is it that stops them? British serial killing peaked in 1986, when four serial killers were active simultaneously. So did Thatcherism and the changes it brought to British society create the circumstances for potential killers to become actual killers? How has the pattern of serial murder changed during the last decade which has been characterised as a period of 'austerity'?

In order to identify those groups that need protecting from those who wish to prey on them, we need to look at the people who have been victimised by serial killers over the last 130 years. Overwhelmingly, as we shall see below, just five groups have been targeted. But before I explore who becomes a victim and why, I must first define what I mean by 'serial killer'.

Serial killers defined

Definitions of 'serial murder' change over time and between different countries. However, most criminologists in Britain would suggest that a murderer should have killed three or more victims over a period of greater than thirty days to be labelled a 'serial killer'. This allows us to differentiate serial killers from spree murderers, such as Michael Ryan at Hungerford in August 1987, who shot and killed sixteen people; Thomas Hamilton at Dunblane, who shot and killed sixteen children and their schoolteacher in March 1996; and Derrick Bird, who killed twelve people in Cumbria in 2010 before taking his own life. This simplistic time period/numeric definition has generated considerable debate. For instance, some criminologists, especially in the USA, believe that serial killers can be defined as such if they commit just two murders, as long as those crimes occurred at different locations and, crucially, that there was no relationship between the victim and the perpetrator. But these stipulations are far too prescriptive. In the British context they would exclude perpetrators such as Dennis Nilsen and Fred and Rosemary West, who had prior relationships with many of their victims and committed their crimes in the same location each time.

Perhaps because definitions of serial killing are so problematic, there have been few attempts to devise a typology of serial murders. The most comprehensive remains that devised by two American criminologists, Ronald Holmes and James DeBurger (1988). Having analysed four hundred serial murders, they concluded that there are four main types of serial murderer: visionary, mission, hedonistic and power/control (although a killer might display characteristics of several of these categories). A visionary killer is impelled to murder because he has heard voices or seen visions demanding that he kill a particular person or category of people. The voice or vision may be interpreted by the killer as belonging to a demon or to God. A mission killer has a conscious goal in his life to eliminate a certain identifiable group of people. He does not hear voices or see visions and his mission is self-imposed. A hedonistic killer murders his victims simply for the thrill of it – because he enjoys it. The thrill becomes an end in itself. The final category of serial killer receives gratification from the complete control he has over the victim. He experiences pleasure and excitement not from sexual acts carried out on the victim, but from his belief that he has the power to do whatever he wishes to another human being who is completely helpless to stop him.

Other typologies have been suggested: for example, that there are 'place-specific' serial killers who murder in particular physical locations, such as hospitals or nursing homes. And attempts have been made to understand the behaviour of serial killers from the perspective of their 'intrinsic' or 'extrinsic' motivation. Does the drive to kill lie outside of their personality (as with 'hit men' or body-snatchers) or deep within their psychological make-up? Ronald and Stephen Holmes (1994) concluded that most serial killers are motivated by intrinsic considerations, but that it is useful to try to understand what a killer has to gain from committing a crime, either materially or psychologically. They suggest that most serial killers murder for psychological reasons, and that

> in interviews, many have told us that the principal motivating factor in their killing was that they simply enjoyed killing. Others have stated that they were motivated by the intense feeling they got out of holding the fate of other persons in their hands. The more a person kills, the greater becomes his need to experience those feelings of gratification or power. The feeling becomes more than a compulsion, it becomes an addiction.

Sadly, those who have been murdered by serial killers to satisfy that addiction are rarely mentioned in histories of the subject; and even though I have set out to redress the balance they sometimes get a raw deal in this book, too. By this I mean that I have included in the text only those serial killers who were tried and convicted at court for murdering three or more victims within my timeframe; and I have counted only the victims that formed part of the court case against them. I have therefore excluded murderers who were charged, arrested and convicted of one or two murders, even if there are strong suspicions that they killed many more people, although I have now been able to amend the text to account for later convictions. There are three exceptions to these general rules: Harold Shipman was convicted at his trial of murdering fifteen people, but a subsequent public inquiry held him responsible for the deaths of 215 in total, so this is the figure that I use throughout; John Haigh was convicted for a single murder but was undoubtedly responsible for five others, so I have set his total at six; and, finally, I have included Stephen Akinmurele, who murdered five elderly people in Blackpool and on the Isle of Man between 1995 and 1998, but who committed suicide whilst on remand at HMP Strangeways and so never came to trial. The inquiry into Shipman's activities raised suspicions that he might have committed a total of 260 murders, but as the extra forty-five could not be proved I have not included them in my analysis. Similarly, it is often suggested that Dennis Nilsen, Peter Sutcliffe, Robert Black and the Wests committed more murders than are generally attributed to them, but I have included only the murders for which they were convicted at court.

Spates of murders can sometimes be attributed to a single killer, but for any number of reasons that killer is never caught. It is generally assumed that Patricia Docker, Jemima McDonald and Helen Puttock were all murdered by the same man – nicknamed 'Bible John' by the press – in Glasgow in the late 1960s, but as he was never apprehended those three women will not appear again in this book. In 1996 Strathclyde Police exhumed the body of a man in the hope that a DNA match might prove conclusive. It did not. And in December 2004 further DNA samples were taken from a number of suspects in their early sixties. Again the murderer was not found, although I have argued that convicted serial killer Peter Tobin is more than likely to have been 'Bible John'. In London the murders of eight sex workers between 1959 and 1965, attributed by the media to 'Jack the Stripper', have never been solved, although there is evidence to suggest that these murders could have been the work of the Welsh child killer Harold Jones. While I have excluded these two anonymous serial killers, I have bent my own rule to include Jack the Ripper, simply because he and his crimes are the foundations of the phenomenon that is at the heart of the book.

Further exclusions come from cases where a series of murders has taken place that is widely assumed to be the work of a serial killer, but when the killer is caught he is charged and convicted of only one crime. For example, Raymond Morris was convicted of the murder of seven-year-old Christine Darby in 1968, but he is suspected of having murdered two other young girls, Diane Tift and Margaret Reynolds. However, to redress the balance I have included the cases of Paul Brumfitt and Theodore Johnson, even though they stretch the definition of 'serial killer'. Brumfitt was convicted of murdering two men in 1979 and served fifteen years for those crimes. Having been released, he murdered again in February 1999. Although cumulatively he murdered enough people to be considered a serial killer, the gap between the second and third murders might seem too great for Brumfitt to be categorised in such a way, but his case is important as it raises issues surrounding the possibility of the rehabilitation of this type of killer. Johnson murdered his wife and two former partners between 1981 and 2016. I have now also been able to include the cases of Robin Ligus and Angus Sinclair. However, as with the case of Michele De Marco Lupo, an Italian who killed four men between 15 March and 18 April 1986 in London, I have excluded any serial killers who were not born or raised in Britain. I have also not included British serial killers who committed their crimes overseas, such as John Scripps, who murdered three people in Singapore and Thailand, and has the dubious distinction of being the last person to be hanged in Singapore, in April 1996.

I do not dwell on the twenty-six murders committed by Peter Dinsdale. Dinsdale – who changed his name to Bruce Lee – was an arsonist who confessed to murdering in the course of setting fire to various buildings and dwellings. He was detained indefinitely under the Mental Health Act in 1981. His crimes were prolific but his targets were mostly random, perhaps reflecting his state of mind. Lee's conviction remains controversial and the Criminal Cases Review Commission (CCRC) referred the case back to the Court of Appeal in 2019. Finally, I do not describe in any detail the rather opportunistic murders committed by Archibald Hall and Michael Kitto, or those of Trevor Hardy (but see A Guide to Further Reading). Hardy, who only come to wider public attention as a serial killer through my own research, is of interest and deserves greater consideration than this history can accommodate.

An overview of British serial killing

Having set the scene and explained my rationale, we may now move on to those serial killers who form the basis of this book. The table below gives brief details of the forty-one killers and their 409 victims. If I could discern no pattern in the killer's choice of victim I have labelled their murders as 'random'. I have also tried to be sensitive before describing a victim as a 'sex worker' or identifying their sexuality. My 'common sense' rule of thumb was to describe a victim as 'elderly' if they were aged sixty or over.

Name	Year Tried	Occupation	Victims	Number
'Jack the Ripper'	N/A	Unknown	Sex workers	6
Thomas Neill Cream	1892	Doctor	Sex workers	3
George Chapman	1903	Publican	Women	3
George Smith	1915	Petty criminal	Women	3
John Haigh	1949	Businessman	Random	6
Reginald Christie	1953	Clerk	Women	6
Peter Manuel	1958	Petty criminal	Random	8
Michael Copeland	1965	Soldier	Young person/ gay men	3
Ian Brady/ Myra Hindley	1966	Clerk/ Typist	Children/ young people	5
Patrick Mackay	1975	Gardener	Elderly women/ priest	3
Donald Neilson	1976	Builder	Men/ young woman	4
Trevor Hardy	1977	Petty criminal	Young women	3
Archibald Hall/ Michael Kitto	1978	Butler/ Unemployed	Acquaintances/ employer	5
Peter Dinsdale	1981	Unemployed	Random	26
Peter Sutcliffe	1981	Lorry driver	Women/ sex workers	13
Dennis Nilsen	1983	Civil servant	Gay men	15
John Duffy/ David Mulcahy	1988 2001	Unemployed	Women/ young person	3

Name	Year Tried	Occupation	Victims	Number
Kenneth Erskine	1988	Unemployed	Elderly	7
Beverly Allitt	1993	Nurse	Children	4
Colin Ireland	1993	Unemployed	Gay men	5
Robert Black	1994	Van driver	Children	3
Fred West/ Rose West	1995	Builder/ Housewife	Young people/ family member	10
Peter Moore	1996	Cinema owner	Gay men/ random	4
Steven Grieveson	1996	Unemployed	Young men	3
Stephen Akinmurele	1999	Barman	Elderly	5
Harold Shipman	2000	Doctor	Elderly	215
Paul Brumfitt	1980/ 2000	Labourer	Men/ sex worker	3
Anthony Hardy	2003	Unemployed	Sex workers	3
Levi Bellfield	2008/ 2011	Doorman	Women/ child	3
Mark Martin	2006	Unemployed	Homeless women	3
Steve Wright	2007	Van driver	Sex workers	5
Colin Norris	2008	Nurse	Elderly	4
Peter Tobin	2009	Odd-job man	Women	3
Stephen Griffiths	2010	PhD student	Sex workers	3
John Cooper	2011	Labourer	Random	4
Theodore Johnson	1981/ 1993/ 2018	Mechanic	Women	3
Stephen Port	2016	Chef	Gay men	4

As this table graphically illustrates, the victims of British serial killers are almost always drawn from just five groups: the elderly, gay men, children, young people who have left home, and sex workers. Of course, there are often overlaps between these very broad categories. For instance, the term 'young person/people' is used to indicate those who have left home and are attempting to make their own way in the world. Some of these people might have been gay, while others might have been working as a sex worker at the time of their death. In such circumstances, if the killer focused on a particular type of victim, they will be listed in that way, although some killers were 'indiscriminate' – they killed whoever they encountered. For example, the Wests concentrated their efforts on young women who had left home, while Dennis Nilsen was more interested in gay men.

Overwhelmingly, the vast majority of victims have been female. However, gay men have also been regular targets of serial killers, especially in the latter part of our time-frame. Perhaps this suggests something about the persistence of homophobia at a time when homosexuality is no longer illegal, same-sex marriages are commonplace, and openly gay men can become the object of considerable public affection and admiration. It is worth noting here that while four of the serial killers – Peter Moore, Dennis Nilsen, Steven Grieveson and Stephen Port – were open about their homosexuality (although Grieveson only after his arrest), we do not know if Michael Copeland was gay. Colin Ireland, on the other hand, suggested that he chose to kill gay men simply because they were vulnerable to attack, and therefore would allow him to achieve his primary objective of becoming famous.

It is important to acknowledge that the elderly have been attacked more regularly than any other group by British serial killers. As indicated, I apply this term to victims who were aged sixty or over, although we should note that this somewhat totalises, rather than helps to reveal the many ways that the elderly live their lives today in Britain. Some 241 elderly people have been murdered by serial killers – admittedly 215 of them by one man – a figure that constitutes approximately sixty per cent of the total number of victims since 1888. This appalling statistic should make us address the conditions in which the elderly live in our society, although this has yet to happen, even in the aftermath of Shipman.

Next, it is interesting to note that, almost without exception, British serial killers are white men. There are no Asian and only one black perpetrator on this list, even though black and ethnic minorities have comprised a significant proportion of British society since the end of the Second World War. Similarly, only three women – Myra Hindley, Beverly Allitt and Rosemary West – appear, and two of them killed in conjunction with male partners. I do not include on my list Joanna Dennehy – who was convicted of the murder of three men in 2013 and which are sometimes dismissively referred to as 'the Peterborough Ditch murders' – as these were committed in a ten-day 'spree'. She is therefore not a serial killer.

We can also see that serial killing has been rising steadily since 1888, despite there being relatively few victims between 1960 and 1972 and between 1999 and 2009 and more recently, and the total absence of a serial killer in Britain in the 1920s and 1930s. It is also obvious that the numbers of both serial killers and their victims rise as the timeframe moves closer to the present. There have been four distinct phases: 1888–1914, Victorian/ Pre-war; 1915–45, Inter-war; 1946–78, Post-war; and 1979–present, Thatcherism/Consensus. The first phase produced three serial killers and eleven victims; the last has so far produced twenty-six serial killers and 351 victims (with the two phases roughly comparable in terms of time).

Statistically, 1986 is fascinating as four British serial killers (as well as Michele De Marco Lupo) were active during the year. John Duffy murdered all three of his victims (and in 2001 his accomplice, David Mulcahy, would also be convicted of these murders), Kenneth Erskine killed seven, Robert Black murdered ten-year-old Sarah Harper, and Harold Shipman killed eight people.

The year 1986 falls in a period covered by an excellent and comprehensive analysis of murder in Britain, and it is instructive to use this research to compare the general characteristics of those who have been the victims of serial killers with those who were murdered during this period. Danny Dorling, now Professor of Geography at Oxford University, but at the time working at the University of Sheffield, analysed the 13,140 people – on average 1.8 murders per day – who were murdered in Britain between January 1981 and December 2000 (Dorling, 2005). He concentrated on who were killed – and in what circumstances – rather than the murderers. His research reveals that serial killing is a quite different phenomenon from the everyday reality of British murder.

Murder in Britain, 1981–2000

What can be discovered by comparing murder and serial killing during this period? Most immediately obvious is the fact that there is a gender imbalance. Dorling notes that males are roughly twice as likely as females to be murdered, and that a quarter of all murders during this period were of men between the ages of seventeen and thirty-two. Disturbingly, the age/gender group with the highest murder rate is infant boys under the age of one. In later years, a male's chances of being murdered doubles between the ages of ten and fourteen, doubles again between fourteen and fifteen, and again between fifteen and sixteen, and again between sixteen and nineteen. Thereafter, for men, the odds of being murdered return to those of a sixteen-year-old only at age forty-six, and to those of a fifteen-year-old only at age seventy-one.

All of this is markedly different from the general pattern in relation to those who were victims of serial killers, even though Dorling's figures include any victims of serial killers who were known at the time of his research. (His analysis does not include those people murdered by Harold Shipman, which came to light later. Shipman's figures are included in the tables and analysis in this book because, although they appear to skew the figures, they represent the actions of our most prolific serial killer.) Most obviously, the gender/age imbalance is reversed, with serial killers frequently targeting women and the elderly. Dorling notes that murder occurs in a particular social context, with poverty being a high-risk factor: the poorer you are, the more likely you are to be murdered. Furthermore, in 2000 the murder rate for men under thirty-five was increasing. Dorling feels this was due to the polarisation of society, which led to inequality, reduced opportunity and increased hopelessness. All these factors then contributed to rising levels of violence, fear and murder. He claims that the murder rate tells us something about 'society and how it is changing', and suggests a reason why those born since 1964 have increasingly become murder victims: 'The summer of 1981 [when someone born in 1964 would have left school] was the first summer for over forty years that a young man living in a poor area would find work or training very scarce, and it got worse in the years that followed. When the recession of the early 1980s hit, mass unemployment was concentrated on the young, they were simply not recruited.'

Dorling goes on to argue that the murder rate of this age group of men has to be viewed through their relationship to these wider social, economic and political issues, noting that the most common way to be killed in Britain was with a knife or a broken bottle:

> Behind the man with the knife is the man who sold him the knife, the man who did not give him a job, the man who decided that his school did not need funding, the man who closed down the branch plant where he could have worked, the man who decided to reduce benefit levels so that a black economy grew, all the way back to the woman who only noticed 'those inner cities' some six years after the summer of 1981, and the people who voted to keep her in office.

Given all of this, it seems fair to conclude that serial killing and murder in general are two very different phenomena, today and historically, even if both should be seen against the background of a changing social context. But does this contrast between murder and serial killing fully explain the public fascination with serial killers, or might other factors also be at work?

Popular culture, the werewolf and the serial killer

In 2007 a search of amazon.co.uk using the words 'serial killer' produced a list of 1,067 DVDs, 357 books (including two of my own), thirty-two CDs and fourteen videotapes. A similar search in 2019 generated even more products, including a serial killer colouring book. This was but a fraction of the list generated by the word 'murder' – 16,169 books, 3,526 DVDs, 799 CDs and 252 videotapes – but it nevertheless highlights our fascination with those who repeatedly kill. Of the hundred bestselling books in Amazon's (largely academic) criminology section, twelve related to serial killers or their detection. A similar exercise with Google produced 2,600,000 websites devoted to serial killers, with the two most popular being crimeandinvestigation.co.uk – which targets all adults with an interest in crime and gives daily TV listings of programmes that might be of interest – and serial killers.com. The latter site reminds visitors:

> Since the beginning of civilization there have always been people missing a few too many brain cells, and become a parasite to society. Feeding on the pain and misery of innocent human prey. The mind of a psycho can be a fascinating yet horrifying thing. Below are links to profiles and movies of some of the most famous killers in history. Disturbing as they may be, in order for you to still be here you must be intrigued, so continue your trip into the twisted minds of some of society's biggest plagues.

While we might wonder whether this site is itself 'feeding on the pain and misery of innocent human prey', there is clearly a market for the posters and films it sells. How are we to make sense of the popularity of serial killing, which seems to deny the personal and social suffering that the phenomenon produces? How are people able to gain pleasure and satisfaction from such an awful reality?

Peter Morrall (2006), of Leeds University, attempts to answer these questions by using the 'mythical werewolf' as a 'suitable metaphor for personal and social ambivalence regarding murder'. He suggests two ways of understanding the disjunction between the suffering that murder produces and the satisfaction that it seems to generate in those who buy the books and watch the DVDs. The first of his propositions is that globalisation has driven all human life into the market place, so all human life – including murder – has become a commodity that can be bought and sold. Murder thus simply becomes another consumable product (although this hardly explains why this product is consumed in such large quantities). Morrall's second proposition employs Freud's observation that violence and sex drive all human behaviour and suggests that there is something sensual and erotic about murder: images of pain, torture and suffering can be both intolerable and tolerated because of their erotic quality. In short there is an attraction to the repulsive.

More recently Scott Bonn has questioned 'why we love serial killers', and suggests that they have become 'celebrity monsters' in our culture. Their total disregard for life shocks our humanity, to the extent that we want to discover what it is that drives them to repeatedly kill. Why so many women, as opposed to men, want to understand this phenomenon remains a moot point, but I have suggested that this might be a legacy of Clarice Starling, who for many of my female undergraduates has become almost an aspirational (if fictional) figure.

All of this brings us back to the quote from Edmund Burke that opens this chapter, and specifically to his assertion that people often find pleasure in the pain of others. Such *schadenfreude* (which literally translates as 'joy of damage') is the most obvious way to explain why society gains pleasure from the pain caused by murder, why it is that we take such a malicious interest in the agony of our fellow human beings. We sometimes also describe this as 'co-activation' – two different and opposing feelings operating at the same time. But while this is probably as good an explanation as any for our collective fascination with murder and specifically serial killing, it does not excuse, far less celebrate, that fascination. If the lure of serial killing leads only to the chronicling of ever more gruesome, spine-tingling and fetishistic details about the killers and their modi operandi, then we do nothing to counteract Morrall's 'werewolf'. That is why I have attempted to write this book from the perspective of the victims.

Against the 'medico-psychological' tradition

Many authors who have tackled this subject have certainly done so through altruistic motives, but they have almost always written about the phenomenon from the perspective of the serial killer himself. In this 'medico-psychological' tradition the killer becomes pathologised through a relentless search for some clue in his past that might explain why he 'became' a serial killer. But there are some major problems with this approach, the first being that it relies, to some extent at least, on evidence provided by the serial killer himself. And is it possible to believe anything that a serial killer tells you?

In my work with serial offenders and serial killers, I encountered two distinct groups. The first – who comprised the majority – had invariably developed a very robust and self-serving view as to why they had killed. Yet, repeatedly, the opinions and emotions they expressed were socially constructed to suit the nature and circumstances of their arrest, conviction and imprisonment. Their explanations for their crimes were designed to engineer a favourable prison transfer; or were rooted in the forlorn hope that they might one day be considered for parole; or sometimes were simply developed to give them an acceptable sense of 'self'. More than this, when the explanations for their actions were investigated in depth they did not provide any great insight. Rather, they were issues that each and every one of us has faced at some time in our lives. Who has not felt lonely, or bullied, or excluded as a child?

Who has not been saddened by the end of a close and loving relationship? Who has not had to face the death of a beloved parent or grandparent? Who would not like to be given a little more credit for one's achievements, and a little less criticism for one's failings? Would such everyday – almost mundane – life events be enough to push us to 'kill for company', as Brian Masters (1986) claims Dennis Nilsen did? And while some serial killers – such as Robert Black, who abducted, sexually assaulted and killed at least three young girls in the 1980s – have undoubtedly endured appalling childhoods, filled with abandonment and abuse, is that enough to explain (let alone excuse) their crimes, especially when so many others have had similar experiences but have not gone on to kill?

Serial killers who are prepared to talk about their murderous behaviour regularly construct a picture that is far removed from the reality of events. For example, after his arrest for a series of murders in the 1970s, Peter Sutcliffe was interviewed repeatedly by Yorkshire Police. He appeared forthcoming, but as Michael Bilton (2003), the leading expert on the murders, has commented: 'it is now wholly evident that he was grossly deceitful and manipulative'. Specifically, Sutcliffe sought to hide any sexual motive for his crimes, and instead painted a picture of himself as simply mad in the hope of influencing every aspect of his trial and minimising his sentence.

Similarly, before taking his own life, Fred West left 111 pages of autobiography. However, as Professor David Canter (2003) explains, anyone hoping to use this to unearth clues for why West killed would be disappointed. This would come as no surprise to John Bennett, the detective in charge of the West investigation. After his arrest, West's interviews with the police amounted to 145 tape recordings that were transcribed into 6,189 pages of text. Nevertheless, since his retirement, Bennett has commented: 'West's interviews were worthless except to confirm that nothing that he said could be relied upon as anything near the truth' (Bennett and Gardner, 2005). Gordon Burn (1998) – one of West's most perceptive biographers – is more blunt, dismissing him as a 'bullshitting liar'. He explains that West would talk 'palaver while apparently talking the truth. Laying out and simultaneously covering up.' And even if serial killers are more honest than Sutcliffe or West, they provide little or no explanation for the phenomenon as a whole.

The second group that I encountered were the mirror opposite of the first. They never talked about what motivated them to commit murder, and they kept their secrets well guarded. The most extreme example of a serial killer who refused to talk was Harold Shipman. Just after his conviction in April 2001 for the murder of fifteen of his patients, West Yorkshire Police interviewed Shipman with respect to other suspicious deaths of people who had been in his care. In the transcript of the interview, the interviewing officer displays his exasperation at the outset by saying that no answers or opinions will be provided by Shipman in this or any future interview. This proves to be an astute prediction as Shipman immediately turns his chair to face the wall and closes his eyes. He remains like that throughout the interview, not responding in any way as a series of photographs of his victims are held in front of his face and he is questioned about their deaths. As the interviewing officer predicted, Britain's most prolific serial killer never did discuss why he killed 215 elderly people. Ultimately, like Fred West, he chose to commit suicide in his cell at HMP Wakefield in January 2004, rather than reveal the circumstances that led him to murder.

So, to apply Gordon Burn's phrase about Fred West more generally, one group of serial killers 'lays out' and another group 'covers up'. Some talk endlessly – although not necessarily coherently – while others refuse to, or possibly cannot talk at all. Bearing this in mind, using what serial killers say, or do not say, as a means to explain their actions is fraught with problems, which is one of the reasons why I distrust the approach adopted by the FBI in the late 1970s and early 1980s.

The 'structural' tradition

In *Hunting Humans* (1986) the Canadian social anthropologist Elliott Leyton argues that concentrating on individual serial killers from within the medico-psychological tradition fails to account for cultural and historical realities. Dangerous and deranged individuals are a constant feature over time and between cultures, but not every culture experiences serial murder. Furthermore, within any given culture there can be long periods when there are no serial murders and then, for no obvious reason, suddenly an explosion of the phenomenon. Leyton's observation therefore also reinforces the importance of analysing why Britain had no serial killers during the 1920s and 1930s, while in the same period Germany had twelve; and why there were so many British serial killers in the 1980s. Leyton – who focuses on North America – feels that the cultural and historical specificity of serial killing cannot be understood simply in terms of a greater or lesser number of dangerous personalities existing in society at any one time. Rather, the phenomenon has to be seen as the product of socio-economic systems that cannot reward the efforts of all, and thus may dangerously marginalise certain groups.

Leyton's argument holds true for Britain as well as America.

An explanation for British serial killing cannot be found in analysis of the individual murderers. Instead, their crimes need to be assessed within the context of the development of the socio-economic structure of Britain since 1888. As the gap between the 'haves' and the 'have-nots' has widened, so too have the numbers of serial killers and their victims.

Given this, it should come as no surprise that most of the victims of British serial killers have belonged to marginalised groups in our culture: the elderly, gay men, sex workers, children and infants, and young adults trying to find their feet away from the comfort of home. These people are the focus of this book.

Criminological methods

This is a book of criminology, and its primary concern is with the crimes committed by serial killers. However, it is also a book about history. By looking at the wider societal forces that produced the victims of serial killers in Britain, we should be able to discern and interpret patterns in our recent past. In turn this should help us to understand our present, and hopefully allow us to mould a brighter future.

Several standard academic categorisations are applied to serial killers in criminology, and these are useful in any discussion of the phenomenon. So throughout this book I shall refer to 'organised' or 'disorganised' killers, detail whether they were geographically 'transient' or 'stable' in the locations of their crimes, and explain whether their choice of victim was 'fixed' or 'indiscriminate'.

I maintain a regular correspondence with several serial killers, having met them during my time as a prison governor. Of course, one has to approach anything they might say with caution, but I still feel it is valuable to try to gain some insight from them. I have tried to learn how and why they chose their victims, primarily to see if that choice helped them to avoid detection. I am also interested in how their knowledge of police procedures or forensic science assisted them in remaining free to commit more crimes. Some of the information they have provided contributes to this book.

The reader may want me to name names, but I shall resist that temptation for two reasons. First, to do so would inevitably mean that sections of the book would focus on a single serial killer rather than the phenomenon as a whole, because I would be obliged to outline the depth of my relationship with the correspondent, how we first met, how open they are about their crimes, and so on. Such concentration on individuals is something I am keen to avoid. Second, as I have stressed, I am much more interested in the victims of serial killers, rather than the murderers themselves. Keeping my correspondents anonymous helps to maintain that focus. However, since his death in HMP Full Sutton in 2018, it has become well known that one of my correspondents was Dennis Nilsen.

To build the stories of serial killers' victims I have used a voluminous secondary literature to complement any contemporary records that exist, primarily reports of the murders as they appeared in *The Times*, the *Guardian* or other newspapers. Official inquiries initiated after a series of deaths have also proved to be useful sources of information. One such was the Allitt Inquiry, which investigated the murder of four children and a number of serious assaults by the nurse Beverly Allitt in 1991. In the earlier chapters I have utilised anthologies of primary sources to try to make sense of Jack the Ripper and the other Victorian and Edwardian serial killers.

In addition to interviewing and corresponding with serial killers themselves, I have spoken to many people from the groups that have been their principal targets. I conducted research about the protection offered by the police to gay men and women in Birmingham, and for three years I coordinated a research programme on behalf of the Children's Society. In prisons I have interviewed older inmates in a bid to understand how the elderly cope in a social structure that was specifically designed for the young and mobile. In late 2006 I advised Sky News on a series of murders of young women working in the sex industry in Ipswich, and through that I witnessed at first hand the police investigation and the manner in which the murders were reported by the media in general. This proved to be an invaluable experience for a variety of reasons, chiefly because it allowed me access to the crime scenes and to the red-light area of Ipswich, where the journalists interviewed a number of sex workers. This primary research with the broadcast journalist Paul Harrison was unanticipated and at times distressing, but it allowed me to test several of the theories at the heart of this book.

Wherever possible I relate the individual narratives and biographies of the victims of serial killers, gleaned from both contemporary newspaper articles and true crime accounts. My intention is to connect the reader to their lives, in the hope that they no longer seem distant and anonymous, but instead become humanised and, consequently, are given some dignity. By providing these pen pictures of people who are rarely seen within either popular accounts or serious academic discourse about serial killing, I wish to create a different interpretation by looking at who is victimised and under what circumstances. Unfortunately, however, this has not always been possible.

Nicci Gerrard (2004) – writing about the murders of Holly Wells and Jessica Chapman in Soham, Cambridgeshire, by Ian Huntley – suggests that 'in the single narrative, we extrapolate wider meanings'. She then goes on to argue: 'One life will engage our personal sympathies while a whole plethora of statistics will not. We need to imagine what it is like, need to identify in order to properly care. Through stories we impose patterns, make meanings, give beginnings and endings, because we cannot bear a world or self without them.'

But the victims of serial killers have rarely garnered as much attention as the two girls killed in Soham. Being on the margins of society for one reason or another, they frequently leave little or no record from which the details of their lives might be reconstructed – no letters, diaries or autobiographies, no websites dedicated to their memory. They are unlikely to be the subjects of television documentaries or feature films. Some victims do not even have a name: they are identified in police records simply by their physical characteristics, such as the colour of their hair, the condition of their teeth, perhaps a tattoo. We know a lot about Lucy Partington, who was killed by Fred West, principally because she was a cousin of the novelist Martin Amis, who has since written movingly about her life. In stark contrast, many of the Wests' other victims were not even reported as missing to the police.

This lack of understanding and information – including an absence of photographs – about the lives of the victims has contributed to a popular and academic over-concentration on the serial killers themselves. Information and images – if not necessarily understanding – about the murderers abound, so this book is a modest attempt to remind us that the people they killed should not be reduced to mere numbers on a list. I admit it is a 'modest attempt' because I have not been able to do full justice to the lives of those who have been victimised by serial killers, and for that I apologise. However, I have attempted to explain how their individual circumstances created their social vulnerability, which thereafter facilitated their murder. Details of those circumstances are often sketchy and incomplete, no matter how much research is done, but by exploring them I hope to create a link between those killed in the 1880s and those who were murdered many years later. This might tell us something of the society that Britain has become since 1888, and reveal who possesses power and who does not.

Of course, forty-one serial killers and 409 victims do not comprise a very large sample on which to build an argument. (By way of comparison, it has been calculated that there have been almost 600 serial killers responsible for at least 4,000 deaths since 1900 in the USA.) However, I believe that analysis of this small sample is worthwhile – and any conclusions that are drawn are valid – for two reasons. First, the serial killer 'industry' is now so omnipresent in popular discourse that it is vitally important to start its deconstruction by shifting focus from the individual to the social. Looking at the victims is an ideal place to begin that process. Second, as serial killing is a unique phenomenon, we have a responsibility to probe every aspect of it in order to understand it more clearly. Attempting to explain serial killing at the social level is not an easy task, but by analysing the victims we can at least begin to discern wider patterns at work in society. In doing so, we might gain a deeper understanding of how we have all helped to create serial killers.

Some readers will certainly be angered by the argument that is at the heart of this book. After all, society has been wedded to the concept of 'personal responsibility' of the offender (and especially the serial killer) for some time. 'Responsibilising' the individual offender has been a key element of successive governments' approaches to law and order. So my attempt to replace the 'individual' with the 'social' in relation to serial killing will not chime well with politicians who have sought to blame and pathologise the individual while exonerating the society in which that individual resides.

That said, I am by no means attempting to let serial killers 'off the hook'. Nor am I trying to blame society for every sin. My point is that those who want to kill repeatedly are able to do so only when the social structure in which they operate allows it to happen by placing value on one group to the detriment of others. Only in these circumstances, when communities become fractured and anxious, with people feeling isolated and distanced from one another, when bonds of mutual support have been all but eradicated, can those who want to kill large numbers of their fellow human beings achieve their purpose.

The prevalence of serial killing usefully reveals the limits of our current social arrangements, and the inadequacy of our protection of the poor and the vulnerable. Children, young people living away from home, gay men, sex workers and the elderly are the prime victims of serial killers only because we have created a society where all of these groups might also become victims of a socio-economic system that does not place value on their lives, and routinely excludes them from the protection of the state.

Chapter Two

'Hacked beyond recognition': Jack the Ripper

> When the stolid English go in for a scare they take leave of all moderation and common sense. If nonsense were solid, the nonsense that was talked and written about those murders would sink a Dreadnought.
>
> Sir Robert Anderson, *The Lighter Side of My Official Life* (1910)

Jack the Ripper is by far the most popular subject of the hundred bestselling books in Amazon's criminology list, so it is with some trepidation that I dip my toe into territory that remains one of the most obsessive preoccupations of the true crime genre. Some of the best-known titles – which amply describe the books' contents – are: *The Complete History of Jack the Ripper*; *Uncovering Jack the Ripper's London*; *Jack the Ripper: The Facts*; and *Portrait of a Killer: Jack the Ripper – Case Closed.* And Jack's influence is not confined to books. In 2009 Amazon listed thirty-four DVDs, twenty music CDs, a video game and an assortment of toys and games in which his name appeared. In the latter category, for example, it was possible to purchase a Jack the Ripper 'action figure', with the promise that 'This faceless villain comes alive with MEZCO TOYZ 9-inch Jack the Ripper roto-cast figure. Jack is fully articulated and comes complete with appropriate accessories including five knives, satchel, hat, and cloth cloak.' If all of that is not enough, you can join a walking tour to 'retrace the steps of the "Ripper", visiting the murder sites, the haunts that were frequented, such as the famous pub the Ten Bells in Whitechapel. Put your amateur sleuthing skills to the test and try and solve the mystery.' Jack was voted the 'Worst Briton over the Last 1,000 Years' in a poll conducted for *BBC History* magazine's February 2006 issue, beating, among others, Titus Oates, King John and Oswald Mosley to the title.

Keying 'Jack the Ripper' into Google in 2020 produced 28,200,000 hits, with the most comprehensive link being casebook.org, which claims to be the 'world's largest public repository of Ripper-related information'. The website's mission statement is written by Stephen P. Ryder:

> In the past 110 years, the name 'Jack the Ripper' has become synonymous with evil and misogyny, eliciting images of foggy nights and gas-lit streets in the minds of millions worldwide. The mass media and entertainment industries are largely responsible for the popularity of the subject, but they are also to blame for many of the myths and misconceptions which have crept in among the facts of the case. Sloppy research performed by those motivated by personal dreams of fame and greed has only added to the mire. Though this situation has recently been aided by the valiant efforts of a handful of diligent researchers, the myths persist, the lies repeated, and the facts of the case remain hidden beneath a cloud of

> confusion. It is our hope that the information provided by Casebook: Jack the Ripper will help scatter this cloud and, perhaps, finally allow a glimpse into that most elusive aspect of the mystery: the truth.

Sir Robert Anderson, the detective in charge of CID at the time of the murders, might well have appreciated Ryder's attempts to find a way through the 'cloud of confusion' – or, as Anderson would have it, 'nonsense' – that has surrounded the case for over a century. Ryder concludes by imploring readers to 'remember that the whole of this fantastic mystery revolves around the deaths of five women whose lives were as precious and as ephemeral as our own . . . do not ignore their humanity, as the Ripper did, but embrace it. Only then can you truly appreciate the tragedy of the case. Only then can you understand why the search must continue.'

This seems an acceptable justification for the existence of Casebook: Jack the Ripper. However, I am still wary about joining in the rush to uncover the identity of a historic serial killer, and my caution has become magnified since the publication of Hallie Rubenhold's *The Five: The Untold Story of the Women Killed by Jack the Ripper*. Rubenhold's research has made me much more sensitive about simply labelling these women as 'prostitutes', although I would suggest that evidence does exist that they may have been selling sexual services on the nights that they were murdered. These sensitivities notwithstanding, along with Emilia Fox, I presented a BBC1 documentary in 2019 called *Jack the Ripper – The Case Re-Opened* which allowed me to taste first hand the public's fascination with this historic sequence of crimes. And, during the making of the programme, we were able to engage the services of trainers on HOLMES – the Home Office Large Major Enquiry System – which had been first developed in the wake of the murders committed by Peter Sutcliffe. We ran what is known as 'the Whitechapel docket' through this information retrieval system and this established – definitively – that Martha Tabram was Jack's first victim. This allowed us to undertake some new geo-profiling and to establish where Jack might have lived. As a result I named a suspect whom I believe to be Jack the Ripper.

I was quick to realise that this did not end the public's fascination with Jack the Ripper – if anything it merely added to it. And, coming as it did in the wake of the publication of Rubenhold's book and an almost virulent reaction to what she argued, especially by online commentators, I want to explain how I approached this case, so that others may follow my logic and see if they agree. Stewart Evans, a trustworthy Ripper expert, initially guided me through the competing suspects and helped shape my thinking, and I also reached out to Paul Begg for his view about Rubenhold's research. So too I corresponded with the historian Judith Flanders and Dr Julia Laite at Birkbeck College, University of London who has been at the forefront of research about the sale of sexual services in the late nineteenth century. Of course any conclusions that I have reached are my own.

Sources and suspects

One advantage of the obsessive public interest in Jack the Ripper is that most of the primary sources relating to the so-called Whitechapel Murders (1888–91) have now been collected and are freely available in the public domain. Of these anthologies, the most valuable is *The Ultimate Jack the Ripper Sourcebook: An Illustrated Encyclopaedia* (2000) by Stewart Evans and Keith Skinner. This includes all the Scotland Yard reports, witness statements, press accounts and other Home Office files. I also found Paul Begg's *Jack the Ripper: The Facts* (2004) helpful, given that it tries to place the murders within a historical context. Begg states that eighty-five new books have been published about Jack the Ripper since the centenary of the murders in 1988. Most, if not all, of them have proposed a name for the killer.

Visitors to casebook.org can vote for these prime suspects. At the time of writing, James Maybrick led the way with 9,862 votes, followed by Francis Tumblety with 7,805 votes, Walter Sickert with 7,587, then a collection of suspects under the heading the 'royal conspiracy', who garnered 6,918 votes. Each of these has been proposed by a recent bestselling book: for example, Maybrick – a Liverpool-based cotton trader who died in 1889 – is supposedly the author of a diary in which he 'confesses' to the murders. However, the diary has become the subject of numerous claims and counter-claims in respect to its authenticity. Meanwhile, Tumblety emerged as a suspect through the diligent research of Stewart Evans and his co-author Paul Gainey in *Jack the Ripper: First American Serial Killer* (1996). While he may have been suspected at one stage by Scotland Yard, he was a very unlikely Ripper: physically enormous, gay and with a distinctive moustache, he would have been (as Begg comments) 'as conspicuous in the East End as a brass band at a funeral'. Nevertheless, Evans remains convinced that Tumblety should not be ruled out, especially as he was certainly in Whitechapel at the time of the murders.

The artist Walter Sickert is put forward as a suspect in *Portrait of a Killer: Jack the Ripper – Case Closed* (2002) by the novelist Patricia Cornwell, who states, 'I knew the identity of a murderer and I couldn't possibly avert my gaze.' Her use of modern forensic techniques to unmask the suspect is admirable, but she concentrates all her efforts in this field, which I believe undermines her case. For instance, while the last acknowledged Ripper victim was Mary Jane Kelly, who was killed on 9 November 1888, Sickert lived on until well into the twentieth century. As Cornwell freely admits, most serial killers do not stop killing until they are apprehended or die, but she gets round the apparent paradox by suggesting that Sickert 'kept killing. His body count could have been fifteen, twenty, forty before he died.' She also claims that he killed children and young people as well as prostitutes. I disagree. Cornwell produces convincing evidence that the artist was obsessed with Jack the Ripper, and it is possible that he even wrote several letters to the police claiming to be the murderer. However, hoax letters are a common feature of many high-profile murder cases. Perhaps the most telling argument against Sickert being Jack the Ripper, though, is that he was out of the country for much of September 1888, when several of the murders occurred.

Another prime suspect is part of the 'royal conspiracy', Prince Albert Victor. Some theories suggest that the prince was the murderer himself; others that the killings were committed to protect his reputation. Notable among the books pointing the finger at Albert Victor is Stephen Knight's *Jack the Ripper: The Final Solution* (1976), and he also features in several films, most recently *From Hell*, starring Johnny Depp. However, the prince was not in London when several of the murders were committed: he was in Yorkshire when Mary Ann Nichols was murdered; in Scotland with Prince Henry of Battenberg when the 'double event' occurred; and in Norfolk when the final murder took place. So Albert Victor could not have been Jack the Ripper, but Knight claims that a 'Freemasons' conspiracy' evolved to cover up the fact that the prince had fallen in love with a young Catholic woman called Annie Crook. He allegedly married her in secret and together they had a child, who was put into the care of Mary Jane Kelly after the prince had been sent to India and Annie Crook locked up in an asylum. As can be seen from the casebook.org poll, these claims are popular, but there is no evidence whatsoever to support them.

Although these modern books often draw unsupportable conclusions, they can be rich in detail and insight, and so are worth consulting. The same is true of late Victorian biographies and autobiographies by several of the principals involved in the case. Robert Anderson's *The Lighter Side of My Official Life* (1910) is idiosyncratic but provides an almost official view of contemporary Jack the Ripper suspects (albeit twenty-two years after the event). Meanwhile, Walter Dew's *I Caught Crippen: Memoirs of Ex-Chief Inspector Walter Dew CID* (1938) covers the author's early career and his attendance at Miller's Court, where Mary Jane Kelly was murdered. Sir Melville Macnaghten's *Days of My Years* (1914), published just before the outbreak of the First World War, is useful, as are trial excerpts from 1903 relating to the murders committed by George Chapman. (The latter was also suspected of being Jack the Ripper, principally because he had arrived in London from Poland shortly before the murders commenced in 1888.) More recent books, such as David Canter's *Mapping Murder* (2003), reminded me to keep asking criminological questions based on what we now know about serial killing and more recent serial killers. Canter explores whether the geography of Whitechapel might provide clues to the killer's identity. And today we are also able to construct a fairly sophisticated profile of the type of person who committed the murders, based on which victims were chosen, what was done to them, and how their bodies were discarded. This has been attempted by 'the FBI's legendary mindhunter' in John E. Douglas and Mark Olshaker's *The Cases that Haunt Us: From Jack the Ripper to*

Jonbenet Ramsey (2000), and while profiles of serial killers can often be very subjective, there can be little doubt that Jack the Ripper's victims and what happened to them provide us with a number of clues that are worthy of consideration.

Mary Ann Nichols – first of the 'canonical five', or should there be 'six'?

The Whitechapel Murders and the crimes of Jack the Ripper are often presumed to be one and the same thing. However, the police files on the Whitechapel Murders begin with the murder of Emma Smith on 3/4 April 1888 and end with the murder of Frances Coles on 13 February 1891. In total, eleven murders are included in these files, but how many of them should be attributed to Jack the Ripper? The standard answer to this question is five, starting with the murder of Mary Ann Nichols on 31 August 1888, then: Annie Chapman on 8 September; Elizabeth Stride and Catherine Eddowes in the early hours of 30 September; and finally Mary Jane Kelly on 9 November. Jack the Ripper therefore fits our definition of a serial killer: he killed three or more victims in a period greater than thirty days.

Of course, some argue that other murders were also committed by him: Patricia Cornwell, for example, believes that Martha Tabram's murder on 7 August was committed by Jack the Ripper. It would now appear that Cornwell was right. Martha, a mother of two boys who had divorced her husband in 1875, was soliciting on the night of her murder with her friend Mary Ann Connelly, who was more popularly known as 'Pearly Poll'. Both women would appear to have been alcoholic. On the night of her murder Martha and Mary Ann were seen drinking in a local pub with two men who are usually referred to as 'soldiers', because they seemed to have been wearing uniforms. The two women parted with their respective clients – Mary Ann to Angel Alley and Martha to George Yard Buildings. Martha's body was later found with thirty-nine stab wounds – many concentrated on the lower abdomen and vagina, and her body had been sexually posed after her death. Despite the police organising a number of identity parades at various military barracks, Mary Ann was never able to identify the man that had been drinking with Martha.

Murders of similar victims tend to be linked to a known serial killer, but most Ripper scholars had only attributed five rather than all eleven victims to him because of a confidential memorandum written by Sir Melville Macnaghten in February 1894. Macnaghten, who had joined the Metropolitan Police Force as Assistant Chief Constable CID in June 1889, wrote this memo in response to a newspaper claim that Jack the Ripper was a recently detained lunatic called Thomas Hayne Cutbush. In it, Macnaghten states unequivocally that 'the Whitechapel murderer had five victims – & 5 victims only'. He then names the 'canonical five' and expressly dismisses Martha Tabram as a Ripper victim. This has usually been used as the basis of attributing only five victims to Jack, even though Macnaghten joined the Met after the Ripper murders had ended. The conclusions reached by HOLMES in 2019 should make us reconsider if Macnaghten got this aspect of the case right.

What do we know of the 'five'? Mary Ann Nichols was also known as 'Polly'. She was born on 26 August 1845 to Edward Nichols, a locksmith, and his wife Caroline, who worked as a laundress. The family lived in Shoe Lane, off Fleet Street. In January 1864 Mary Ann married an Oxford-born printer called William Nichols at St Bride's Parish Church in Fleet Street, and between 1866 and 1879 they had five children. While this indicates that their marriage was publicly fruitful, it was also privately stormy, and it broke down completely one year later. William suggested that this was a result of Mary Ann's alcoholism, but her father denied that she was a heavy drinker, suggesting instead that the marriage failed as a result of William having an affair with the nurse who looked after Mary Ann during her last pregnancy. Whatever the truth, Mary Ann moved out of the family home in September 1880 and went to live in the Lambeth Workhouse, where she stayed for some nine months, and where she would return periodically over the next eight years.

At first, after their separation, William continued to support Mary Ann, but he eventually stopped the payments. When the parish authorities tried to collect more maintenance money from him, he explained that his wife had deserted her children, taken up with another man, and was now earning her living as a prostitute. He won the case, and at the time of her death he had not seen Mary Ann for three years.

Between April and July 1888, Mary Ann worked as a domestic servant in the home of Mr and Mrs Cowdry in Wandsworth, a job found for her by the matron of the Lambeth Workhouse. She was sufficiently proud of this new role to tell her father about it in a letter of May that year: 'I am settled in my new place, and going on all right up to now. My people went out yesterday, and have not returned, so I am in charge. It is a grand place inside, with trees and gardens front and back . . . they are teetotallers, and religious, so I ought to get on.' It is logical to presume that the matron had deliberately placed Mary Ann in a situation where she would not have access to alcohol, but unfortunately this plan backfired. On 12 July Mrs Cowdry sent Mary Ann's father a postcard to say that she had stolen clothing worth £3 10s. and absconded. At the time of her death, Mary Ann was living in a doss house, known as the White House, in

Flower and Dean Street, where men and women were allowed to sleep together.

Mary Ann was five feet two inches tall, with a dark complexion, brown eyes, brown, greying hair, high cheekbones and discoloured teeth. Her associates viewed her as a very clean woman who tried to keep herself to herself and rarely talked about her affairs. This might suggest something of the regret she must have felt for the children she had left behind. On the night that she died she went out drinking in the Frying Pan in Brick Lane, but by 1.20 a.m. she was in a lodging house in Thrawl Street, where she was asked for fourpence for her bed. She did not have the money so was turned out. In all likelihood, then, she was murdered while trying to earn enough cash simply to secure a bed for the night.

Later, Mary Ann was spotted by Mrs Emily Holland, with whom she had once shared a room in Thrawl Street. Emily described her former roommate as drunk and said she found her slumped against the wall of a grocer's shop. According to her statement, Emily tried to persuade Mary Ann to go home with her, but Mary Ann wanted to earn her doss money, so she staggered up Whitechapel Road and into Buck's Row – known today as Durward Street – where she met her death.

The circumstances in which Mary Ann was found are now so well known as not to need repeating here. Of greater relevance are the injuries that she suffered, given that these might afford an insight into the state of mind of her killer. Mary Ann was found with two bruises on her face, one on each side. There were two cuts to her throat – one four inches long, the other eight inches – both of which were so deep as to reach the vertebrae of her neck. There was also bruising on her abdomen, and on her right side three or four cuts running downwards – a contemporary account claims that the 'lower part of the person was completely ripped open'. All of the wounds had been inflicted with a sharp knife. While not commented upon by the coroner, several newspapers reported that Mary Ann might have been wearing a ring, which had been removed by the killer.

It would seem fair to conclude that Mary Ann turned her back to her murderer – possibly intending to have intercourse in this position – and that this gave him the opportunity to cut her throat. As Patricia Cornwell notes: 'His position behind her would have prevented him from being splashed by the arterial blood that would have spurted out of her severed left carotid artery. Few murderers would choose to have blood spattering on their faces, especially the blood of a victim who probably had diseases – at the very least, sexually transmitted ones.' Cutting his victim's throat would also have left her unable to scream, allowing him more time to mutilate his dying victim. This suggests that Jack the Ripper was 'act focused' – he wanted to kill his victims quickly – and was not interested in prolonging the process by which they died. He sought a dead victim, so thereafter he could feed his fantasies with an inert body.

Paul Begg notes that all of the murders (with the exception of Elizabeth Stride's, when the Ripper was disturbed) were 'characterised by extensive mutilation of the victim, the womb being the target of his attacks'. Dr Llewellyn, who conducted the full post-mortem examination on Mary Ann, thought that her killer must have had at least some, albeit crude, anatomical knowledge. His opinion has been used as supporting evidence by many of those who propose doctors or people with a medical background as the murderer. However, as Cornwell points out, 'this isn't surgery; it is expediency, or grab and cut'.

Finally, there is no evidence that the killer engaged in sex with Mary Ann, or indeed with any of his future victims.

The 'canonical five'

Name	Age	Occupation	Time of Murder	Place of Murder	Alcoholic
Mary Ann Nichols	43	Sex worker?	Friday, 2.30 a.m.	Street	Yes
Annie Chapman	48	Sex worker?	Saturday, 6.00 a.m.	Street	Yes
Elizabeth Stride	44	Sex worker	Sunday, 1.00 a.m.	Street	Yes
Catherine Eddowes	46	Sex worker?	Sunday, 1.45 a.m.	Street	Yes
Mary Jane Kelly	24	Sex worker	Friday, early morning	House	Yes

As the table above indicates, there is a striking degree of similarity between the five victims: they had all, at some time, worked as sex workers (although there remains debate about Eddowes), all had problems with alcohol, and they were all – with the exception of Mary Jane Kelly – in their forties. Annie Chapman, the second victim, was born Annie Smith in September of either 1840 or 1841. Her father, George, was a soldier in the Life Guards. Annie's first job seems to have been as a domestic servant, and in May 1869 she married a coachman named John Chapman. Together they had three children, but Annie drank heavily and her 'dissolute habits' eventually led to the couple's separation in 1882. She was given an allowance of ten shillings a week by her ex-husband, but when he died in 1886 that came to an abrupt end. Thereafter, Annie drifted from one relationship to another, and she tried to support herself by selling matches and flowers bought at Stratford Market. Her friends described her at the time of her murder as 'addicted to drink'. However, it was only when her ex-husband died that she was forced into sex work which, as Rubenhold shows, merely reveals the precarious nature of life in late Victorian England for working-class women and therefore how we have to be careful to define what we mean we describe someone as a 'prostitute'.

On the night of her murder Annie had been drinking in the Britannia public house on the corner of Dorset Street, near where she had been staying at a lodging house. She returned to her lodgings, and, like Mary Ann Nichols, was asked for money for her bed. She did not have it but told the warden – Tim Donovan – that he should not let out her bed because she would return soon enough with the cash. Donovan stated that Annie was drunk but was walking straight. There were also some unsubstantiated reports that she went on to the Ten Bells pub on the corner of Fournier Street. In any event, Annie was found dead, lying on her back, in the rear yard of 29 Hanbury Street. Her throat had been cut through to the spine, and a portion of her small intestine and abdomen was lying on the ground over her right shoulder, but still attached to her body. Begg describes the remainder of her injuries: 'from the pelvis the uterus and its appendages, with the upper portion of the vagina and the posterior two-thirds of the bladder, had been entirely removed'.

Elizabeth Stride and Catherine Eddowes were killed just over three weeks later, on the same night. This is often described as the 'double event', a phrase used in a postcard purportedly written by Jack the Ripper on 1 October 1888. Elizabeth was murdered first; then, just forty-five minutes later, Catherine was killed. Their murders are of particular significance because both seem to have been witnessed.

Elizabeth Gustafsdotter was born in Sweden in November 1843. She emigrated to London in February 1867, after inheriting sixty-five Swedish krona from her mother's estate. This seems to have been an attempt to put the past behind her, as she had already been arrested by the Swedish police for prostitution. She married a carpenter named John Stride in March 1869, and soon they were running a coffee shop together. However, John suffered ill-health, and in January 1879 Elizabeth asked the Swedish Church in London for financial assistance. John was admitted to Poplar Workhouse in August 1884 before being sent to the Poplar and Stepney Sick Asylum, where he died of heart disease two months later.

The Strides' marriage seems to have broken down three years before John's death, with Elizabeth's heavy drinking reportedly the principal cause. She spent time in the Whitechapel Workhouse infirmary, and would eventually be sentenced to seven days' hard labour for being drunk and disorderly and soliciting on 13 November 1884. She liked to tell people that her husband and two of her children had died in a shipping accident in 1878, and Cornwell notes that Elizabeth had 'led a life of lies, most of them pitiful attempts to weave a brighter, more dramatic tale than the truth of her depressing, desperate life'. Begg suggests that she might also have masqueraded as another woman, Elizabeth Watts, and she certainly had a variety of nicknames, among them Long Liz, Hippy Lip Annie and Mother Gum.

After the collapse of her marriage, Elizabeth lived on and off with a man named Michael Kidney. By all accounts it was a stormy relationship, with Elizabeth disappearing for days or weeks at a time: 'It was the drink that made her go away,' claimed Kidney after Elizabeth's death. Support for this statement comes in the form of the numerous appearances that Elizabeth made before the magistrates. For example, she was charged in February and October 1887 and February and September 1888 with being drunk and disorderly and using obscene language. Kidney and Elizabeth parted company for the last time on 25 September – just five days before her death. As a result, he was initially suspected of her murder.

Elizabeth was seen drinking in the Bricklayer's Arms in Settles Street on the night of her death, and she may have been sold a bunch of grapes by one Matthew Packer between 11 p.m. and midnight, although none were found in her stomach during her post-mortem. Her body was discovered in a passageway beside 40 Berner Street, which had been converted into the International Working Men's Educational Club. That night about a hundred people had turned up at the club to debate 'Why Jews Should Be Socialists', with most not leaving before 11.30 p.m. Several others stayed on to drink until well after midnight. Clearly, then, people must have been around when Elizabeth was attacked on Berner Street. In particular, Israel Schwartz followed a man into the street from Commercial Road. He saw the figure approach Elizabeth – who was standing outside the gates of the club – stop, exchange a few words with her and then assault her. Schwartz thought it was a domestic dispute, so he crossed the street to avoid becoming involved. He then saw a second man leave a pub on the corner and light his pipe. Next he heard someone shout 'Lipski' – a reference to a notorious Jewish murderer who had been hanged the previous year – which might have been intended to scare off Schwartz. He did indeed run away – as did the man with the pipe – but he reported all he had witnessed the following day at Leman Street police station.

If Schwartz is to be believed, he undoubtedly saw the man who murdered Elizabeth Stride, and he provided the police with a description of Jack the Ripper. Schwartz stated that the man was approximately thirty, short – about five feet five inches tall – with broad shoulders, a fair complexion, dark hair, a full face and a small moustache. He was wearing a dark jacket and trousers and a black peaked cap.

Because of the presence of Schwartz and/or the man with the pipe, or possibly due to the arrival several minutes later of Louis Diemshutz, who worked at the club as a steward, this time the killer did not linger over his victim's body. He cut Elizabeth's throat, but her body was not mutilated in any way. Unfortunately for Catherine Eddowes, that meant the killer had unfinished business that night.

Catherine Eddowes – also known as Kate Kelly – was born in Wolverhampton on 14 April 1842. Her father was a tinplate worker and her mother a cook, and the family moved to London when Catherine was just one year old. Nevertheless, she spent some of her childhood back in Wolverhampton, and she would eventually find work there as a tinplate stamper. However, she was fired from that job and ran off to Birmingham, where she stayed with an uncle who made boots and shoes. Again, though, this did not work out, so she returned to Wolverhampton in 1861, where she met and set up home with a former soldier called Thomas Quinn. The couple had a son, moved to London, and then three further children were born. However, Catherine's heavy drinking and fiery temperament had destroyed the relationship by 1880, when she turned to sex work, although this is challenged by Rubenhold and by Laite. She moved into a lodging house called Cooney's in Flower and Dean Street, where she met John Kelly. He denied at the time that Catherine was involved in prostitution, but admitted that she sometimes drank to excess – she was charged with being drunk and disorderly in September 1881.

On the day of her death, Catherine had again been drinking heavily enough to be arrested by PC Louis Robinson at 8.30 p.m. She was taken to Bishopsgate police station to 'sleep it off'. Just before one o'clock the following morning the station sergeant asked PC George Hutt to check if anyone could be released. By this time Catherine was sober, so she was freed by Hutt, who asked her to shut the station door on her way out. 'All right. Good night, old cock,' she said as she walked into the early hours of the morning, just as Elizabeth Stride's body was being found.

Catherine seems to have gone in the opposite direction to Flower and Dean Street, and eventually she must have wandered into Mitre Square, where her body was found. By all accounts, the square was poorly lit, but the patrolling PC Watkins reported nothing unusual at 1.30 a.m., when he was on his rounds. However, just five minutes later, a commercial traveller in the cigarette business named Joseph Lawende noticed a couple standing at the entrance of a passageway leading to the square. Lawende described a woman wearing clothes that matched those worn by Catherine that night. Strangely, at the inquest into Catherine's death he did not give a description of the man who was with her, but *The Times* provided a brief pen picture, and the Home Office files contain a full description that can only have come from Lawende. Perhaps the police were trying to keep Lawende's information out of the public domain in the hope of using the intelligence he provided to trap the killer.

In any event, Catherine's body was discovered by PC Watkins when he returned to Mitre Square on his beat at 1.45 a.m. As he was later to tell the *Star* newspaper, Catherine had been 'ripped up like a pig in the market . . . I have been in the force a long while, but I never saw such a sight.' The attack had been ferocious: her throat had been cut; after death her killer had mutilated her face and abdomen; her intestines had been cut out and placed over her right shoulder; and her left kidney and uterus had been removed. The damage to Catherine's face – the tip of her nose and her ear lobes had been cut off, and her cheeks slashed – was clearly deliberate. As Cornwell observes: 'the face is the person. To mutilate it is personal.'

A search was made of the area near where Catherine's body was discovered and some graffiti was found. Again, this has become part of Jack the Ripper folklore. It reportedly read, 'the Jews are the men that will not be blamed for nothing', but there is no way of knowing if it was connected to the murders or had been in existence for some time.

The last of the 'canonical five' was Mary Jane Kelly, also known as 'Black Mary', 'Ginger' and 'Marie Jeanette Kelly'. By far the youngest of the victims, her body was found at 13 Miller's Court, Dorset Street. Her murder was unusual because she was not murdered in public, and the extensive injuries inflicted upon her indicate that the killer was able to spend some considerable time with Mary Jane's body after her death. More than any of the other murders, this one represents the ultimate expression of Jack the Ripper's hatred of his female victims. By the time of her death, Mary Jane would have been all too aware that there was a killer walking the streets of Whitechapel murdering women – some of whom may also have sold sexual services. However, she continued to sell sexual services, a simple fact that highlights the desperation of the young women who were involved in the sex industry in late Victorian Britain.

In his autobiography Walter Dew claimed that he knew Mary Jane well by sight, and said that most of her contemporaries would have described her as pretty. Born in Limerick, Ireland, she had spent some of her childhood in Wales, and at sixteen had married a mineworker who was killed three years later in an explosion. After this tragedy she moved to Cardiff, where she first seems to have become involved in prostitution. Eventually she made her way to London. By April 1887, she was in a relationship with a porter called Joseph Barnett, but at the time of her murder their relationship had begun to cool, perhaps because Barnett disapproved of her work as a prostitute. As a result, Barnett lived apart from Mary Jane, who was renting a room in Miller's Court from a well-known East End pimp called John McCarthy.

There are several conflicting witness testimonies relating to when Mary Jane was last seen alive, and with whom she was seen entering Miller's Court. But there is no doubt about what happened to her after her death, with the police taking photographs of both Mary Jane's body and the interior and exterior of 13 Miller's Court. Dew noted simply: 'there was little left of her, not much more than a skeleton. Her face was terribly scarred and mutilated.' Indeed, her ears, nose, cheeks and eyebrows had been partly removed. Dr Thomas Bond – who conducted Mary Jane's preliminary post-mortem at the crime scene – described the state of her body:

> The legs were wide apart, the left thigh at right angles to the trunk & the right forming an obtuse angle with the pubes. The whole surface of the abdomen & thighs was removed & the abdominal cavity emptied of its viscera. The breasts were cut off, the arms mutilated by several jagged wounds & the face hacked beyond recognition of the features . . . the viscera were found in various parts viz; the uterus & kidneys with one breast under the head, the other breast by the right foot, the liver between the feet, the intestines by the right side & the spleen by the left side of the body. The flaps removed from the abdomen & thighs were on a table . . . the Pericardium was open below & the Heart absent.

When Mary Jane was buried ten days later at Shoreditch Church there were three large wreaths on her coffin, two crowns of artificial flowers and a cross that bore the words: 'A last tribute of respect to Mary Kelly. May she rest in peace, and may her murderer be brought to justice.'

Jack the Ripper – a profile

Today, if the police were faced with a series of murders such as those that have just been described, they would have access to a wealth of forensic expertise that was not available to their Victorian counterparts. There would be a mass of DNA evidence available for analysis, fingerprints, CCTV camera footage, and mobile phone records. The police would also be able to call upon profilers, who would suggest that the characteristics of the murderer could be deduced from a carefully considered examination of his offences. In other words, the offence characteristics – how the crime was committed, why the victim was chosen, and manner in which the body was dismembered – would give us insights into the type of person that the offender was likely to be. In particular, a profiler would look carefully at five areas: the crime scene; the nature of the attacks; forensic evidence; a medical examination of the victim; and finally the victim's characteristics.

Based on this type of analysis, the US Federal Bureau of Investigation (FBI) – where modern scientific profiling began – suggests that offenders can be characterised as either 'organised' or 'disorganised'. An organised offender does a great deal of planning: he wears gloves, carries a rope or handcuffs to subdue the victim, and typically is very much in control of the crime scene. As a result, he leaves few clues such as fingerprints, blood or semen. The FBI claims that these offenders have a specific personality type: they are invariably intelligent, sexually active and competent, and they are likely to have a partner. They will probably be working in a skilled or semiskilled job, and to all intents and purposes they will appear 'normal'. However, this mask of normality obviously hides a deeply antisocial personality. Organised offenders tend to follow reports of their attacks in the media, and they are often prompted to commit their offences because of anger and frustration in their personal lives.

On the other hand, disorganised offenders do not plan their crimes. Their actions are sudden and random, so they will use whatever comes to hand to commit the offence. For example, a disorganised offender might tie up his victim with her own scarf or underwear. He will stab or bludgeon using weapons found in the vicinity of the crime scene and will put little effort into concealing evidence: often the victim's body is simply abandoned, rather than hidden. The offender is likely to live alone – or with his parents – and usually he commits his crimes within his home area. He will be socially and sexually immature, will often have a history of mental illness, and is likely to offend while frightened or confused.

In the case of Jack the Ripper I would note that there was no evidence of sexual assault and that he was 'act focused' – all of his victims were killed quickly. He did not torture them while they were alive; but when he had time to be alone with a dead victim, he mutilated her abdomen and sometimes her face. He removed body parts, and sometimes took other 'trophies', such as Mary Ann Nichols' ring. Obviously, the attacks on the abdomens of his victims have sexual overtones, but I would suggest that Jack the Ripper was not sexually competent, and consequently was single. While he murdered women who sold sexual services, his choice of victim does not seem to have stemmed from a desire to buy those services. Rather, prostitutes, unlike most women at the time, would simply allow him to get sufficiently close to commit his crimes. Interestingly, he committed most of his murders in the street, which meant that he usually did not have much opportunity to be alone with his dead victims for any length of time before being disturbed by passers-by. This meant he only fully accomplished his goal in the case of his final victim, Mary Jane Kelly, whom he murdered indoors and so was able to mutilate at his leisure. He also never seemed to give much thought to his escape route, or indeed how he would dispose of his victim's body. All of this suggests that he was a disorganised killer, who had no plan and merely sought out any random opportunity to kill. When he did have the time to be alone with a victim, Mary Jane Kelly, the mutilation of her body was so comprehensive that her identity was virtually obliterated.

I feel the timing of his attacks was also significant. They always occurred in the early hours of the morning on a Friday, Saturday or Sunday. This would seem to indicate that he had some form of unskilled work that occupied him during the week, and that the opportunity to be alone – that is, away from those who knew him, were related to him, or were living with him – came only during the weekend. However, we should remember that Martha Tabram was murdered on a Tuesday and that her killer had been in the company of another man. All of the attacks also occurred in a very narrow geographical area, which strongly suggests that he lived locally – he was too disorganised to travel any great distance. It seems reasonable to assume that he had lodgings near to Buck's Row, where his first victim, Mary Ann Nichols, was killed. He surely had somewhere to return to after each attack, where he could clean himself and perhaps hide while the police conducted house-to-house searches.

I would suggest that Jack the Ripper was a white man of limited intelligence and education, under the age of forty-five. From the nature of his offences, it seems highly unlikely that he would have been interested in writing letters to the press.

There is also no real evidence of any medical training or surgical knowledge in his crimes; rather, he seems to have been curious about female internal organs. Finally, the nature of the murders he committed suggests that he was insane.

If we accept the broad parameters of this profile – which is not far removed from others that have been conducted in the past – we can start to rule out some favourite suspects. First, the prime suspect James Maybrick does not fit this profile in any way: he lived in Liverpool rather than locally; he was ill; he was older than the profile suggests; and he would surely have planned any attacks far more carefully than the man who was disturbed while murdering Elizabeth Stride and was spotted with Catherine Eddowes. Whatever the truth about his diary – and in all likelihood it is a forgery – Maybrick is therefore a very unlikely candidate for Jack the Ripper. Nor, as I have indicated earlier in the chapter, should we 'close the case' and blame Walter Sickert. Even if he did write letters to the press claiming to be the Ripper, a profiler would say that such an action points more to his innocence than to his guilt.

So, having dismissed two of the principal suspects, who are we left with?

Eyewitness testimony

At least two people saw Jack the Ripper and provided descriptions to the police: Israel Schwartz, who saw Elizabeth Stride being assaulted in Berner Street; and Joseph Lawende, who spotted Catherine Eddowes with her killer in Mitre Square. Their descriptions are remarkably similar. As we know, Schwartz recalled seeing a short, stocky, thirty-year-old with a moustache who was wearing a black cap with a peak. *The Times* reported that Lawende witnessed a man of shabby appearance, about thirty years of age, five feet nine inches tall, with a fair complexion and a small moustache, wearing a peaked grey cloth cap. The Home Office files relating to Lawende's description go into more detail (and knock a couple of inches off the height, bringing it more in line with Schwartz's description): 'aged about thirty, five foot seven or eight, of fair complexion, with a fair moustache, of medium build, wearing a pepper-and-salt-coloured loose jacket, a grey cloth cap with peak of the same colour, and a reddish handkerchief tied in a knot around the neck, and having the appearance of a sailor'.

Sir Robert Anderson outlined where the police's attention was focused in light of these descriptions:

> One did not need to be a Sherlock Holmes to discover that the criminal was a sexual maniac of a virulent type; that he was living in the immediate vicinity of the scenes of the murders; and that, if he was not living absolutely alone, his people knew of his guilt, and refused to give him up to justice. During my absence abroad the Police had made a house-to-house search for him, investigating the case of every man in the district whose circumstances were such that he could go and come and get rid of bloodstains in secret. And the conclusion we came to was that he and his people were certain low-class Polish Jews; for it is a remarkable fact that people of that class in the East End will not give up one of their number to Gentile justice.

When his book was published, Anderson was criticised for the anti-Semitism of this passage, and he had to justify his observations in various contemporary newspapers and magazines. However, amid the controversy, an even more significant passage was largely overlooked, both at the time and for the next seventy-seven years: 'the only person who had ever had a good view of the murderer unhesitatingly identified the suspect the instant he was confronted with him; but he refused to give evidence against him'.

In 1987 the so-called 'Swanson marginalia' were discovered and received considerable publicity in the *Daily Telegraph*. Chief Inspector Donald Swanson was placed in overall charge of the Whitechapel Murders inquiry in September 1888. He retired in 1903 but kept in touch with his former colleague, Sir Robert Anderson, who later gave Swanson a presentation copy of his memoirs. At some point Swanson made a series of pencil comments in the margins, but of specific interest are those appended to the section quoted above, where he has written: 'and after this identification which suspect knew, no other murder of this kind took place in London'. He also notes that 'this identification' took place at the 'Seaside Home where he had been sent by us with great difficulty in order to subject him to identification, and he knew he was identified'.

The 'Seaside Home' is now presumed to be the Convalescent Police Seaside Home in Hove, which was opened in 1890. It seems that the police had a suspect and forced him to visit Hove, where he was officially identified, presumably by either Lawende or Schwartz. Swanson claims that this confrontation put an end to the murders because thereafter the suspect knew that he would be watched closely by the police. Further details are then given in the marginalia: 'in a very short time the suspect with his hands tied behind his back, he was sent to Stepney Workhouse and then to Colney Hatch and died shortly afterwards – Kosminski was the suspect – DSS'. Of course, if this is true, it answers a question that is often raised about Jack the Ripper: as he was never caught, why did the murders not continue into the 1890s?

The identification of Kosminski (no first name is given) brings us back to the confidential Macnaghten memorandum. In this, Macnaghten first states that 'no one ever saw the Whitechapel murderer' (which, of course, contradicts what has just been described), but then he mentions three people, 'any one of whom would have been more likely than Cutbush to have committed this series of murders': Montague Druitt, whom he describes as a doctor, Kosminski (like Swanson, Macnaghten does not include a first name) and Michael Ostrog. However, a generation of research has been able to demonstrate conclusively that neither Montague Druitt nor Michael Ostrog could have been Jack the Ripper. For example, although Druitt committed suicide in late 1888 and was in all likelihood insane, he seems to have taken his own life after being sacked from a teaching job at a school in Blackheath for sexual impropriety. While these issues make him an interesting suspect, research by Paul Begg has demonstrated that Druitt was playing cricket on the day after Mary Ann Nichols was murdered, and ten days after Mary Jane Kelly had been hacked to death he was present at a board meeting of his cricket club and gave no cause for concern. Thereafter he successfully represented the family business in an appeal held before Lord Chief Justice Coleridge and justices Manisty and Hawkins. None of this suggests the mental state of a man who had only recently obliterated Mary Jane. Whatever caused Druitt to take his own life, it seems unlikely that it was a result of his being Jack the Ripper. Meanwhile, Ostrog was a career criminal who spent most of his life in prison for a series of opportunistic thefts. Nothing in his record suggests that he could display the type of violence that was perpetrated against the Ripper's victims, and Begg goes as far as to say that the 'mystery is why anyone ever thought that he might have been [Jack the Ripper]'.

Macnaghten describes Kosminski as 'a Polish Jew, & resident in Whitechapel. This man became insane owing to many years indulgence in solitary vices. He had a great hatred of women, especially of the prostitute class, & had strong homicidal tendencies; he was removed to a lunatic asylum about March 1889. There were many circs [*sic*] connected with this man which made him a strong suspect.'

Kosminski

Two primary sources – Anderson's autobiography and Swanson's marginalia – provide us with details about someone they strongly suspected of being Jack the Ripper. Allied to these we also have Macnaghten's memorandum. In effect, all three tell the same story: a Polish Jew living in the heart of the murder area who had people to look after him was responsible for the murders, and he was eventually committed to an asylum on account of his 'solitary vices' by his family in 1889. A thorough search of asylum records by the author Martin Fido (2001) unearthed only one Kosminski who was admitted at this time – a young man named Aaron – and no other Kosminski has ever been located. So it is likely – although not certain – that this was Anderson and Swanson's suspect, even though some of the details that each provides are at odds with what we know from historical records.

Aaron Kosminski was born in Poland in 1865 and came to England as a seventeen-year-old in 1882. He lived with his brother Woolf at 3 Sion Square, a small street near Mulberry Street in Whitechapel. He was a barber, Jewish and unmarried. In July 1890, and on the instruction of his brother, Kosminski was admitted to the Mile End Old Town Workhouse as a way of controlling his behaviour, prior to being moved to a number of asylums. The reason given was 'two years insane' – that is, since

1888 – with the cause being 'self abuse'. He was then institutionalised for the rest of his life, dying in March 1919.

Various medical notes catalogue Kosminski's time in several asylums, describing his 'mania', 'delusions', 'hallucinations' and 'incoherence'. One comments on Kosminski's belief that 'he is guided and his movements altogether controlled by an instinct that informs his mind'. Others record that he once threatened to kill his sister. When he was admitted to the Leavesden Asylum in April 1894, his next of kin was recorded as his mother, who was living at 63 New Street, off New Road, in Whitechapel.

Unfortunately, the medical notes tell us little more about Kosminski, and they certainly do not provide an insight into his state of mind in 1888. However, they do suggest that he was incapable of looking after himself, and that his family could no longer cope with his mania – perhaps after he threatened to kill his sister. It is also worth pausing to consider the cause of his committal – 'self abuse' – which clearly meant excessive (perhaps even public) masturbation. This would now be described as hypersexuality – known to the Victorians as 'satyriasis' – and is characterised by an abnormal and compulsive need for frequent genital stimulation. However, no sexual or emotional satisfaction is ever gained by the sufferer, who may also succumb to bipolar disorder during periods of mania.

We should also reflect on the murder of Martha Tabram. Martha had been drinking with her friend Mary Ann and both had left in the company of two men, who were believed to have been soldiers. No soldier was ever identified by Mary Ann. Is it straining the historic record too much to suggest that this second man might have been Woolf Kosminski?

Was Aaron Kosminski Jack the Ripper? There is no way to be certain, although he was clearly a strong suspect at the time. Furthermore, he fits our modern-day profile of Jack the Ripper, based on the crimes that he committed: Kosminski was sexually incompetent, insane and protected by people until they could do so no longer. He also lived locally, which puts him in the same bracket as the vast majority of serial killers. They are literally 'the bloke next door', rather than a prince, a famous artist or a Liverpudlian who travelled to London to commit his crimes. The 'Ripper industry' has largely been built on myth and fantasy, and the wilder the hypothesis the more successful the book or film tends to be. However, a cold, rational look at the facts of these awful murders does not lead to a royal conspiracy or to any other 'celebrity suspect', but rather to a sad, disturbed, anonymous immigrant from the East End.

Six murdered women

While we can never be sure that Kosminski was Jack the Ripper, we do know the identities of the murderer's victims. Their stories reveal much about the risky nature of life led by working-class women in late Victorian times, and how easy it was for them to slip from relative comfort to abject squalor. For example, the lives of Mary Ann Nichols and Annie Chapman turned when maintenance payments from their former husbands stopped. Their lives – and those of the Ripper's other three victims – became dominated by the need to earn fourpence for a bed for the night, a task made all the more difficult by their addiction to alcohol. This latter dependence also often brought them into contact with the police: of course, Catherine Eddowes was released from the local station just before her murder. All of the 'canonical five' were problem drinkers, and some of them were clearly alcoholic. Selling sexual services either on a casual or more regular basis provided them with the means to keep their bodies and souls together, and with just enough to buy more alcohol. Each of them probably 'led a life of lies', to borrow Cornwell's phrase, in order to hide the desperation of a reality that kept them working the streets even when they knew there was a killer on the loose.

Five women's need to make money to feed an addiction made them enormously vulnerable to attack by a ruthless serial killer. It is a pattern that has been repeated many times over the last 130 years. Alcohol would eventually be replaced by heroin and crack, but the simple need to earn enough cash for the next drink or fix creates a sad and desperate connection between those who died at the hands of the Ripper and those who would become victims in the years that followed.

Chapter Three

'Women were his preoccupation': George Smith, George Chapman, Thomas Cream

> That the principle which regulates the existing social relations between the two sexes – the legal subordination of one sex to the other – is wrong itself, and now one of the chief hindrances to human improvement, and that it ought to be replaced by a principle of perfect equality, admitting no power or privilege on the one side, nor disability on the other.
>
> John Stuart Mill, *The Subjection of Women* (1869)

In 1851 the philosopher John Stuart Mill wrote to his fiancée Harriet Taylor to protest against the laws that would govern their impending marriage, which in effect amounted to a 'civil death' for Harriet. Simply by marrying, every woman's existence was surrendered under the common law doctrine of 'coverture' – literally, 'concealment'. Harriet's legal personality would be subsumed by the legal personality of her husband. A married woman could not sue or be sued unless her husband was also party to the suit; she could not sign a contract unless her husband joined her; she could not make a valid will unless her husband agreed to its contents. A husband also assumed legal rights over his wife's property, as well as any property that she subsequently inherited. Even a wife's personal possessions – including all of her clothing and any money that she might have saved or earned – passed entirely to her husband. Furthermore, a woman's body was held to belong to her husband, and it was only in 1891 that a High Court ruling denied a husband the right to imprison his wife in pursuit of his conjugal rights. The husband decided where the couple should live – often taking his new bride away from her family and friends – how their children should be brought up, and virtually every other aspect of their relationship. Most men saw nothing wrong with these 'rights'. By contrast, Mill gave Harriet 'a solemn promise never in any case or under any circumstances' to enforce them.

Unfortunately, Edith Pegler married a serial killer rather than a philosopher. She applied for a job as a housekeeper in Bristol in July 1908, and a few weeks later her new employer, George Joseph Smith, proposed marriage. Of course, she had no idea that her charming new fiancé was a convicted bigamist and fraudster, nor that he would eventually resort to murder. He roamed around the country – ostensibly 'on business' – rarely sending Edith any money to buy food, and demanding that she communicate with him only through the Woolwich Equitable building society. However, he always came home eventually, so she went back to live with him at his request. She dutifully moved with him from Bristol to Bedford, then to Luton, Southend-on-Sea, Croydon, Walthamstow, Tunbridge Wells and Bath. Every time he returned from his travels he would entertain her with stories of his money-making schemes – buying and selling Chinese figurines, oil paintings, and jewellery, then pumping the profits into property. He would sometimes bring her clothes, and tell her that baths were dangerous for women, especially women with weak hearts. When Edith was cross-examined at her husband's trial for the murder of three 'wives' – the true source of his income – she denied all knowledge of the other women. And when she was asked, almost incredulously, 'You went back to him when he asked you to go back?', she simply replied, 'Yes.'

Edith's straightforward reply reflects the legal and social position of women at the turn of the twentieth century. The Married Women's Property Acts of 1870 and 1882 had made a small attempt to redress the balance, but women were still denied the right to vote, they could not join most professions, and they had very limited access to higher education, all of which left them under intense pressure to 'marry well'. After all, the average wage for a single, working-class woman was well below subsistence level. Legal rules, social convention and economic structures conspired to force women into marriage and then ensured that they would be entirely dependent upon their husbands. In 1871 nearly 90 per cent of women between the ages of forty-five and forty-nine were currently or had been married. Edith Pegler remained with her husband because she had no other option in a hierarchical culture that was dominated by men – some of whom turned 'civil deaths' into actual ones. 'Power' and 'privilege' still rested firmly with the male of the species half a century after John Stuart Mill had called for 'perfect equality'.

This chapter is concerned with the ten women who were killed between 1891 and 1915 by Dr Thomas Neill Cream, George Chapman (who was born Severin Antoniovich Klosowski) and

George Joseph Smith. Both Cream and Chapman were once also thought to have been Jack the Ripper. Chapman's association with the Ripper originates with an offhand comment made by Inspector Frederick Abberline, who led the police investigation in Whitechapel between September 1888 and March 1889. Abberline is supposed to have congratulated the arresting officer in the Chapman case with the words, 'I see you've got Jack the Ripper at last.' He then tried to explain away Chapman's and the Ripper's markedly different modi operandi in the *Pall Mall Gazette*. The link between Cream and the Ripper is even more tenuous. It stems from the facts that he also murdered prostitutes and is reported to have said, 'I am Jack the . . . ' as the drop fell on the scaffold at Newgate on 15 November 1892. However, he was in prison in the United States between 1881 and 1891, serving a life sentence for murder. There is a much stronger link between Cream and Smith: the former's trial set a precedent in allowing cumulative evidence that indicated a 'pattern' to be admitted in court, and this was applied in Smith's case. Today, *Rex v. Smith* is still the determining case cited by lawyers who wish to introduce evidence of similar crimes.

It has been very difficult to reconstruct the lives of the women murdered by Cream, Chapman and Smith. However, as usual, the lives of the murderers themselves have been analysed extensively. Most of the literature relating to this trio attempts to demonstrate that their murderous intentions can be explained by carefully considering issues in their pasts, so all three life stories have been diligently researched. W.T. Shore, for example, who published the proceedings of Cream's trial in 1923, thought it was 'necessary to give his biography in as full as detail as possible' in order to understand the crimes that he had committed. We learn that he was a 'fast' and 'extravagant' medical student, who nevertheless taught Sunday school, and that he was given enough money by his father to maintain a 'stylish carriage and pair'.

As for Chapman, we know all about his early life in Nargornak, Poland, and that, at the age of fifteen, he was apprenticed to a surgeon in Zvolen. From there he joined the Russian Army before emigrating to England, where he changed his name. E.R. Watson, who published Smith's trial papers in 1922, notes that the murderer 'early displayed criminal tendencies . . . [and] speedily took to evil courses', serving time in prison before joining the Northamptonshire Regiment. Watson also muses on Smith's 'extraordinary power over women', claiming that his attraction was the result of 'a certain magnetism about the eyes' and even suggesting that he may have hypnotised his victims. In conclusion he says: 'George Joseph Smith was undoubtedly a male whose love for mastery over women, including the infliction on them of humiliation . . . approached the pathological limit where the normal masculine desire merges into sadism.'

These early theories about the motivations of killers – coming as they did when the disciplines of criminology and psychology were first emerging – mark the start of the medicopsychological tradition. Ever since, the story of the serial killer – rather than those of his victims – has become the means by which we try to understand the phenomenon of serial killing. The stories of those who died, and what characterised their lives, have all but disappeared. No one bothered to collect biographical information about their childhoods, schooldays, relationships, hopes or aspirations. Yet, if we were to look more closely at these details, we would undoubtedly see clear patterns emerging. Using a structural approach by focusing on the place of women in late Victorian and Edwardian society affords a much fuller explanation of why three men were able to kill repeatedly. And it certainly provides more insights than any number of interesting but speculative psychological theories about their individual motivations.

Because I have discussed prostitution and what drove women to it extensively in the previous chapter, I shall not dwell here on the crimes committed by Cream. Rather, I shall discuss at length the cases of Chapman and Smith, whose victims suffered from a more discreet, but no less oppressive, form of subjugation.

'You don't know what he is'

By October 1895, Mary Isabella Spink had been left by her husband because she was drinking far too much: it was suggested that she had 'intemperate habits'. She was short and plump, with blonde hair cut like a boy's, but she was far from destitute, having been left six hundred pounds by her grandfather – a common way to try to overcome coverture. Around this time she met George Chapman and they started a relationship. However, neither Mary nor George was free to marry. Mary had not been divorced by her husband, and Chapman seems to have been married at least twice before taking up with her. So, rather than risk being charged with bigamy, Mary and Chapman never attempted to marry in any official sense. Instead, they told their circle of friends that they were to wed, and on the appointed day simply drove off in a carriage around Hastings. They returned some hours later to be showered in confetti. Thereafter, they lived as husband and wife, and Chapman even 'adopted' Mary's ten-year-old son, Willie. Mary subsequently gave what remained of her inheritance to her new 'husband' so that he could open a barber's shop.

This business did not work out as well as they had hoped, perhaps because it was in the wrong part of Hastings, so Chapman leased another shop in George Street. He also hit on an idea for attracting customers: Mary was musical, so Chapman hired a piano on which she could entertain clients while they were being shaved. These 'musical shaves' proved to be very popular, a successful piece of entrepreneurship based on Mary's talents and her willingness to make something of the life that she shared with Chapman. In this respect, according to the account of Chapman's trial written by H.L. Adam in 1930, Mary was a 'social pioneer. Lady hairdressers were unknown at the end of the last century, yet Mrs Spink lathered all her husband's customers; later she even on occasions tried shaving them.' This perhaps gives an indication of what Mary might have achieved in a different age and culture.

We know some other details of the couple's life in Hastings. Chapman bought a small sailing boat, the *Mosquito*, with the profits from the second barber's shop. He boasted that he would one day sail it across the English Channel to Boulogne, but he never had the nautical skills to achieve such a feat. Nevertheless, he was always 'appropriately dressed' in sailing costume when he took the boat out on the water. This desire to look and act the part was a prominent feature of Chapman's personality. He had even changed his name in order to assimilate better into the culture of England, taking his surname from a former girlfriend, Annie Chapman. To him, it must have seemed far more suitable than the Polish Klosowski. 'Consistent mendacity was one of Chapman's main characteristics,' wrote Adam, with Chapman regularly boasting not only of his sailing prowess but of his sporting expertise and big game adventures. There was a restlessness in him, displayed by his constant desire to move on both socially and geographically. He clearly wanted to improve himself, but rather than taking the time to master a particular skill, he tended simply to fabricate stories of his successes and achievements.

On one occasion the *Mosquito* capsized and Chapman and Mary had to be rescued. This may have been a first, botched attempt by Chapman to rid himself of a 'wife' who was no longer wanted or needed, having served her purpose in setting him up in business. Chapman had a history of adultery before he met Mary, and by now he had started to flirt with a domestic servant called Alice Penfold, telling her he was single and the owner of a piano shop. He had also taken over the lease on a public house called the Prince of Wales in Bartholomew Square, off City Road, in London, and it seems he asked Alice to join him there. But Mary was still in the way, so Chapman started looking for a new means to eliminate her, one from which she could not be rescued. He had gained a rudimentary medical training in Poland, so understood something about chemicals and their effects on the human body. Probably using this knowledge, he purchased some tartar emetic from one his customers, a local chemist called Davidson.

Tartar emetic is a poisonous crystalline compound derived from potassium antimony, and it is extremely toxic unless used in very small doses. The Victorians used it as an expectorant in the treatment of parasitic infections, and as a way to loosen and clear mucous and phlegm from the respiratory tract. Given the toxic nature of the compound, Davidson fixed a label to the bottle that he gave to Chapman that clearly stated: 'Poison. Tartar Emetic. Dose – one-sixth to a quarter. To be taken with Caution'. Chapman duly signed Davidson's 'poisons book' on 3 April 1897 – as was required by law – probably believing that the book would not come back to haunt him because he and Mary would soon be leaving Hastings, to run the Prince of Wales in London.

In spite of her history of drinking, up to this point Mary's health had never been a cause for concern. So, as Adam puts it, 'it was astonishing, therefore, that, after only a few months of life at the Prince of Wales, this long spell of good health should completely break down'. This hardly does justice to the pain that Mary must have experienced, for tartar emetic produces severe vomiting, diarrhoea and debilitating abdominal pain.

Even a small dose of the drug – a white powder that is easily soluble in water – can be lethal, and Mary was almost immediately confined to bed after Chapman started to poison her. He engaged a neighbour, Martha Doubleday, to nurse his wife and to help at the bar. She persuaded Chapman to call in the local GP, Dr Rogers, who would eventually be much criticised at Chapman's trial.

Mary finally died on Christmas Day 1897. Chapman, 'in the eyes of those who were present at the end [gave the impression of being] an attached husband, prostrated with grief'. In reality, of course, Chapman had once again acted to propel himself forward, this time not just by changing his name or by staging a sham wedding but by murder, while all the time appearing to those around him to fit in and be just like them. However, there may have been some raised eyebrows when he overcame his grief sufficiently to open the Prince of Wales that Christmas Day, and when he dispatched his adopted son Willie to the Shoreditch Work house a little later.

After Mary died, Chapman advertised for a barmaid. Elizabeth Taylor – known as 'Bessie' – applied and got the job. (By this time, it seems that Alice Penfold had wisely decided to have nothing more to do with Chapman, even though she had unwittingly provided his motive for murdering Mary.) Bessie had been a domestic servant, and was the daughter of a cattle dealer from Warrington called Thomas Parsonage Taylor. Chapman soon proposed to her, and in early 1898 the pair performed a similar charade to his previous 'marriage' to Mary. Thereafter, again just as Chapman had done with Mary, they lived as husband and wife.

We know little about Bessie, other than the fact that she enjoyed cycling, which she used to practise outside the Prince of Wales. Chapman – as ever, desperate to fit in – seems to have become a keen cyclist, too: he rode with the local police cycling team when they went on outings. Soon, though, he gave up the lease on the Prince of Wales and moved with Bessie to a pub in Bishop's Stortford called the Grapes. At this point Bessie's health began to deteriorate. The couple did not stay at the Grapes for long, moving back to London to take up the lease on the Monument Tavern in Union Street. It was here, on 13 February 1901, that Bessie died. Her death certificate listed the cause of death as 'exhaustion from vomiting and diarrhoea'. She was buried back in Cheshire, some five miles from where she had been born. It seems likely that Chapman – yet again playing the grieving widower – wrote the inscription on her gravestone:

> Farewell my friends, fond and dear,
> Weep not for me a single tear,
> For all that was and could be done
> You plainly see my time has come.

In reality, of course, her 'time' had been accelerated by the actions of Chapman, who had discovered a highly effective way to dispose of unwanted 'wives'. There was no obvious motive for his killing of Bessie, though, so perhaps Adam's conclusion that Chapman's '*idée fixe* [was] the pursuit, the capture and destruction of women' is correct. He does seem to have relished the pursuit and capture of women, but once the reality of making a life with them was under way he was determined to find a way out, even if that meant resorting to murder.

Soon another barmaid started working for Chapman. Maud Marsh applied for the job in August 1901, when she was living with her parents in Croydon. Maud's mother Eliza – who was suspicious of Chapman from the start, and would prove an excellent prosecution witness at his trial – travelled with her to the interview at the Monument Tavern. As ever, Chapman was plausible, saying that he was a widower and that a family was currently living above the pub – a lie told to encourage Eliza to allow her nineteen-year-old daughter to stay at the tavern. Maud took the job and within a few weeks Chapman was starting to woo her with presents, such as a gold watch and chain. Several months later, they were 'married'. Eliza was far from happy, though, and perhaps for the first time Chapman had to face a family that refused to accept his bland assurances that a ceremony had taken place. Maud's mother demanded to see the marriage certificate, but of course none could be produced. However, in attempting to protect her daughter, Eliza may simply have hastened her demise. It seems that Chapman was understandably very worried by the enquiries she was making.

There was another motive for this murder, too. Before Maud fell ill, a new barmaid called Florence Raynor had begun to work for Chapman. As usual, he could not resist flirting with her, and even asked her to move with him to the United States. At Chapman's trial Florence – who did little to discourage these advances – claimed she pointed out, 'You have your wife and don't want me.' At which point Chapman snapped his fingers and described how he 'could give her [Maud] that and she would be no more Mrs Chapman'. Very soon afterwards, Maud began to suffer from dreadful abdominal pains, sickness and diarrhoea.

Prior to this point Maud and her sister had gone for a walk together and Maud had started to cry before confiding that Chapman beat her regularly and declaring, 'You don't know what he is.' So when Maud's sister and the rest of the family came to the tavern to nurse her the tension must have been considerable. Chapman, though, insisted that he should still prepare everything she ate and drank. Eliza ensured that Dr Stoker – a local GP who had previously attended to Bessie – was called in to examine her daughter, but he remained baffled as to what might be causing the illness. Maud was eventually sent to Guy's Hospital, where she made a brief recovery. However, having returned home, her health deteriorated throughout the autumn of 1902. Fearing the worst, Eliza called in her own doctor, Dr Grapel from Croydon, to consult with Dr Stoker. At first, he too was baffled, but on his return to Croydon he telegraphed Stoker to suggest that Maud was being poisoned. But he came to the correct conclusion too late: Maud died on 22 October 1902, just fourteen months after meeting Chapman.

Grapel's telegraph at last prompted Stoker into some action: he refused to sign the death certificate. Three days later, Chapman was arrested, and a post-mortem revealed that Maud had nearly seventeen grams of 'tartarated antimony' in her stomach. A fraction of that amount would normally be lethal. The bodies of Bessie and Mary were subsequently exhumed: Bessie had over twenty-three grams of antimony in her stomach; and even though Mary had died five years previously, there was still over a gram in hers.

While awaiting trial in his cell, Chapman continued to play the dutiful husband. In a move that angered Maud's family, he sent a wreath of lilies, tuberoses, camellias and pink chrysanthemums, all tied up with a violet ribbon, to the funeral. There was also a card stating, 'In Memoriam', and below that the inscription: 'From a devoted friend, G.C.'

Adam reports that the judge at the trial, Mr Justice Grantham, 'embarked on a severe censure of the entire [medical] profession ... This reproof was occasioned by the invariable failure of doctors to detect, and incidentally frustrate, the operations of the secret poisoner.' Furthermore, Grantham noted that when Mary died in 1897:

> Dr Rogers actually gives a certificate for something which could not, by any possibility, have been the cause of her death, and by that certificate prevents any examination being made, and if it was not that, fortunately, in this country at any rate, cremation is not the usual system – if it had been, by no possibility, could these poisonings have been discovered, and I hope it will be taken as a warning that our churchyards should not be shut up, and that people should not say we should not bury in the churchyard.

The jury took precisely eleven minutes to find Chapman guilty of murder. He was executed on 7 April 1903.

Doctors, lawyers, landlords and, of course, a husband (albeit a fake one) dominated the lives of these three women and created the circumstances in which they were made vulnerable. That vulnerability was then scandalously exploited by Chapman, but the simple truth is that all men benefited from a culture that gave them legal, social and financial power and precedence over their wives.

George Smith's modus operandi

There are many similarities between George Chapman and George Joseph Smith. Both used aliases, with Smith at various times calling himself 'George Love', 'George Rose', 'Henry Williams', 'Charles Oliver James' and 'John Lloyd'. Both were restless, always moving from one place to another and rarely staying put for any length of time. In the criminological literature relating to serial killers this practice would earn them the label 'geographically transient'. Chapman was born in Poland and lived in the USA before settling in England, while Smith talked of emigrating to Canada or the USA, but all of their crimes were committed in England. Whereas nowadays a geographically transient killer might roam from state to state or country to country, in Chapman and Smith's time simply moving from town to town helped them evade detection. Their relocations never amounted to more than a few hundred miles, but just by crossing a county boundary, and moving into a different police force area, they could leave their earlier crimes behind.

However, their greatest similarity was in their choice of victim. Both targeted women, with Chapman going through his sham marriage ceremonies and Smith bigamously marrying his future victims in a church or register office. For example, Smith legally married Beatrice Thornhill in Leicester in January 1898, but less than a year later he married an unidentified 'Miss' at St George's, Hanover Square Registry, London. Thereafter he spent two years in prison, prior to marrying Edith Pegler in Bristol in 1908. At least that marriage was legal (by then, Smith had divorced Beatrice Thornhill), and he would remain officially married to Edith for the rest of his life.

Nevertheless, on 17 September 1914, Smith married Alice Reavil, a domestic servant whom he had met in Bournemouth only nine days previously. Alice's story – which she told in full at Smith's trial (Watson, 1922) – graphically demonstrates the speed with which he worked, what he hoped to gain and how devastated his surviving victims were on discovering his fraud.

> On 7 or 8 September I was in the gardens on the front, sitting on a seat, when a man came and spoke to me ... We had some

> conversation, in which he said he admired my figure. After an hour's conversation, in which he informed me he was an artist, and had £2 per week from some land in Canada, he made an appointment for 6 p.m. the same evening. I met him as arranged; he did not tell me where he was staying; I never knew. Next day I met him as arranged, and he then told me his name was 'Charles Oliver James'. He said he had been to Canada and his agents sent him money. He also said he understood I had some money. I met him every evening ... after the third or fourth day of our acquaintance he asked me to marry him, and I consented, and he said he would put his money with mine and he would open an antique shop ... he asked how much money I had, and I said about £70 odd, and some furniture, including a piano. He asked me to sell them, and I decided to ... We went to the registry office and were married by special licence.

It is worth pausing here to assess Smith's methods in more detail, and to reflect on the wider significance of what Alice described. Note the lies that Smith told – starting with his name, but also his claims that he had a regular income, that he was an artist and that he had entrepreneurial goals. An antique shop must have seemed aspirational to Alice, as would stories of Canada and the agents who sent Smith his fictitious weekly income. However, all his talk of money was designed merely to get Alice to reveal details of her own savings and property. Smith quickly – on the third or fourth day – turned the conversation to a marriage proposal. The speed with which it was accepted surely reflects the importance of marriage for a woman locked in a hierarchical, paternal culture. Furthermore, Alice did not hesitate to sell her piano and other items because being married was far more important than any number of possessions. Having sold everything she owned, she raised just £14 – the equivalent of about £1,000 today.

Alice continued her story with details of what happened after she married Smith:

> We … went to 8 Hafer Road, Battersea Rise [Wandsworth, London] where he had taken two furnished rooms … on the way he showed me a lot of bank notes, and he asked me for my £14 to put in the bank with his. I gave it to him. When we got to our lodgings … he produced a post office withdrawal form for me to fill up to draw all my money from the bank. I filled it up, and added, 'with interest to close account', and we went out together to post it … he put it in the box. All my clothing was at this address, and was kept in four boxes … On 21 September we went to the post office, Lavender Hill, to obtain the money … he told me to ask for all £1 notes, but they gave me four £10 notes and two £5 notes, and the remainder in £1 notes and cash. In all I received £76 6s and some coppers. He picked up the notes and the cash – the odd six shillings. I never saw the notes again.

Alice explained that they returned to their lodgings in Battersea Rise and paid the bill with a view to moving on to new premises the following day. Smith also arranged for their newly packed possessions to be taken to a locker in Clapham Station. At Smith's trial, Alice related what happened the following morning:

> On 22 September we left the house … we got on a tramcar, and on the way he spoke of Halifax, Nova Scotia, and asked me if I would like to go. He took some penny fares, and we got off at some gardens. We walked through the gardens,

> and on getting to the other end he said he was going to the lavatory, and asked me to wait. I did so, and waited about an hour. He did not return, so I returned to 8 Hafer Road, and found the attached telegram waiting for me. [It read, 'Wait home for letter. Next post – James.']

The letter was clearly designed to stop Alice reporting the day's events to the police. Obviously, she would have feared that something had happened to Smith, but with this cunning device he eased her concerns and, more importantly, gave himself the opportunity to escape. While Alice waited for the post, Smith travelled to Clapham Station and removed all of their possessions. He then returned to Edith Pegler in Bristol, where he gave his ever-loyal wife Alice's trousseau! Alice sadly concluded her evidence: 'the result on my meeting with [the] prisoner was that I was left with only a few shillings and the clothes I was actually wearing. What he had taken consisted of the whole of my life's savings.'

However, Alice was lucky, because she was defrauded in the middle of his period of killing. He had already claimed the lives of two 'wives', and shortly after running out on Alice he would murder a third.

'I suppose I may go with my husband'

George Smith married Bessie Mundy on 26 August 1910 and killed her in July 1912. Of the three murders he committed this first one is perhaps the most tragic, because it reveals something of the desperation of women in Bessie's position in Edwardian England. She was thirty-three in 1910, living comfortably in Weymouth on the proceeds of some £2,500 left in trust for her by her father, who had been a bank manager. Bessie received her income from the trustees, headed by her uncle, who sent her eight pounds a week. Smith – styling himself Henry Williams – told Bessie that he was a thirty-five-year-old bachelor and a picture restorer. Interestingly, Smith regularly presented himself as a painter, or as involved in the art world in some capacity. He might have thought this afforded him some cachet, or perhaps he concluded that it would allow him to breach normal social conventions and thus swiftly become intimate with his intended victim. It certainly worked in this case, as Smith quickly gained Bessie's confidence and they married soon after their first meeting. On their wedding day he instructed a local Weymouth solicitor called Wilkinson (who would give evidence at the trial) to request a copy of the trust's papers from the Mundys' family solicitor. However, the trust had been set up well and Smith apparently could not find a way to get his hands on his new wife's inheritance. Consequently, he had to make do with what Bessie had in the bank, around £150, and in her lodgings. Just over two weeks after their marriage, he absconded from Weymouth, leaving Bessie to clear up the mess. It would be almost two years before she met her husband again.

In a remarkable coincidence, they were both in Weston-super-Mare in spring 1912. Bessie was staying at a local boarding house called Norwood House, which was owned by a friend of her aunt, Mrs Sarah Tuckett. On 14 March Bessie went out to buy some flowers and en route she spotted her missing husband looking out at sea. Of course, an alternative reading is that this meeting was no coincidence. Smith might have thought he had devised a way to access Bessie's trust fund, had somehow found out where she was staying, and had travelled there to be 'discovered' by her. Whatever the truth, he had some explaining to do about why he had left Bessie in Weymouth, an abandonment that must have caused her severe embarrassment within her social circle. The reunited couple visited a local solicitor, Wadsworth Burrow Lillington, of Baker and Company, on the day of their chance meeting. Years later, Lillington provided some details of Smith's smooth talking at the latter's trial:

> He began by informing me that he had been for some time seeking his wife, and that he had that day casually met her in the street. He then explained to me the circumstances in which he alleged he had left his wife in Weymouth. He said that he believed at the time, although it had subsequently proved to be incorrect, that he had contracted a contagious disease, that he feared to communicate it to his wife, and that therefore he thought it better that he should leave her.

It is impossible to say whether Bessie believed this story to be the truth, or if she merely wanted to believe it, but she was sufficiently convinced to take him back (in spite of the obvious implication in Smith's statement that at the time of their marriage he had contracted a venereal disease). Having made his confession, Smith asked Lillington to write to Bessie's uncle in the hope of establishing better relations between them.

Lillington duly did so.

At the trial, Lillington was asked to describe Bessie's demeanour during this meeting. The solicitor replied that she was in the 'assenting manner. I should say that she had very little indeed to say, except that she did reply to any question that I put to her. I think she volunteered the statement that she had forgiven the past.' Bessie's 'assenting manner', her reluctance to speak unless spoken to and her forgiving nature were all esteemed qualities of the idealised wife in early twentieth-century Britain. They were also perfectly consistent with the doctrine of coverture – Bessie's (supposed) husband had certain rights over her that were upheld by the law of the land. The fact that they went to a solicitor on the day of their apparently coincidental meeting suggests that Smith was fully aware of these rights, and it explains why Lillington did very little to challenge such an incredible story.

Of course, Bessie could have behaved differently. She did not have to give Smith the benefit of the doubt. But as a middle-class woman schooled in the formalities of Edwardian culture, she had to try to make her marriage work, even though that marriage was to a man she had not seen for nearly two years. On the other hand, Bessie's landlady was much less forgiving of Smith: Mrs Tuckett was far from impressed by him, his return or any explanation that he offered. She also telegraphed Bessie's aunt to inform her of what had happened. Reading between the lines, she had clearly tried to stop Bessie leaving with Smith. Mrs Tuckett and Smith seem to have had an argument, and Smith had then used it as a pretext to move on. Bessie had told her landlady, 'I suppose I may go with my husband', to which Mrs Tuckett had reluctantly replied, 'I cannot hold you back, you are thirty.'

Mrs Tuckett never saw Bessie again, although Smith wrote to her the following day. In his letter he mentioned the 'heated argument' that had taken place, and said that, 'for the sake of peace', he and Bessie had left. The letter continued:

> All I propose to state at present beside that which has already been stated by Bessie and myself before the solicitors that it is useless *as the law stands* [emphasis added], and in view of all the circumstances, together with the affinity existing between my wife and self, for any person to try and part us, and dangerous to try and do us harm or to try and do us harm or endeavour to make our lives miserable ... Bessie shall soon

> have a settled, comfortable home and be happy with me. I trust there are many many years of happiness before us.

Here again we can detect Smith's familiarity with the law: he knew how it protected him as a 'husband'. There are also some threats, which indicate that Smith was dangerous as well as educated.

The couple moved to the other side of the country, Herne Bay, where Smith took further legal advice about Bessie's trust fund. Counsel's opinion was sent to him on 2 July 1912. It suggested that if mutual wills were made – each favouring the other – then Bessie's fund would come to Smith if she died and he survived her. This amounted to Bessie's death warrant. A mere five days after the mutual wills were drawn up, on 13 July, Bessie was found drowned in her bath. By the end of the year Smith was in possession of all of Bessie's estate.

How Bessie came to be drowned in her bath was still a matter for speculation several years later, when Smith was brought to justice. The record of his trial states simply that he used 'certain means' to drown his victims, but no elaboration is offered. Perhaps Watson feared that by publishing the details he might encourage what we would now call 'copy-cat' crimes. However, the authorities knew how Smith had managed to drown Bessie without leaving any tell-tale bruising. An experiment was undertaken in early 1915 by the pathologist Sir Bernard Spilsbury and Detective Inspector Arthur Neil. Using a nurse in a bathing suit as their guinea pig, they discovered that if they pulled her ankles in the air while she was sitting in the bath, her head would slip under the water and she could not move. This experiment was so 'successful' that it took some thirty minutes of artificial respiration before Neil and Spilsbury were able to revive the nurse!

'The money is payable on demand'

Smith would kill two more 'wives' in this manner: Alice Burnham, whom he married on 4 November 1913 and who was dead by 12 December that year; and Margaret Lofty, whom he married on 17 December 1914 and murdered the following day. As is obvious from these dates, the frequency of Smith's crimes increased as he became a more competent killer – a trend that can be found with most serial killers. Furthermore, the time between 'marriage' and murder decreased markedly: Bessie was killed after nearly two years, Alice survived for only five weeks and Margaret was murdered just hours after her marriage. This does not reveal that Smith preferred Alice to Margaret and so gave her a stay of execution. Rather, it indicates that he needed time to extract money from her family.

Alice was twenty-five years old when she married Smith. She lived in Aston Clinton in Buckinghamshire, where her father Charles was a fruit grower. A stout but healthy woman, she worked as a nurse. Her family did not like Smith, although no reason is given for their antipathy in the trial papers, which merely state that Charles thought Smith was 'evil' and did not like his behaviour. As a result of the family's opposition, Smith and Alice travelled to Southsea, and they were married in Portsmouth register office. This time, Smith used his own name on the marriage certificate. The day before the wedding he had insured Alice's life for five hundred pounds – although the relevant paperwork was not completed until 4 December – and four days after that she made a will in favour of her husband. Smith also started to extract money from the Burnham family.

Charles had given Alice a promissory note for a hundred pounds to be paid on her marriage, and Smith now set out to obtain this money. However, Charles did not give in easily, so Smith wrote to him, complaining of his new father-in-law's 'obdurateness, contempt and remorse ... what earthly right have you to scorn your daughter in these ways?' It seems that Charles had previously written to Alice to suggest that Smith should not be given access to the promissory note. But Smith was having none of it, and threatened: 'It is mentioned in the letter Alice received on the 11th instant that as I have an income – the £100 and interest should stand over. A more foolish and illegal action I have never heard. The money is payable on demand, failing which I will take the matter up myself without further delay.'

Nevertheless, Charles still delayed giving Smith any money, which infuriated his son-in-law. He also made enquiries into Smith's background, approaching a Mr Redhead of Horwood and James solicitors to see if he could establish anything about Smith's past. Having got wind of this, Smith wrote to Charles on 24 November, sarcastically claiming: 'my mother was a Buss horse, my father a Cab-driver, my sister a roughrider over the arctic regions – my brothers were all gallant sailors on a steam-roller'. Three days later he wrote again, this time with more menace: 'I do not know your next move, but take my advice and be careful.'

Meanwhile, Alice had written to her father to ask him to release the money as promised. Charles finally relented, perhaps because of Alice's request but more likely because Smith had the law on his side and would surely win any court case brought on the matter. In his evidence at Smith's trial, Charles explained: '[on the] advice of my solicitor I drew up a cheque for the money which I owed to my daughter'. This was cashed on 1 December 1913. Eleven days later, Alice was found dead in her bathtub in Blackpool, where the pair had moved from Southsea.

Margaret Lofty was thirty-eight when she married Smith just over a year later in Bath. On their marriage certificate Smith used the name 'John Lloyd' and claimed he was a land agent.

Margaret's father was the late Reverend Fitzroy Fuller Lofty, who died in 1892, leaving a widow, a son and two other daughters. She worked as a companion to elderly ladies in cathedral cities, but clearly aspired to a better life through marriage. However, she had been disappointed in love the year before she met Smith, when she discovered that the man she was courting was already married. Perhaps this goes some way towards explaining her eagerness to engage with Smith. She seems to have guessed that her mother and sisters would not have approved of Smith, so she married him clandestinely. By the time of the ceremony, Smith had already persuaded Margaret to take out a life assurance policy with the Yorkshire Insurance Company in Bristol for the sum of seven hundred pounds. The newly married couple immediately left Bath for Highgate, where Smith had booked rooms. The next morning Margaret visited a firm of solicitors in Islington to make her will, in which she bequeathed everything to her new husband. Later she withdrew all of her savings from the Muswell Hill post office. That evening she took a bath.

Death by drowning in their baths of three newly married brides in as many years produced sympathetic notices in various regional newspapers. However, the relatives and friends of Smith's first two 'wives' – as well as Sir Arthur Conan Doyle – were suspicious of the supposedly grieving husband, and they took their concerns to the police. Smith's money-making scheme finally began to unravel as several regional forces put two and two together, and he was eventually arrested on 1 February 1915. Watson notes that at his trial 'women thronged round him in the dock . . . at the Old Bailey the police had special instructions to make it as difficult as possible for women to be present'. His charisma failed to save him, though, and he was executed seven months later at HMP Maidstone.

Watson's description of Smith's trial is part of his attempt to paint a picture of personal responsibility that centres on the 'mysterious powers' that Smith supposedly used to seduce women. This is entirely consistent with the medico-psychological tradition of theorising about serial killers. Watson is less keen to acknowledge that Smith was merely a grotesque reflection of the male-dominated, hierarchical culture of late Victorian and Edwardian Britain; and that his 'mysterious powers' were not unique to him, but rather commonly enshrined in the law, customs and practices of the times. To achieve his ends, Smith had been obliged to deal with male lawyers, insurance agents, estate agents, bankers and a host of other professionals. Yet none of these highly educated men had thought that his actions and demands were unusual or suspicious. Wadsworth Burrow Lillington, for example, carried out his client's demands to the letter in spite of the fantastic nature of the story he had just been told. Moreover, Smith himself was fully aware of his legal rights in relation to his wives' property, and he wasted no opportunity to inform others of those rights if the situation demanded it – as it had with Charles Burnham.

So George Smith's 'mysterious powers' were not so mysterious after all: they were simply the ruthless exercise of power based on gender and marital status. Any single woman, especially one past the normal 'marrying age', could not afford to ignore the attentions of a suitor, no matter how recently they had met, nor how obsessively interested he seemed to be in her finances.

'Wretched women'

Louisa Harris – also known as 'Lou Harvey' – was picked up by a man outside St James's restaurant, London, on 20 October 1891. She then spent the night with him at a hotel in Berwick

Street. She told the man that she was 'a servant, but that was not correct', because Lou earned her living by selling sexual services. Her need for money had recently become more desperate because her partner – Charles Harvey, 'an omnibus man' – had lost his job only a few days previously.

During their night together, Lou's client told her that he was a doctor from the United States. No doubt hoping to impress her, he casually mentioned that Lou might like to move there with him. In the morning, he noticed that Lou had some spots on her forehead, and he said he could provide her with some pills to remove the blemishes. They arranged to meet later that day on the Embankment, near Charing Cross Station, from where they would go on to the Oxford music hall. But Lou was suspicious, so decided to bring Charles Harvey along for protection.

She was right to be worried. Her client was indeed a doctor, but he was also an arsonist, abortionist, blackmailer and convicted murderer (of an elderly man in the United States). He had also already murdered two prostitutes since arriving in England at the beginning of the month, having recently been released from prison in Illinois. Thomas Neill Cream had qualified at McGill University in Canada, and he spent some time doing postgraduate work at St Thomas's Hospital in London in 1876, prior to being admitted to the Royal Colleges of Physicians and Surgeons in Edinburgh in 1877. According to W.T. Shore, who edited his trial papers, Cream 'embarked upon his career of murder and medical malpractices with a quite adequate knowledge of medicine and surgery'. He was also a drug addict, and in all likelihood insane.

Lou met up with Cream as planned, with Charles watching from a safe distance. However, Cream explained that some pressing medical matters at St Thomas's meant he could not attend the music hall immediately, so would have to catch up with Lou later that evening. He had remembered the pills, though, so he took Lou to the Northumberland Arms, where he bought her some wine and figs, which he told her to eat after she had taken the tablets. She pretended to swallow the pills, but cleverly palmed them before throwing them away. Thinking that she had taken the medicine, Cream gave her five shillings for a cab and said he would meet her later. Of course, he never showed up, and it would be another three weeks before Lou saw him again – this time in Piccadilly Circus. He didn't remember her at first, but after he had taken her to a pub in Air Street he asked her name. It gradually dawned on him who she was, whereupon he turned smartly on his heel and walked away.

Cream's modus operandi was to poison his victims with pills laced with strychnine. As would have been the case if Lou had swallowed the tablets, he was never present when they died. This allowed him to create an alibi, and meant he did not have to witness the distressing effects of strychnine poisoning. According to Shore, Cream gained pleasure from 'a mixture of sexual mania and sadism. He may have had a half-crazy delight in feeling that the lives of the wretched women whom he slew lay in his power, that he was the arbiter of their fates.' An associate who knew Cream well would later write in the *St James's Gazette*: 'Women were his preoccupation, and his talk of them far from agreeable. He carried pornographic photographs, which he was too ready to display . . . he was a degenerate of filthy desires and practices.'

Of course, Cream was not the first and would not be the last serial killer to seek out the services of prostitutes, who would be more willing than other women to indulge a client's sexual peccadilloes. The fact that Cream showed acquaintances pornographic pictures suggests that he was either an exhibitionist or a very poor judge of Victorian social convention and morality.

Such a lack of judgement was no doubt exacerbated by his drug taking and mental illness.

In total, Cream murdered four 'wretched women', all by strychnine poisoning: Ellen Donworth, Matilda Clover, Alice Marsh and Emma Shrivell. He also attempted to murder Violet Beverley but she, like Lou Harvey, was suspicious and survived simply by refusing to swallow the 'American drink' he had prepared for her. We know only a few details about each of Cream's victims.

Matilda Clover was 'a pleasant-looking young woman, with somewhat prominent teeth'. She was twenty-seven at the time of her death, a single mother of one son, and lodged in two rooms on the top floor of a house in Lambeth Road, owned by a Mrs Phillips. As it was rather delicately put at Cream's trial, Matilda was 'in the habit of bringing men back with her' to her lodgings, and there is some evidence to suggest that Mrs Phillips was running a brothel. Lucy Rose, a servant who worked in the house, testified at Cream's trial, and her evidence gives some indication of the agonising death all four women must have suffered. She was woken by loud screams coming from Matilda's rooms, and on investigating further:

> I found her lying across the foot of the bed with her head fixed between the bedstead and the wall. She told me that she had been poisoned by pills given her by the gentleman. She was apparently in great agony. During her agony she screamed as if in great pain. There were moments when she appeared to have relief, and then the fits came on again. When the fits were upon her she was all of a twitch. She said once she thought that she was going to die, and she said that she'd like to see her baby.

Ellen Donworth was nineteen when Cream poisoned her, while Alice Marsh and Emma Shrivell, 'two unfortunate girls who had come up from Brighton', were twenty-one and eighteen, respectively. Cream enjoyed some bottled beer and tinned salmon in Alice and Emma's rooms before he poisoned them. They survived just long enough to explain what had happened.

After he had killed each of his victims, Cream attempted to extort money from various people he claimed were responsible for the murders. He also wrote strange letters to, for example, the Deputy Coroner of East Surrey, informing him of his theories. He claimed that Frederick Smith, the heir to the W.H. Smith's retail empire, had killed Ellen Donworth, and that Earl Russell and the royal physician Sir William Broadbent were responsible for two of the other murders. This narcissistic desire to gain celebrity from the murders that they have committed is common in many serial killers, and often helps in their arrest. Cream was ultimately caught because he attempted to blackmail a fellow lodger and doctor, Walter Joseph Harper. When the police visited their shared lodgings they quickly identified not Harper but Cream from descriptions provided by his dying victims. He was arrested on 3 June 1892 and executed at Newgate on 15 November that year.

Cream's story is significant not because he was Jack the Ripper (as I have mentioned, he could not have been), nor because he is a classic example of the 'power/control' serial killer typology. Rather, he is of interest for structural reasons. People like Thomas Neill Cream have existed in every society throughout history, and many of them will have wanted to exert their power and control over others by killing them. However, such people are able to achieve that objective only at certain points in history and in specific locations. At other times and in other places they find it impossible to murder repeatedly, and thus are denied the opportunity to become serial killers. Tragically for the ten victims who have featured in this chapter, in late Victorian and Edwardian England the law, social conventions and customs, and especially the economic status of single women, conspired to allow deranged, dangerous men to murder time and time again.

Chapter Four

'Corpses don't talk': English murder, English miracle

> Of course I still saw only a handful of criminal cases each year. Murder is not rife in England, as it is in some countries: it is comparatively rare. The London area, which has more than its fair share, gets only about 50 murders a year; and only about 150 to 160 cases – the figure has been remarkably constant since the beginning of the century – occur annually in the whole of England and Wales.
>
> Keith Simpson, *Forty Years of Murder* (1978)

George Smith murdered his third victim, Margaret Lofty, on 18 December 1914 – a month or so after the first Battle of Ypres. Thereafter, for almost three decades, until Reginald ('Reg') Christie started his killing spree with the murder of Ruth Fuerst in August 1943, no serial killers were active in Britain. This remarkable fact is both fascinating and important, as it might provide a clue to how we could avoid spates of serial murder in the future. The British figures are even more noteworthy when compared with the number of serial killers who were active in Germany in the same period: between 1920 and 1940 there were a dozen documented cases of German serial killers, including the so-called 'Vampire of Düsseldorf', Peter Kurten, who was charged with nine murders in April 1931; Fritz Haarmann, who killed twenty-four male prostitutes in Hanover between 1919 and 1924; and Bruno Ludke, who may have murdered as many as fifty-one people over a fifteen-year period that began in 1928.

So how are we to explain our lack of serial killers when the Weimar Republic (1919–33) and the Third Reich (1933–45) had so many? What was it about our culture at that time that deterred serial murderers, while the Germans encountered them on such a regular basis? Keith Simpson, the first Professor of Forensic Medicine at London University, suggests that it was simply a consequence of the relative lack of murder as a whole in Britain between the two world wars. This phenomenon was even noted at the time, with *The Times* suggesting that murder was so fully under control that only 'one . . . baffled the police in 1937'. British inter-war crime figures generally and the murder rate in particular have been investigated repeatedly ever since. Some historians and criminologists describe what happened as the 'English miracle', given that the country's rising population was not matched by an increasing crime rate. Moreover, the comparative stability in the recorded crime figures can be traced even further back: for example, in 1857 there were 91,671 indictable offences recorded by the police; in 1906, despite a doubling of the population accompanied by rapid industrialisation and urbanisation, the number of recorded crimes stood at 91,665. Can this be explained simply by the development of forensic science and the increasing competence of the police deterring potential criminals, including serial killers, from committing crimes? Or were there broader forces at work?

How much murder?

According to *Criminal Statistics*, the annual compendium of recorded crime produced by the Home Office, in 1935 there were

> Known to the police 87 cases of murder of 101 persons aged one year or over. In 41 cases, involving 50 victims, the murderer committed suicide; in 44 cases, involving 49 victims, two of whom had died following an illegal operation, 47 persons were arrested. In 2 cases involving 2 victims, 1 of whom had died following an illegal operation, no arrest was made.

Of the forty-seven people who faced a criminal trial: three were discharged; one died while on remand in prison; six were found to be insane; six were acquitted; fourteen were found guilty but insane; eight were executed; seven had their death sentences commuted to life imprisonment; one was sent to Broadmoor; and the final defendant had his conviction quashed at the Court of Appeal.

These statistics give an appearance of certainty, finality and order. They also indicate the power of the state to punish the crime of murder, and so provide a form of reassurance to the public that this offence is taken seriously: perpetrators will be apprehended and face trial, and justice – up to and including execution – will be meted out on behalf of the murderer's victim or victims. In dispensing this justice, no doubt the state hoped that potential murderers would be deterred from committing a similar crime; and that the public would believe that murder was controlled by the machinery of the criminal justice system.

However, the extent to which this is true is debatable. For instance, what are we to make of the fact that so many murder suspects (more than half in 1935) committed suicide or were found to be insane? Furthermore, why do the statistics catalogue only victims over the age of one? Above all, what conclusions should we draw from longer-term trends that seem to indicate a century of stability? On average, there were only fifty murder trials in England and Wales each year between 1914 and 1939, and in only five of the 104 years between 1862 and 1966 were there fewer than 120 murders or more than 179. For example, between 1900 and 1924 there were on average 149.40 murders each year, and between 1925 and 1949 that average was almost identical at 148.76. As the compiler of the *Criminal Statistics* for 1925 remarked:

> Figures as to murder always attract interest. For the past fifty years, during which time the population has increased from twenty-four millions to thirty-nine millions, the number of murders in each year coming to the knowledge of the police has remained almost stationary at about 150 cases per annum, of which for many years past about fifty have been murders of infants aged one year and under.

This author does at least reveal the number of very young children who were murdered each year, although these would have been classified as 'infanticides' as a result of the Infanticide Act of 1922, and would have attracted a lesser penalty than murder. He also seems to confirm the stable pattern of murder that has been described. But is that pattern a 'remarkable miracle' or merely the result of statistical sleight of hand?

The historian Howard Taylor (1998) has been at the forefront of trying to interpret these crime figures and has come to a startling conclusion: they have been doctored; or, as he more carefully puts it, they are a 'public illusion'. Specifically, Taylor claims that a combination of the Treasury's unwillingness to fund prosecutions – which meant that local ratepayers had to meet as much as half of the cost of each prosecution – and the 'gatekeeping' role of the police kept criminal prosecutions artificially low. He maintains that the police did not press for large numbers of prosecutions because that would have made them seem inefficient. So they carefully screened allegations and reports of crimes, and thereby dictated the number and range of offences and offenders that were prosecuted. This applied to every type of offence, but especially murder, where the costs of prosecution were particularly high. As a result, Taylor suggests that there was a quota for the number of murders that the police would allow to be prosecuted each year. Consequently, he says that most murders went uninvestigated, with many suspicious deaths instead recorded as suicides, accidents, death by misadventure, or death through natural causes.

In particular, 'suicide' increased dramatically throughout the period that the murder rate remained stable – especially after the First World War – and neither of these phenomena can be explained by the rising population. Perhaps there is an element of what might now be termed 'post traumatic stress' in relation to suicides after the war, but the numbers being considered are marked. For example, in 1856, 1,314 suicides were recorded; by 1939, this figure had risen to a staggering 5,054. Looking more closely at the statistics for the later year gives us an insight into the 'public illusion' that Taylor describes. According to various coroners' inquiries, there were 618 suicides but no homicides using poison; 706 suicides but only twenty-nine homicides by hanging or strangulation; 247 suicides and ninety fatal accidents but only twenty-one homicides involving firearms; 787 suicides and 813 accidents but no homicides by drowning; and, finally, 422 suicides and fifteen accidents but only twenty-two homicides involving cutting or piercing instruments. The implication is clearly that murders were often recorded as 'suicides', which leads Taylor to conclude that 'it was an open secret that most murders and suspicious deaths were not investigated'.

Some evidence for how this worked in practice has been provided by Robert – later Sir Robert – Mark, who in 1972 became Commissioner of the Metropolitan Police. Back in 1937, bored with his job in the warehouse of the carpet manufacturer James Templeton and Co. in Piccadilly, Manchester, Mark decided to join the Manchester Police. In his autobiography (Mark, 1978), he remembers that in his first few years of service, 'I did . . . pick up a few points on policing, one of which illustrates well the ingenuity and practicality of the police in those days.' Specifically, he recalls that:

> On the border of Openshaw and Clayton with Droylsden there was a canal lock, a favourite place for suicides. Providing that the beat officer found the body and no members of the public were present, two shillings would induce the lock keeper to open the gates to allow the body to be pushed through into the county. I did this once and suffered the indignity of finding the body back on my side of the lock the following morning. I suppose the eventual police amalgamations put an end to that, as well as reducing the tax free perks of the lock keeper.

Although this story is recounted by Mark for comic effect, it does reveal the reality of policing suspicious deaths in the 1930s. Such a death was routinely labelled a 'suicide' as long as that seemed an even remotely plausible conclusion. Furthermore, if possible, the responsibility for any investigation that might have to be made was shifted on to a neighbouring police force by relocation of the body.

Mark – who would make his name by attempting to stamp

out police corruption in the Metropolitan Police – indicates that the practice of trying to move a body to a neighbouring area probably ended with the amalgamation of police forces during the Second World War and subsequently. The manipulation of crime statistics by the police was not so readily abandoned, however. For instance, a future Chief Constable of West Yorkshire, Keith Hellawell (2003), remembers being confronted by a prostitute called Mary while he was a young officer in Huddersfield in the 1960s. Mary had lifted her skirt at the raw recruit to embarrass him, and he wanted to take some action. However, he had 'already arrested one woman for prostitution, but the charge had been refused, and when I asked why I was told that there were no prostitutes in Huddersfield'. Hellawell continues:

> When I repeated my observation, the charge sergeant repeated, 'There are no prostitutes in Huddersfield,' adding, 'because the Chief Constable says so.' That was how history was written. Other fictions were maintained. Crimes were rarely recorded until detected, and by this means we kept the number of recorded crimes artificially low, achieving an almost 100 per cent detection rate. This changed when resources were allocated in accordance with the number of crimes reported. Within a year the recorded crime rate in Huddersfield soared and the detection rate plummeted. So much for the validity of statistics.

Hellawell remains a controversial figure, but his reminiscences smack of honesty and forthrightness, rather than simply courting controversy. In what he reveals we can see how the gatekeeping role of the police served to keep figures for prostitution artificially low in Huddersfield. Refusing to prosecute prostitutes made the problem 'disappear', at least as far as the official criminal statistics were concerned. Of course, the economics of policing – specifically the supply and demand of crime and its detection – could also lead this problem to 'reappear' whenever it suited the police, such as when more crime meant more money for the force.

So does any of this indicate that the absence of serial killers between the wars was merely the result of a failure of the police to record murder accurately? This is, of course, a possibility, but nonetheless very unlikely. For instance, even if the police had not catalogued all murders correctly, surely the press would have filled in the gaps with respect to a serial killer. After all, murder has always aroused great public interest, and a voracious print media has been well aware since the time of Jack the Ripper that stories of serial killing especially boost their circulation. In the 1930s, as at every other time in modern British history, the newspapers were filled with stories of murder, and as usual these proved irresistible to huge audiences. By 1930 circulation for the *Daily Express* and the *Daily Mail* was approaching 2 million, and by 1934 the *Daily Mirror* had reinvented itself as a tabloid, with crime never far off its front page.

In June 1934, for example, the public was gripped by the 'Brighton Trunk Murder'. The cloakroom attendant at Brighton Station had become aware of a foul odour emanating from a trunk deposited there, and on opening it he discovered the torso of a young woman. The following day the rest of her body was found in another trunk at King's Cross Station in London. For the first time, this led the police to appeal directly to the public for information about her identity. As a result, a local Brighton dancer called Violet Kay was reported as missing. The police questioned Violet's lover, Tony Mancini (who gave his name as Cecil Lois England), and then decided to search their lodgings in 52 Kemp Street. They found Violet's body in a black trunk in the cellar, and Mancini was tried for her murder. However, he was ruled out as the killer of the still-unknown woman whose body had been found in the trunks at the railway stations. Amazingly, Mancini was acquitted at his trial, but in 1976 – at the age of sixty-eight – he confessed to the *News of the World* that he had indeed murdered Violet, although he could not be retried for her murder.

The 'Brighton Trunk Murder' might have come straight out of a plot by Agatha Christie, who introduced the Belgian detective Hercule Poirot to her readers in 1920, and then the much-loved Miss Marple in a short story called 'The Tuesday Night Club' seven years later. With these two characters Christie ensured the continued popularity of the 'whodunit' as a literary form that Conan Doyle had pioneered for the preceding generation. Indeed the inter-war years were referred to as the 'golden age' of British crime writing, presided over by Christie and her fellow 'Queens of Crime', Dorothy L. Sayers, Margery Allingham and Ngaio Marsh.

While Howard Taylor is probably right that many 'suicides' of the inter-war period were actually murders, with the press and the public so keen to write and read about murder, it is fairly safe to assume that any serial killer active at the time would not have escaped detection for long. So, if the absence of serial killers in the inter-war period is not simply a statistical fiction, how else are we to account for it?

'There are people who say corpses don't talk, but indeed they do'

These days it is hard to escape forensic science. Hardly a day goes by without news of an offender being caught by a new DNA profiling technique that allows 'cold cases' from years ago to be solved. In books and on TV white-coated scientists have grabbed centre-stage from police officers, psychologists, offender profilers and ageing spinsters with too much time on their hands. Forensic science is now synonymous with certainty, self-discipline, objectivity, truth and justice. More unexpectedly, it has also become glamorous.

Yet, for all this recent interest, we know comparatively little about the origins of the discipline and how some of its pioneers built up their expertise. Sir Bernard Spilsbury – the pathologist who nearly drowned a nurse in a bath to prove a theory – came to prominence during the trial of Dr Hawley Crippen. However, Spilsbury left very few written records in respect to how he went about conducting autopsies, what his relationship with the police was like, or how he prepared himself for cross-examination in the witness box. This is no small omission, for we should remember that 'forensic' is defined as 'of or used in a court of law', so 'forensic science' is simply the application of scientific (usually medical) knowledge to legal problems. However, although Spilsbury is not much help to historians, he was active when forensic science started to be taken seriously by the authorities in Britain. In the 1930s the Home Office begin to issue Forensic Science Circulars to local police forces, and various contemporary departmental committees emphasised the importance of science as a tool in criminal detection. Consequently, the Metropolitan Police established the first specialist, large-scale laboratory in 1935, and under Home Office guidance others were opened in Nottingham in 1936 and Birmingham and Cardiff in 1938. So, did a growing awareness of the role that forensic science might play in combating crime, and the increasing professionalisation of the discipline, contribute to the absence of serial killers during the inter-war years?

Two interesting autobiographies can help to answer this question. The best-known is *Forty Years of Murder* by Professor

Keith Simpson, first published in 1978 as his career was drawing to a close. The second was written by Simpson's secretary, Molly Lefebure: *Evidence for the Crown: Experiences of a Pathologist's Secretary* (1955). 'Miss Molly', as she was known by those who worked with her, notes that 'there are people who say corpses don't talk, but indeed they do . . . and my goodness, how they talk! Everything about them talks. The way they look, the way they died, where they died, how they died.' These two books offer a unique insight into how forensic science developed between the wars, and the role that the forensic scientist played in bringing murderers to justice.

In 1924 Simpson enrolled at Guy's Hospital, London, where he was surprised by the informality: there was no scrutiny of his qualifications, no supporting letters of reference were required, and no formal interview took place. All he had to do was convince the clerk that he had the money to pay the fees, then he was immediately accepted and enrolled. For the next ten years, in addition to his general medical training, Simpson specialised in pathology at Guy's, an education he describes as 'the only sound foundation for a crime pathologist'. He attended his first murder case at the end of 1934 at the York Hotel, opposite Waterloo Station, and fondly remembers how he had to be guided through the procedure by a kindly detective. Later, he recalls: 'When I started to do medico-legal post-mortems in London in the middle thirties, the standards of work were deplorably low.' Specifically, the Coroners' Act of 1926 gave coroners the power to call upon any qualified medical practitioner to perform an autopsy, so many doctors with no pathology training, none of the appropriate equipment and ill-equipped laboratories were asked to conduct post-mortems. Simpson suggests that only a 'handful' of people – including Spilsbury – knew what they were doing and had the necessary training and good instincts with respect to the issues of 'obscure death or insurance, pensions, industrial, suicidal and homicidal cases'.

Simpson also reveals how the Home Office handled criminal evidence that needed to be scientifically evaluated before the opening of their specialist facility in 1935:

> At the time all scientific work was handled by independent experts like Churchill, the firearm dealer, who was a shrewd businessman, jealous of the only competitor in his field, Major Burrard; Roche Lynch, a fine chemist at St Mary's Hospital, persuaded disastrously to undertake glass, hair, fibres, dust and blood-grouping work of which he had no experience whatever; Mitchell, an ink and handwriting expert (the latter has always been mistrusted); and dear old John Ryffel, 'Junior Home Office Analyst' (at sixty), my own teacher at Guy's. It was a quaint and unsatisfactory 'team' to cover laboratory service for the Home Office in crime investigation in England, but it committed no major blunders for nearly twenty years.

We only have Simpson's word that this motley team did not commit any major mistakes, and we have to wonder whether loyalty to colleagues and indeed his old teacher clouded his final assessment. Perhaps a more accurate impression can be gained from the fact that 'blood-grouping work' – one of the staples of contemporary forensic science – was undertaken by someone who had been 'persuaded disastrously' to carry out the task, and that he had no experience at all in this most sensitive area. Of course, Simpson may have exaggerated the level of incompetence to create an impression of 'progress' in forensic science (largely as a result of his efforts) as the century wore on, but his naming of the individuals involved adds a degree of authenticity that is difficult to deny.

With his medical training and pathology background, Simpson soon made his mark. He was joined by two other medically trained pathologists – Francis Camps and Donald Teare – and the trio began to provide medico-legal assistance to various police forces throughout the country. Simpson was appointed Medico-Legal Advisor to the Surrey Constabulary in 1937, and he would become particularly well known through his forensic work during the Second World War. The conflict brought 'a steady flow of rapes (some with strangling and other violence), of assaults (some fatal), of abortions and infanticides, of breaking into "deserted" houses (sometimes with violence), all arising from the changes in life that were thrust by service conditions on ordinary people'.

The 'three musketeers', as Simpson describes Camps, Teare and himself, eventually fell out, and such personality clashes seem to have been a feature of the discipline of forensic science at the time. Simpson did not warm to Spilsbury either, describing the older man as standing 'like a monolith, alone, aloof, respected but unloved; and unmourned too, when he finally committed suicide, in his tiny laboratory in University College, London [in 1947]'. The antipathy between the two is also highlighted by Spilsbury's biographer, who comments that Simpson was 'unstintingly hostile' and never 'missed a chance to sink his fangs into [Spilsbury]'.

It was in 1941 that Simpson first employed Molly Lefebure. She had trained as a journalist before becoming Simpson's secretary, and her autobiography is a marvellous mine of information, providing a richness of detail that the scientifically minded Simpson probably thought irrelevant or perhaps in appropriate. She also sometimes contradicts his memory of events, and in general her account is the more convincing. For example, she says that she worked with Simpson before 'the now famous

Department of Forensic Medicine at Guy's' was established. At that time they were billeted in the curator's office in the Gordon Museum at the hospital, where

> We did all our filing, report writing, correspondence and so forth, amidst a gleaming array of specimen jars in which floated grotesque babies, slashed wrists, ruptured hearts, stomach ulcers, lung cancers, bowel tumours, cerebral aneurisms and the like. Here too we generally took afternoon tea.

This is all very different from the description of clinical and efficient working conditions given by Simpson himself when he published his own book two decades later.

Molly also reveals how some of the specimens ended up in the jars in the curator's office. One day she encountered Simpson in a mortuary conducting the post-mortem on a young window cleaner who had slashed his throat and wrists after being abandoned by his lover. As Molly puts it, 'the wrist wounds were especially fine ones', so Simpson wanted to remove one of them and preserve it for future reference. The only problem was how to transport it back to Guy's, until Simpson hit upon a solution. On her way to work, Molly had bought a pair of gloves: 'So the new gloves went in my pocket, and I tripped out of the mortuary bearing the hand in the pretty little candy-striped paper carrier-bag which a chic shop assistant had given me barely an hour ago.'

This was far from the most macabre trip across London that Molly made with a specimen, and she tended to transport them in anything that was even vaguely suitable. For instance, she once carried a dead baby back to Guy's from Southwark Mortuary in a suitcase. She and Simpson also kept Chief Superintendent Fred Cherrill, head of Scotland Yard's fingerprint department, supplied with specimens from post-mortems. On one occasion Cherrill said, 'I've got one or two bits of a young woman here.' He then started rummaging around in a cupboard in the hope of handing the 'bits' to Molly so that she could take them to Guy's for incineration. However, Cherrill was 'most annoyed at his failure to find the lady, or what portions he had of the lady, and fumed around his office, grumbling, "I know I've got her here somewhere."' Molly's autobiography is full of such stories, which are often given a comic twist. However, they have the ring of truth, and reveal the rather amateurish state of forensic science at the time.

Simpson claimed that he came across only a handful of criminal cases each year. But here we should not only remember the gatekeeping role of the police but note that neither Simpson nor Lefebure mentions every high-profile murder that was committed during the time they worked together. For example, neither describes the case of the 'Blackout Ripper' – the pseudonym given to Gordon Cummins – a spree, rather than serial, killer who murdered four women in five days in 1942. These omissions are all the more remarkable given that Cherrill's fingerprint work was instrumental in bringing Cummins to justice, and that the chief superintendent was close enough to Molly to ask her to become his secretary.

Between the wars, then, forensic science was dominated by only a handful of qualified practitioners, and there was little love lost between them. These experts all pushed the development of the discipline in various directions that suited their own tastes and interests. The practice of forensic science was also very informal, and the widespread establishment of specialised forensic science facilities did not occur until after the Second World War, notwithstanding the opening of the Metropolitan Police Laboratory in 1935. However, there was a growing official awareness that science could aid criminal detection. As a consequence, relationships between the forensic scientists and the police developed rapidly in the 1930s, often prompted by the Home Office. Even so, it is hard to conclude that the development of forensic science and improved detection contributed to the absence of serial killers in Britain during the inter-war years.

So, the next question that must be asked is: was it the police who kept serial killers at bay?

Police forces

The British police do not have a particularly good record when it comes to catching serial killers. Their most obvious and dramatic failings in this respect were revealed by their botched investigation into a series of attacks and murders of women in the North of England between 1975 and 1981. The murderer, Peter Sutcliffe, was interviewed nine times by West Yorkshire detectives before being arrested. The police complained that their investigation was frustrated by poor administration and a lack of technology: specifically, they did not have access to a computer to process and coordinate information received by the Major Incident Room. Also hampering their efforts was the failure of police force areas to share information with one another, given that Sutcliffe killed in more than one region. So when thinking about policing in the inter-war period, it is worth considering the extent to which the police utilised the new technology of their day – such as telephones, telegraphs, radios and the motor car – and whether information was shared across police force areas, and indeed between colleagues from different disciplines within the same area.

Between 1856, when the County and Borough Police Act came into force, and 1964, with the passing of the Police Act, there were three different types of police force in England and Wales, and three different chains of command. First, there was the Metropolitan Police, who were responsible to the Home Secretary; second, the borough forces, such as Liverpool, Manchester and Birmingham, who were responsible to watch committees appointed by local councillors; and finally, the county forces, initially responsible to the police committees of the County Bench, and after 1889 to the standing joint committees of magistrates and county councillors.

Throughout the inter-war years there were regular attempts to centralise control of the police within the Home Office, and consequently to weaken local authority control and influence. The Desborough Committee of 1919 recommended a series of measures intended to bring greater uniformity to the police in the interests of 'good order and efficiency': the establishment of uniform rates of pay, the creation of the Police Federation, the introduction of 'F Division' within the Home Office to oversee, plan and direct the work of the police, and a rationalisation of the borough forces through a series of amalgamations of those boroughs with populations of less than fifty thousand. However, the committee's recommendations were never accepted, and subsequent attempts to abolish the borough forces – such as those made under the auspices of the Royal Commission on Local Government in the 1920s and the Select Committee of 1932 – always failed. A decision in the case of *Fisher v. Oldham* in 1930 ruled that a police constable 'is not the servant of the borough. He is the servant of the State, a ministerial officer of the central power, though subject in some respects, to local supervision and local regulation'. However, the previous year, the Inspectors of Constabulary (another centralising body) had bemoaned the fact that talks to amalgamate the eleven men in the Borough of Tiverton Police with the Devonshire Police had broken down, even though: 'Little island police districts like Tiverton are anachronisms in these days of modern facilities of travel, fenced in as they are by boundaries of which nobody takes any notice.' In 1939 there were still over 180 police force areas, but the onset of war finally persuaded these local fiefdoms to see sense. The Tiverton force voluntarily united with Devonshire, and several similar amalgamations took place around the same time. In 1943 twenty-six forces on the south coast of England were amalgamated into just six.

In the inter-war years the 'little island police districts' had indeed been anachronisms, especially given that the population was becoming increasingly mobile through the spread of car ownership. No longer the preserve of the upper classes, even the working classes could realistically aspire to own a vehicle, while the middle classes often already did. As early as 1921, almost a quarter of a million people owned cars, and the following year the launch of the Austin Seven – which cost £195 to buy and a penny a mile to run – brought the possibility of owning a small family car within reach for the masses. Just before the outbreak of war, the British automobile industry was producing close to 350,000 new cars each year.

This growth in car ownership made offenders far more mobile than they had ever been before, and while the police might take note of police force boundary areas criminals certainly did not. Other new technologies – such as the telephone, telegraph and radio – could have been used by the police to alert neighbouring forces about suspicious characters who might have been heading their way. However, although telephones had been installed in almost every police station in the country by the mid-1930s, the forces were slow to utilise telegraph and radio communication, partly because of the expense of investing in these technologies but also because of the various forces' contrasting organisational cultures and conservatism. As late as 1935, for example, J. A. Wilson, the Chief Constable of Cardiff, was complaining that his city force, which had developed an 'effective wireless system', was surrounded by county forces that took no interest in technological developments. This situation scuppered Wilson's attempts to share intelligence: 'we have offered to cooperate but without success, and as long as things are like that it is impossible to carry out an efficient system of wireless'.

If there were issues of cooperation across police boundaries, there was a similar problem within forces. Specifically, nowadays it is considered crucial that detectives have good working relations with their uniformed colleagues. However, the Royal Commission of 1929 suggested that CID at Scotland Yard regarded itself as 'a thing above and apart, to which the restrictions and limitations placed upon the ordinary police do not, or should not, apply'. Similarly, the Departmental Committee on Detective Work, which reported in 1938, emphasised that detectives should have specialist training, which must have created a barrier between them and their uniformed colleagues. Detectives were also rather thin on the ground: just before the outbreak of war, the fifty-eight county forces had only 581 detectives between them, while the 121 city and borough forces (excluding the Metropolitan and City of London Police) had only 1,198. In light of all this, it seems highly unlikely that improved detection prevented serial killing at this time.

So, if we can discount the contributions of the police generally as well as specialist detectives and forensic science between 1914 and 1943, how else are we to account for the absence of serial killers in this period?

Not just waiting for war

The 1920s and 1930s are relatively close to the present day, and they seem even closer as a result of our easy access to innumerable newspapers, photographs, novels, radio broadcasts and films of the period, not to mention the houses built in the inter-war years that still dominate many urban landscapes. Furthermore, many people alive today were born and grew up in the 1920s and 1930s, and they provide a bridge between then and now through their memories and recollections.

In spite of this wealth of source material, for many the whole period can be summed up in a few images and events: the abdication of King Edward VIII in 1936; huge crowds attending the first Wembley Cup Final; and the General Strike that brought the country to a standstill. The historian and former Labour MP Roy Hattersley (2007) chooses another image 'to represent the hard reality of Britain between the wars':

> The one picture of life in inter-war Britain which is most deeply impressed on the collective memory illustrates the abiding tragedy of men without work ... it is the march that set out for London on 5 October 1936 which is embedded in the national memory. It called itself, and came to be known as, the 'Jarrow Crusade'.

This choice reflects Hattersley's own interests and preoccupations, and his frequent use of the phrases 'inter-war' and 'between the wars' – not to mention the title of his book, *Borrowed Time* – reminds us that historians have tended to view this period as simply the prelude to war. Our knowledge that war with Germany would come in 1939 has led many authors to confine themselves to debating how prepared Britain was for battle, or to what extent the policy of appeasement made the coming conflict inevitable.

Another preoccupation of historians is the mass unemployment that ravaged all the industrialised nations in the period. As the traditional industries of coalmining, steel and shipbuilding declined, many people were forced out of work: for instance, the number of coalminers declined from 1,083,000 in 1920 to 675,000 in 1938, and by the mid-1920s nine out of ten miners in Northumberland, Durham and South Wales had been laid off. Historians writing in the 1980s used such statistics to attack the laissez-faire economic policies of Margaret Thatcher, and the 1930s thus became the 'devil's decade', popularly seen as a time of unremitting decay, deprivation and depression.

However, characterising the period in this way ignores the fact that the majority of those who lived through it became better paid, were better dressed, lived in better houses, increasingly drove motor cars, took paid holidays, watched and attended sports events, went to the cinema, listened to the BBC and generally enjoyed higher standards of living. It also ignores the growth of the professional middle class, and the development of new industries that kept the vast majority of people in work. More than this, in the 1920s and 1930s, those who were in paid employment – whether as professionals, tradesmen or labourers – became culturally more homogeneous, and the aspirations of one group were largely similar, or at least sympathetic, to those of another.

Even the Jarrow Crusade was led by the Mayor and Lady Mayoress of Jarrow, who marched at the head of the column for the first twelve miles. Along the way the marchers were provided with food, shelter and clothing not only by local trade unions but by churches and ordinary members of the public. A service of support for the marchers was held in Ripon Cathedral, and Ellen Wilkinson – Member of Parliament for the borough – marched between twelve and nineteen miles a day with her constituents. The march therefore seemed to demonstrate that people – *all* people – mattered: with universal suffrage having been achieved over the previous two decades, the life of every Briton was now inextricably bound up with that of every other Briton, irrespective of continuing disparities in wealth and status. Class divisions obviously existed, but these did not come close to producing either a fascist or a communist state in Britain at a time when such regimes were being established elsewhere. When war did break out, it was fought by a united people.

People matter

Three factors support the argument that people mattered in Britain in the inter-war years. First, the development of universal suffrage; second, the various initiatives that were aimed at improving the lives of working-class people in terms of health, housing, and benefits made available to them in times of crisis; and, finally, the notion that the state had a responsibility to care for the elderly and educate the young.

As the First World War ended, the Representation of the People Act of 1918 trebled the electorate in the United Kingdom by giving the vote to every man over the age of twenty-one, and to women over thirty who owned property. Over 21 million people were now eligible to vote in the United Kingdom; forty per cent of them – 8.5 million – were women. This extension of the vote to women has often been viewed as a 'reward' for the role they played during the war, for example by working in munitions factories, on farms and even down coal mines or by driving buses. However, a variety of other reasons also contributed to the government's decision, not least the knowledge that it would appease moderate 'suffragists' who might otherwise have supported the type of direct action employed by the 'suffragettes' before the war. The 1918 Act had some serious limitations, though: it still denied the vote to older women who lived in rented property as well as to many women in their twenties who had done much of the war work. Women overall would not receive the vote for another ten years. The Representation of the People Act of 1928 extended the vote to all women over the age of twenty-one, and as a result an extra five million names were added to the electoral register. This 'flapper vote', as it is sometimes called, is often seen as crucial in bringing the Labour government of Ramsay MacDonald to power, although there is little evidence to support such an assertion. Nevertheless, by 1928 women were being viewed politically, legally and socially in a very different way to how they had been perceived in the Edwardian period, a time when they had been subsumed by the legal personalities of their husbands.

Between 1919 and 1922 Lloyd George's coalition government built over 200,000 'homes fit for heroes'. Meanwhile, the Addison Housing Act of 1919 also stimulated house-building by offering subsidies to local authorities to launch construction projects aimed at providing accommodation for working-class families. In 1914 only about 1 per cent of the population rented council homes; by the outbreak of the Second World War that figure had increased to 14 per cent. In total about 4.3 million new homes were built between the wars, and by 1939 almost one family in three was living in a modern house that had been built after 1918. The Addison Housing Act was repealed in 1921, but the principle of offering subsidies to local authorities to build affordable homes for the working classes was maintained in the Chamberlain Housing Act of 1923, the Wheatley Housing Act of 1924 and in further Acts passed in 1930, 1933 and 1935.

It should be stressed that many people still lived in accommodation that was inadequate, that slum clearances were a major preoccupation of various governments during the interwar years, and that house construction still struggled to keep up with demand. However, perhaps for the first time in British history, the government seemed genuinely concerned about the living conditions of the whole population, as did other institutions, such as the Church of England. And that concern resulted in council houses that were brighter and airier, and had more bedrooms and better sanitary facilities than anything built before 1918. For example, by 1939 some 75 per cent of homes were wired for electricity. In turn, those who lived in these houses naturally wanted to take good care of them, and they started to spend more time inside rather than outside. Sales of vacuum cleaners rose from just over 200,000 in 1930 to 400,000 in 1938, while the sale of electrical cookers trebled during the same period. Other changes in society are indicated by the facts that, on the outbreak of war, just under twenty million newspapers were being sold each day, and thirty-four million people had access to a radio. Over eight million radio licence holders tuned in to the BBC, which had begun broadcasting in November 1922.

Better housing conditions certainly contributed to the improved health of the nation. A Ministry of Health had been established for the first time in 1919, and several Public Health Acts were passed in the 1930s. National Health Insurance was introduced in 1911, and while it had its weaknesses, by 1936 nineteen million wage earners were covered by its provisions. They received a small cash payout when they were sick and could not work, enabling them to consult a doctor and receive treatment without charge. There were also more hospitals, more hospital beds, more nurses and more doctors: in 1911 there were 6.2 doctors per 10,000 of the population; by 1941 that had increased to 7.5 per 10,000. The Holidays and Pay Act of 1938 increased the number of people who were entitled to a paid week's holiday from one million in 1920 to eleven million in

1939. No doubt a significant proportion of them spent their week at one of the two hundred holiday camps that now dotted the British coastline. Others might simply have stayed at home, with occasional outings to the pictures for a treat: by the outbreak of war there were over four thousand cinemas, with the average weekly attendance over twenty million.

The Old Age Pension Amending Act was introduced in 1919, and was followed six years later by the Widows', Orphans' and Old Age Contributory Pensions Act, which organised pensions on a contributory basis and, as a result, made them available to many more people. The contributory principle distributed the cost of the pension between the worker, the employer and the state. By 1932, old age pensions of ten shillings a week were being provided to a total of 2,231,016 people aged sixty-five and over, with benefit provisions becoming more liberal and qualifying conditions – such as nationality and residency – becoming less stringent. For men, pension contributions were fourpence ha'penny a week, with the employer paying an equal amount and the state assuming responsibility for any shortfall. As a result, state expenditure on pensions for those aged between sixty-five and seventy increased from £2,703,000 in 1928 to £16,381,000 in 1934.

Young people – and especially their education – became another preoccupation of successive governments. Between 1923 and 1933 a consultative committee chaired by Sir William Henry Hadow produced six reports about the education of young people from nursery school age onwards, making recommendations about the school leaving age, the provision of books in elementary schools and differentiation of the curriculum for boys and girls. Cumulatively, these reports totalled 1,500 pages. Hadow's 1926 report – *The Education of the Adolescent* – recommended a 'regrading of education' so that there would be 'primary' and 'secondary' schools that would be based on 'a fresh classification of the successive stages of education before and after the age of 11+', and proposed that the school leaving age should be raised to fifteen by 1932 (although this would not be achieved until the 1944 Education Act). The curriculum of secondary schools, Hadow suggested, should have 'a certain amount of work bearing in some way upon [the pupils'] probable occupations'.

Of particular significance, Hadow's 1931 report, *The Primary School*, argued for separate infant schools and suggested that a primary school's curriculum should be 'thought of in terms of activity and experience, rather than of knowledge to be acquired and facts to be stored'. It also demanded a maximum class size of forty, special help for those children who were especially gifted or 'retarded', and a training scheme so that teachers might meet the demands of the new primary school system. This system would be described today as 'child centred', so there would be no standard curriculum but rather a focus on project work, which would allow the pupils to solve problems and make discoveries for themselves. In other words, children were to be valued and encouraged because, like everyone else in the 1930s, they mattered.

All of this should not obscure the fact that in the inter-war years many Britons endured considerable hardship and suffering, and significant disparities of wealth continued to exist. The key, though, is to understand that while the working class might no longer have been needed in the shipyards, down the pits or in the steelworks, their labour remained vital. They were simply required in different industries and different locations. Car production, for example, was increasingly concentrated in the South-East of England, so people relocated there from the coalfields of Wales and Yorkshire and the shipyards of the

North-East. This undoubtedly created temporary difficulties, but for those who wanted to find employment, work was still available, and with it a stake in society and the possibility of improving both one's own life and that of one's family.

This is crucial when attempting to explain the absence of serial killers in Britain at a time when there were so many in Germany. As has been shown in this chapter, it is highly unlikely that this was due to better policing or to the development of forensic science. Nor does the 'English miracle' fully explain it. Rather, the sheer scale of state initiatives and the willingness of successive governments to intervene in order to improve British citizens' lives indicate that people mattered in Britain in a way that they did not in the Weimar Republic and especially once Hitler had come to power. Under the Third Reich, Jews, gay people, gypsies, the elderly and the mentally ill were all seen as irrelevant to the state's future and a drain on resources. The authorities' 'solution' to this was extermination, which could be achieved actively, in the concentration camps, or passively, simply by failing to provide these people with any form of state protection. Compare this situation to what was happening in Britain, where an inclusive society was being created, with every citizen viewed as vital to the future development of the nation, and the ties that bound people together becoming all-encompassing. Sport, literature, cinema and the media all helped to create a sense of what it meant to be British, part of which was the notion that one's fellow citizens were important. The government took the lead in fostering this concept by extending state protection to those groups that had previously been forced to manage for themselves as best they could. As they were increasingly viewed as having something to offer, they became more valued and therefore less vulnerable.

The lesson here is that if people look out for one another, and if their lives are valued and protected by the state, then it is much harder for a potential serial killer to achieve his objectives.

Chapter Five

'The more the merrier': Reg Christie, John Haigh, Peter Manuel

> Leave your car outside in the street without lights and the police will be down on you in a flash, but if you're murdering somebody at the bottom of your garden, they'll never discover that.
>
> John George Haigh

John Haigh was a very English serial killer. In the eighty letters that he wrote from prison to his elderly parents – which have never been published before – as he awaited his trial and execution for the murder of Mrs Olive Durand-Deacon in 1949, he comes across as a man preoccupied with the banality of middle-class life. Leaving aside Haigh's largely self-serving explanations as to why he killed Mrs Durand-Deacon – he claimed that a car accident had left him with an insatiable appetite for the taste of blood – the most striking feature of the letters is their incessant discussion of the weather. In March 1949, writing from HMP Lewes, Haigh says, 'the weather has been very good here', and the following month he asks from HMP Brixton, 'Hasn't it been a marvellous weekend? Much too hot and pleasant to be in here.' In May he notes that there had been 'lovely rain. Wonderful sensation', and in June that it was 'marvellous weather for Ascot'. In early July he writes:

> in spite of being overcast there seems little inclination on the part of the clouds to drop any rain. A matter which seems to be causing grave concern in many parts. It amazes me that we have droughts now for years yet no one seems to have any thought of the very simple expedient of building more reservoirs to retain the ample supply of water we get in the winter!

Later in the month he is relieved that there has finally been some rain, and that 'it's much fresher as a result and I have no doubt it will have pleased the farmers'. Just days before his execution he writes, 'It's a wonderful day although the heat is terrific. I don't remember such a succession of torrid weekends for years.'

Is this the authentic voice of 'Middle England', wearily shaking its head? If only more people were like him, Haigh seems to be saying, there would be no more water shortages and summers would be more bearable. He also seems to abhor change and disruption, while cherishing certainty and tradition. He articulates the value system of the middle classes who enjoyed Ascot and worried, as he put it, 'about the shortage of cuckoos this year. Have you noticed it too? Apparently there are not nearly so many about as there usually are.'

There are other obsessions, too: gardening, the royal family, life in general not being as good as it had been in the past. He repeatedly implores his mother to get his father to sort out their lawn, and is in raptures about Princess Margaret – who was on a tour of Italy at the time – writing lovingly of her eyes, and deciding she is 'a bit of a card altogether'. From HMP Brixton he admits, 'Life is much too drab nowadays. No one possesses the capacity for enjoying simple pleasures – they seem much too docile: too wrapped up in forms and encompassed by government restrictions. It's time there was a revolution!' However, presumably to clarify that this would not be a revolution from the left, he writes, 'Thank goodness I'm not a Communist.' He admired Winston Churchill – now leader of the opposition, having been defeated by Clement Attlee in the General Election of 1945 – and deplored the fact that 'these days' Britain was represented abroad 'by uncouth colliery and railway clerks'. Nationalisation was another bugbear, with Haigh worrying, 'Where we are getting to with the railways nowadays goodness only knows. Even they are taking seriously to Rules & Regulations now with the result that they'll get about one train out where they used to get half a dozen before.' He resignedly concludes, 'If [Labour] win the next election – which I doubt – then Britain might just as well fold itself up and disappear quietly into the bottom of the sea.' Haigh was wrong: Attlee's government did win the next General Election, in February 1950, albeit with a much reduced majority. Haigh had been executed seven months earlier. Naturally, he never once complained about the death penalty: to do so would have gone against everything he believed in.

Before being executed, Haigh left explicit and detailed instructions that the green suit he had worn at his trial should be sent to Madame Tussaud's. He had learned that a model of him was to be placed in the waxworks' Chamber of Horrors. He had previously visited the museum with a girlfriend by the name of Barbara Stephens, who later revealed that Haigh had been especially interested in the model of George Smith. She said Haigh had called Smith 'the cleverest killer of the lot' when they had viewed the bath in which Margaret Lofty had been drowned. In an eerie forewarning of how he would dispose of his own victims, Haigh told Barbara that Smith killed his brides in a bath of acid and then 'pulled up the plug and let the body run away'. Of course, this is untrue, but it creates a gruesome link between two serial killers who were executed over three decades apart.

The usual suspects

Although Haigh was the first serial killer since Smith to come before a British court, someone else started his own killing spree before him. Reginald Christie strangled Ruth Fuerst in August 1943, more than a year before Haigh murdered William McSwan. However, Christie would not be caught, tried and executed until 1953. So for five years, between 1944 and 1949, there were two serial killers at large in Britain, both of whom lived in London. There are other connections between Haigh and Christie, too. Both originally came from Yorkshire, the former from Wakefield and the latter from Halifax; both had formal, almost Victorian upbringings, with Christie's father one of the founder members of the local Conservative Party and Haigh's parents both belonging to the Plymouth Brethren; both enjoyed pretending to be someone they were not, sometimes dressing up in a uniform to create the right impression and on other occasions fraudulently forging signatures; and both had extensive criminal records before they started to murder. Searching for a reason as to why both would eventually kill, Molly Lefebure (1958) travelled to Wakefield Cathedral – where Haigh had sung and played the organ – and tried to 'imagine the thoughts and feelings Haigh had indulged in'. She then analyses a photograph of Haigh as a child and suggests:

> It is not really the face of a child that looks at us. It is already the face of John George Haigh ... the appraising, shrewd, cold eyes, the rather hard, cynical mouth, the level brows, the neat nose and self-possessed chin, the eager, go-getting boy on his toes with the smart mind and the unexpected sense of humour – all that is already there, frighteningly so.

Such an assessment is firmly rooted within the medico psychological tradition and is thus open to question. Haigh might well have been 'shrewd', 'appraising' and 'go-getting', and this probably clashed with the religious convictions of his parents, but it is too great a leap to see this as the source of his murderous career. Lefebure says Haigh was a 'snob' who dreamed of a future 'with a large house, a large staff of servants, several first-rate cars, a good social life' and killed to achieve and maintain that lifestyle. But that simply begs the question: why do other 'snobs' – and indeed everyone who dreams of a big house and an exciting social life – not turn to serial murder, too? Moreover, we would normally praise shrewd, appraising go-getters, rather than see them as potential serial killers. Instead of examining their characters in a bid to explain why they killed, it is more important to learn how Haigh and Christie were able to escape detection for so long, which enabled them to kill repeatedly.

The opportunities created by war

For any crime to occur there needs to be a motivated offender who has access to a suitable victim, and an opportunity for that offender to act upon his desire to commit a crime. Such opportunities to offend might be constrained by the presence of formal controls, such as the police, or through the various informal controls that are present when the members of a community feel responsible for everyone who lives within it.

On the other hand, opportunities to commit crimes increase when formal and informal controls are lacking, or when the number of suitable victims grows. Haigh's snide comment at the start of this chapter about the police's priorities indicates that he well understood both their formal control of minor offences and their inability to tackle much bigger crimes, such as murder.

War provided many opportunities for the motivated offender. The blackout ensured anonymity, and a killer did not have to be too careful – or too organised – about disposing of his victims' bodies, given that the Luftwaffe's bombs regularly left many corpses in the streets, or in bombed-out flats and houses. For example, the skull of Christie's second victim, Muriel Eady, whom he had buried with Ruth Fuerst in his garden during the war, was dug up by his dog in 1949. Christie then simply dumped the skull in one of the ruined buildings in St Mark's Road, round the corner from Rillington Place, where he lived. People moved from one place to another regularly during the war – they could be called up, return home to be with their families, or move in search of somewhere more peaceful. In such circumstances communities quickly fragmented, no matter how much the 'spirit of the Blitz' propaganda of the time suggested that everyone was pulling together. No one was surprised if friends, neighbours or even family members disappeared suddenly, often without warning. All of this ensured that most of the victims of serial killers during the war were very different types of people from those who were targeted both before and after.

The war assisted the potential murderer in other ways, too. With most able-bodied men in the armed forces, women were expected to assume less traditional roles, which meant that they were often out and about on the streets, working in factories, driving buses, trams and trains, or 'digging for victory'.

This meant they routinely came into contact with people they would not have met during peacetime. Meanwhile, older men and those unfit to fight also took on new roles and responsibilities: for instance, Christie, who had been invalided during the First World War, was a War Reserve constable. This afforded him the opportunity to pry into other people's business and to visit places that would previously have been off-limits to him. He carried out his duties diligently, earning two commendations during the course of the war. But wearing a uniform and supposedly 'upholding the law' also gave him great freedom of movement and action to pursue his darker objectives. In this he was aided by the fact that, in the chaos of wartime, his earlier criminal convictions had been lost.

In different ways, both Haigh and Christie used these opportunities that the war created to start killing. Christie concentrated on those who would not be missed. Meanwhile, Haigh's horrific but ingenious modus operandi ensured that, while his victims might be missed, their bodies would never be found.

John Haigh – the acid-bath murderer

Haigh's first victim was William McSwan – universally known as 'Mac' – and a very atypical victim of a serial killer. William was the son of a Scottish local government officer called Donald McSwan, who had moved to England to work with the London County Council. Later, Donald had invested all of his savings in an amusement arcade in Tooting. Mac managed this arcade for his father, but as the business expanded the McSwans advertised for a 'secretary/chauffeur' in 1935. Haigh got the job. He did not disclose that he had only recently been released from prison, having served fifteen months for conspiracy to defraud and obtaining money by false pretences. His wife had given birth while he was inside, and the child had been given up for adoption. Mac and Haigh were both twenty-six in 1935, and they developed a friendship based on shared interests in fast cars and good food. Soon they were regulars in the Goat pub in Kensington High Street. A black-and-white photograph exists of Mac from around this time (reproduced in Lefebure, 1958). In it he poses nonchalantly for the camera, his right hand buried in his pocket as he leans against a table, smiling and confident. He is wearing a three-piece tweed suit, with a handkerchief tucked in his breast pocket. His hair is swept to the side, and a neat, pencil moustache graces his rather long, thin face. He looks every inch the fashionable young man about town. No doubt Haigh wished he had the wealth and confidence that Mac seemed to exude.

Haigh worked hard for the McSwans, but in 1937 he was tempted into another fraud. He set himself up as a solicitor, or rather three solicitors – one in Guildford, another in Hastings and the third in Chancery Lane, London. Having drawn up letterheads for each of these firms, he took an accommodation address where he could receive mail. His fraud was ingenious, targeting the stock market and company shareholders. He studied the stock market and looked out for companies that seemed vulnerable to offloading of their shares. Having found one, in his solicitor guise he would write to any shareholders with substantial holdings in the company, claiming to represent the family of another, recently deceased shareholder. He then offered these fictitious shares for private sale at a favourable price. He had raised nearly three thousand pounds before one suspicious shareholder noticed that Haigh's letterhead had no 'd' in 'Guildford' and contacted the police. Haigh was arrested and sentenced to four years, which he served first in HMP Chelmsford and then in HMP Dartmoor.

He was released on licence in 1940, but was soon serving another twenty-one months following a dispute about a refrigerator. This time he was sent to HMP Lincoln, where he conducted biological experiments – dissolving the bodies of field mice in acid that he had stolen from the prison's tinsmith's shop. He was released with this newfound knowledge in 1943. Despite being liable for conscription, Haigh found employment in Crawley, Sussex, as a salesman and bookkeeper for a local businessman called Alan Stephens. He was the father of Barbara Stephens, the woman who visited Madame Tussaud's with Haigh. Stephens' firm made dolls' prams, fancy goods and radio components. Just as he had for the McSwans, Haigh worked hard for Stephens, and soon he had earned enough money to rent a small basement in Gloucester Road, London, and a bedsit in Queen's Gate Terrace. Later, he would also rent a room at the nearby Onslow Court Hotel, which was populated by rich, elderly ladies.

In late summer 1944 William McSwan popped into the Goat in Kensington and bumped into his old friend John Haigh. It is unlikely that this was simply a coincidence – no doubt Haigh had worked out that a visit to their old drinking hole offered the best chance of meeting Mac again. By this time, Mac's parents had sold the amusement arcade and bought several properties in London with the proceeds, although Mac still had to look after some of the old pinball machines. Mac took Haigh to meet his parents in their new flat in Pimlico, and they were delighted to reacquaint themselves with their former, loyal employee.

Mac – like Haigh – was now liable for conscription, and he told his friend that he wanted to 'disappear'. Haigh promised to help, and he was as good as his word. Inviting Mac back to his basement in Gloucester Road on 9 September 1944, Haigh promptly hit him over the head with a length of lead piping, then stripped him of any valuables. The following morning Haigh forced Mac's body into an oil drum – his 'baths' would become more refined over time – which he had filled with hydrochloric acid. Then, just as he had done with the field mice in HMP Lincoln, he waited for the body to dissolve. Later he explained to Mac's parents that their son had gone to Scotland to evade his army call-up, then he forged various letters to the elderly McSwans, supposedly from Mac in Glasgow. He next suggested – again using the device of a letter from Mac – that the McSwans should hire Haigh to collect the rents on their properties. They readily agreed, which allowed Haigh to develop a detailed understanding of the intricacies of their business affairs.

When the war ended the McSwans must have expected their son to return. Knowing this, Haigh decided to dispose of them too, in July 1945. By this time, he had almost perfected his acid-bath technique: he wore a mask to protect himself from the fumes and had constructed a stirrup-pump with which to fill the bath. Within forty-eight hours of their murder, the McSwans had been turned into a ghastly sludge that Haigh flushed down the drain and into London's sewers. He continued to forge deeds, renewed the family's ration books, sold their houses and belongings, and told anyone who asked too many questions that the whole family had moved to America. In all, he raised at least three thousand pounds from obliterating the McSwans, and promptly set himself up at the Onslow Court Hotel, where he could spot other suitable victims.

Next on his list were fifty-two-year-old Dr Archie Henderson of the Royal Army Medical Corps and his wife Rose, a former beauty queen. Lefebure (1958) describes them as 'wealthy members of London society'. Archie was good looking and 'dashing', despite being a 'bottle-of-scotch-a-day man'. More importantly, as far as John Haigh was concerned, he had also been left twenty thousand pounds after the death of his first wife in 1937. Archie had married Rose only a few months later, once she had divorced her first husband, Rudolph Erren, a First World War German fighter pilot. (In the 1920s and 1930s Erren was at the forefront of the development of hydrogen engines, and science prizes are still awarded in his name.) When she married Archie, Rose was a 'sophisticated, worldly brunette ... very good-looking, well-educated. She and the doctor made a striking couple.'

Haigh met the Hendersons when he offered to buy a property from them at an inflated price. He never went through with the deal, and Rose seemed to harbour some suspicions about him, but he soon ingratiated himself into their home in Ladbroke Square. He played piano for them, and over time came to dominate their social life. The Hendersons, like the McSwans, were not typical targets of a serial killer: under normal circumstances too many people would have noticed the disappearance of this 'striking couple' and commented on their absence. But the slow return to normality after the war made them vulnerable to attack by a motivated murderer such as Haigh. In February 1948 the trio took a trip to Brighton, close enough to Crawley for Haigh to invite the Hendersons to see his workshop. There they ended up in an acid bath. However, Haigh then had to deal with Rose's brother Arnold Burlin, who was not easily deflected by the murderer's charm or reassurances.

As he had with the McSwans, Haigh used forged letters to cover his tracks. In the guise of Rose, he wrote to her brother, explaining that she and Archie had gone away to sort out their marriage. The letters were credible because Haigh had acquired so much knowledge of the couple's lives that he was able to infuse them with familiar phrases and personal anecdotes.

Eventually – still pretending to be Rose – Haigh convinced Arnold that the Hendersons were living in South Africa, having fled there after Archie had performed an illegal abortion. Meanwhile, Haigh was following the pattern he had established with the McSwans' estate: he forged various deeds of transfer and sold off the Hendersons' properties and belongings, amassing about seven thousand pounds as a direct result of their murder. However, within six months he was in debt again, and looking for someone else to kill.

Haigh – like many serial killers – became less organised as his number of victims increased. This is probably the result of the serial killer gaining confidence in his ability to kill without being detected, and so becoming less cautious and less controlled about what he is doing. After being caught, many serial killers describe their feelings of 'power' and 'invincibility', not only with respect to the power of life and death that they hold over their victims, but in terms of their ability to evade police detection. On the other hand, their lack of caution may be due to an increasing disconnectedness from the morality that guides 'real life', which leads to ever more unrestrained behaviour. We do not need to 'enter the mind' of a serial killer to appreciate how bizarre it must be to spend one's life killing people and then disposing of their remains, while all the time appearing 'normal' to one's friends and acquaintances, discussing the weather, work, current affairs, or the latest trials and tribulations of family members. The net effect is that many serial killers – including Haigh – start to kill more frequently; and as the gap between each murder narrows, the chance of detection increases.

Olive Henrietta Helen Olivia Robarts Durand-Deacon – a widow worth £36,000 – was a fellow resident of the Onslow Court Hotel. One night she and her friend Mrs Birin took the table next to Haigh's in the hotel's dining room, where they discussed the manufacture of artificial fingernails. By the end of the evening, Mrs Durand-Deacon had invited Haigh to go into business with them. Sensing an opportunity, he accepted. Then, on 17 February 1949, he persuaded Mrs Durand-Deacon to visit his workshop in Crawley. He picked her up in his car outside the Army & Navy Stores in Victoria Street, London, no doubt in a bid to keep the trip a secret: if they had met at the hotel, they might well have been spotted by the other residents. In Crawley Haigh shot Mrs Durand-Deacon in the back of her head, stripped her of her valuables, and dumped her trussed-up body in the acid bath. He then casually went to Ye Olde Ancient Priors Teashop for a poached egg. Later, the manager remembered some of their jocular conversation.

Unfortunately for Haigh, though, Mrs Durand-Deacon's absence was soon noticed by her friend Mrs Constance Lane, another of the Onslow Court Hotel's residents. On his return, she asked Haigh about the trip to Crawley. Haigh said that Mrs Durand-Deacon had failed to appear at the Army & Navy Stores, and he feigned concern about what might have happened to her. Over the next few days, Mrs Lane grew more concerned, and eventually she decided to report the disappearance to the police. As usual exuding supreme confidence, Haigh offered her a lift, and the pair went together to Chelsea Police Station. Here, Haigh met his nemesis – Woman Police Sergeant Alexandra Lambourne. She was immediately suspicious of the charming and glib Haigh, and some basic checks with the Criminal Records Office at Scotland Yard uncovered the extent of his criminal past. Thereafter, police searches of the workshop in Crawley revealed his acid-bath paraphernalia, while in his attaché case they found identity cards, ration books and other personal papers related to the McSwans and the Hendersons. The forensic pathologist Keith Simpson also noticed some dentures, a piece of pelvis and some foot bones in the strange sludge that lay around the yard of the workshop. Faced with the inevitable, Haigh confessed all. He even invented other murders in support of his defence that he had developed an insatiable taste for blood.

Unusually in the case of a serial killer, Haigh's victims were all missed almost as soon as they had been murdered. The concern of family and friends for relatives, neighbours and acquaintances generally imposes a degree of informal control over the activities of would-be serial killers. And, as we have seen, Haigh had to work hard to conceal his crimes. Arnold Burlin quizzed him repeatedly about the whereabouts of his sister Rose. He even went so far as to arrange an emergency SOS broadcast by the BBC to ask Rose to return home from South Africa because their mother was critically ill. Constance Lane was similarly worried about the sudden disappearance of her friend, Mrs Durand-Deacon, and had enough sense to report her suspicions to the police. The elderly McSwans' concern for their son was only assuaged by the letters Haigh forged and sent to them. Indeed, it was Haigh's skill as a forger and fraudster that allowed him to evade detection for so long. He kept suspicious family members and friends at bay by exploiting his intimate knowledge of the lives of the McSwans and the Hendersons, while his understanding of the law allowed him to profit from the murders he committed. But all of this was possible only because of the opportunities that the war and its aftermath provided.

Haigh, then, was an exception to the rule, and he needed extraordinary circumstances to achieve his ends. Typically, if a murderer targets people who are fully integrated into society, concerned families and friends will raise the alarm before he is able to kill again.

10 Rillington Place

Reg Christie was a much more 'typical' serial killer because he concentrated his murderous efforts on people who would not be missed. His disposal of the bodies was more mundane, too: he buried the first two in his garden; hid his wife Ethel's body under the floorboards of their house in Rillington Place, Notting Hill, London; and deposited his last three victims' corpses in an alcove in the house. Christie was not a mobile killer: he murdered his victims in a very specific location, which made him a forerunner of both Dennis Nilsen and the Wests, who similarly used their homes and gardens for their crimes. The phrase 'house of horrors' – which was regularly used by the press when reporting both the Wests' Cromwell Street home and Nilsen's Cranley Gardens flat – was coined for 10 Rillington Place, which the Christies occupied from 1938.

Lefebure (1958) provides a detailed description of Christie's garden:

> A typical London one, with dark, weedy earth in which proliferated flower-pot shards, dry sticks and old mutton bones. There was a 'rockery', which was little more than a collection of broken bricks, and a lawn, which comprised a very small mud patch on which struggled for existence several unkempt tufts of grass. Honeysuckle, jasmine, ramblers and forsythia each spring made further dejected efforts to clamber over the sooty garden walls.

One day in 1946, while Christie was digging in the garden, he unearthed part of a human femur belonging to one of his first two victims. Rather than throwing away his find, he used it to prop up a rickety trellis on the right-hand side of the garden. This arrangement would remain in place for the next seven years, even though the garden had by then been searched by detectives investigating the murders of Beryl and Jeraldine Evans. No one noticed the improvised buttress, lending support to Haigh's observation that the police will diligently look out for minor traffic offences while missing murders at the bottom of a garden.

In addition to his wife Ethel, Christie murdered Ruth Fuerst, Muriel Eady, Rita Nelson, Kathleen Maloney and Hectorina MacLennan. He also probably murdered Beryl and Jeraldine Evans, although he was never convicted for these crimes. His first victim – Ruth Fuerst – and his last three were all sex workers. Ruth came to England in 1939 to train as a nurse. However, by 1943, now aged twenty-one, she was working in a munitions factory and supplementing her income by selling sexual services to American servicemen, and possibly to Christie. In his job as a War Reserve constable – a role that earned him the nickname the 'Himmler of Rillington Place' – Christie visited the cafés and bars where many vulnerable young women were earning a living by picking up male customers. He met Ruth several times, and on the last occasion she accompanied him to Rillington Place. Ethel was away in Sheffield, visiting her family, and it may have been a telegram announcing that she was on her way home that prompted Christie to kill Ruth and bury her in the garden.

Christie came into contact with Muriel Eady because they worked at the same radio factory in Acton after he gave up his job as a War Reserve constable. According to Lefebure (1958), she was a 'respectable woman' who lived with an aunt and had a steady boyfriend. The Christies seem to have socialised with the couple, so it was probably not unusual for Muriel to visit Rillington Place. In October 1944, while Ethel was again visiting her family in Yorkshire, Christie convinced Muriel that he had a cure for catarrh and invited her round.

Muriel's absence was reported to the police, but at the time such disappearances were not necessarily viewed as suspicious – especially now that V1 rockets were raining down on London. Almost 2,500 of these flying bombs hit the capital and the South-East, killing nearly 9,000 people and injuring thousands more. They created panic, and many Londoners chose to leave the city, often with little warning. This may even have been the reason for Ethel's visit to Sheffield. While she was gone, Christie simply exploited the opportunities that the chaos of war provided.

Contemporary descriptions of Ethel Christie cast her as a rather innocent, naïve and put-upon woman who was totally dominated by her husband. Although Lefebure (1958) admits that it is 'almost impossible to discover what she is really like', she goes on to describe Ethel as 'plump, big-bosomed, rather pleasant-looking, sentimental and by nature kind and cheerful, she went shopping, cooked, kept the home reasonably tidy and was completely under her husband's thumb'. Nevertheless, Christie waited until Ethel was away before murdering his first two victims, so perhaps she exercised some form of informal control over him. After her death on 14 December 1952 the number of murders committed by Christie spiralled, and the gap between them decreased: there was a gap of some fourteen months between the murders of Ruth Fuerst and Muriel Eady, but he would kill his wife and his final three victims in the space of only four months. As we have noted, this is typical behaviour for many serial killers. It seems that Christie felt he had nothing left to lose after he killed his wife. After his arrest he commented simply, 'The more the merrier.'

Christie seems to have been interested in necrophilia. It has been suggested that he gained sexual pleasure from strangling his victims and then having sex with them either at the moment of their death or just after they had died. He would often convince the women that he brought back to Rillington Place to inhale gas, which they believed was a medicinal mixture to cure various ailments. This rendered them unconscious and so allowed Christie to ravish them at his leisure. Three of the victims who were found in the house were diapered, and these nappies had seminal stains on them. The exception was Ethel: it seems that Christie had not had sex with her for some time before her death. Strangulation usually leads to defecation and/or urination, so – in a memorable phrase of Martin Fido (2001) – the nappies reveal that Christie was both 'filthy and fastidious'. All three of the women hidden in the alcove – Rita Nelson, Kathleen Maloney and Hectorina MacLennan – were found with large amounts of semen in their vaginas.

Rita, Kathleen and Hectorina were killed between January and March 1953. Lefebure (1958) captures something of the disconnectedness that Christie must have been experiencing at this time. She suggests that by the autumn of 1952 he had entered 'a fantastic undergrowth world, a limbo-lost, a nightmare place'. Even so, the only women he could victimise – apart from his wife – were prostitutes. And there might have been two more if Mary O'Neill and Helen Sunderland had not escaped Christie's attentions. Mary met Christie on 23 January 1953 and went back to Rillington Place with him, where he demanded sex and suggested that she would 'not be missed' if he killed her. Keeping her wits, Mary informed Christie that a friend knew precisely where she was. Helen told a similar story, but would later claim that her relationship with Christie had never been sexual.

After his arrest, Christie's story changed so many times that it is impossible to be certain what happened to Rita, Kathleen and Hectorina. He suggested that all three made advances to him. For example, he claimed that Kathleen – who was drunk – spotted him in the street and demanded a pound from him; when he refused she followed him home, asking for more money all the time. He said that he offered Rita and Hectorina lodgings, but once at Rillington Place they made sexual advances towards him. Of course, this was all self-serving nonsense.

Lefebure (1958) provides some uncharitable descriptions of the three women, based on what emerged at their autopsies. Rita had 'poorly kept, scarlet-varnished finger-nails; her toenails too had been painted'; Kathleen had 'been drinking before her death'; and Hectorina was a 'somewhat tatty young person – her hands and feet were poorly kept, her fingers nicotine-stained'.

While Christie took care when disposing of the bodies of his first three victims – burying Ruth and Muriel in the garden and prising up the floorboards for Ethel – it seems that he was wholly out of control by the early months of 1953, using the highly unsuitable alcove to store the bodies of Rita, Kathleen and Hectorina. Cunningly, he used this lack of control as the basis for his defence – pleading insanity. It is therefore difficult to believe anything he said once he was in custody. This makes it especially difficult to analyse the most controversial part of the Christie case: the question of whether he killed Beryl and Jeraldine Evans in 1949, and was thus responsible for the execution of an innocent man.

Timothy, Beryl and Jeraldine Evans

In 1948, ten years after the Christies had moved into 10 Rillington Place, Timothy Evans and his wife Beryl started renting the top-floor flat. At the time they had been married for less than a year and were expecting their first baby, Jeraldine.

The twenty-four-year-old Evans had an IQ of just seventy. He drove a van for a living, drank a lot, and was known as a habitual liar who concocted self-aggrandising fantasies about his background. Unsurprisingly, given his poor mental development, he found it difficult to read. Beryl, who was just nineteen, enjoyed a close relationship with her husband's two sisters. However, the Evanses' marriage was stormy, with frequent rows about debt, and neighbours commented that Timothy had hit his wife.

In August 1949 Beryl invited a friend by the name of Lucy Endecott to come and stay. They shared the flat's only bed, which forced Timothy to sleep on the floor. His mother arrived and Lucy was persuaded to leave, but by this time it seems that Timothy had fallen in love with her. He was so infatuated that he threatened to throw Beryl out of the window before following Lucy out of the flat. Before long, though, he returned to Beryl, who quickly discovered that she was pregnant again. By the end of November 1949 both Beryl and Jeraldine were dead, and Timothy had been arrested and charged with their murder. Four months later, he was sent to the gallows.

Given what we now know about Christie, this seems an astonishing coincidence: two murderers living simultaneously at the same nondescript address. Can we really believe that Christie – who by this time had already committed two murders – had nothing to do with the deaths of Beryl Evans and her daughter? The controversy has raged ever since Christie's arrest and trial. Soon two inquiries and two parliamentary debates were being held in a bid to discover whether an innocent man had been sent to the gallows for a crime he did not commit. However, nothing was resolved conclusively, and two opposing camps still debate the issue: the first claims that Evans was completely innocent; the second accuses him of the murder of either Beryl or Jeraldine.

F. Tennyson Jesse's (1957) *Trials of Timothy John Evans and John Reginald Christie* and Ludovic Kennedy's (1961) *10*

Rillington Place come down in favour of Evans's total innocence. Kennedy is particularly scathing about the inquiry undertaken by John Scott Henderson – the Recorder of Portsmouth – who was given only eleven days to review the case at the conclusion of Christie's trial. Henderson concluded that Evans did indeed strangle his wife and daughter, disregarding the fact that Christie had confessed to Beryl's murder as well as several other points that should have been in Evans's favour, such as the duration of the police interviews with him. To Kennedy, the inquiry seemed like a 'put up' job to support the police who had arrested, interviewed and charged Evans, and was therefore prepared to let a miscarriage of justice go unchallenged. Henderson subsequently issued a supplementary report to his original, but he did not change his opinion that Evans was guilty.

In 1966 the success of Kennedy's book led Home Secretary Roy Jenkins to appoint Sir Daniel Brabin to re-examine the case. He concluded that there was 'reasonable doubt' over Evans's guilt in relation to the murder of his daughter. As a result, Jenkins granted Evans a 'free pardon' – an amazing decision given that Brabin also concluded that Evans had killed Beryl.

John Eddowes has been at the forefront of refuting Jesse's and Kennedy's version of events with *The Two Killers of Rillington Place* (1994). (It should also be noted that his father Michael published a book that was sympathetic to Evans, *The Man on Your Conscience: An Investigation of the Evans Murder Trial* (1955).) Eddowes benefited from the public release of a number of papers relating to the case, which showed that Evans was a violent man who had attacked Beryl throughout their marriage. This image was far removed from John Hurt's portrayal of Evans in the film version of Kennedy's book, where he was presented as an innocent simpleton. In addition, Eddowes demonstrated that the police had not planted any evidence on Evans and proved that Beryl's body had not been raped after her death, which one might have expected if Christie had been the culprit.

Given these conflicting theories, what should one conclude? That is a difficult question to answer because both Timothy Evans and Reginald Christie were habitual liars who changed their stories repeatedly. Evans made four statements to the police relating to the murders of his wife and daughter: at first he admitted that he had killed them, but then he withdrew that statement. Christie's confession is untrustworthy too, however. He hoped to avoid the gallows through his plea of insanity, and clearly thought that claiming as many murders as possible would support his defence. As a result, he later confessed to killing Jeraldine as well as her mother.

On balance, I feel that Christie is the more likely of the two to be responsible for the murders of Beryl and Jeraldine. In 1949 Christie had murdered twice before; Evans, despite being violent and unpleasant, had not. In criminological terms, that alone makes Christie the far stronger suspect. Furthermore, Beryl and Jeraldine were strangled, which was Christie's preferred method of murder. As the murders of Ruth Fuerst and Muriel Eady indicate, Christie was adept at exploiting his circumstances to locate his victims. It seems that the arrival of Timothy Evans and his family at 10 Rillington Place merely provided him with another opportunity to kill and escape justice.

Peter Manuel and the opportunities of crime

While Haigh and Christie used the opportunities that war and its aftermath created to find suitable victims, Peter Manuel committed property and sexual crimes, then killed the people he had robbed or raped. Manuel – who was born in New York to Scottish parents – moved to Britain in 1932 when he was five, living in Coventry and then in Scotland. He was first arrested for burglary at the age of twelve, spent the next few years in and out of reform school, and was sent to jail aged just sixteen for the sexual assault of a school employee. Further sentences for burglary and rape would follow before he settled with his parents in Birkenshaw, in the east of Glasgow, in 1953. Over the next five years, Manuel would murder at least seven people. The true figure is difficult to determine for a number of reasons. Manuel confessed to and was charged with killing seventeen-year-old Annie Knielands, whose body was found on the fifth fairway at East Kilbride Golf Club in 1956, but the trial judge ordered that the jury find him not guilty on that count. His murder of Sydney Dunn – a taxi driver in Newcastle-upon-Tyne – was not tested in court. And there are suspicions that he may have been responsible for a total of fifteen murders. Unusually for a serial killer, Manuel was indiscriminate about his victims, who included middle-aged men and women, teenage girls and a young boy.

In the autumn of 1956 Manuel was on bail for a theft from a local colliery. Seeing his temporary freedom as an opportunity to commit more crimes, he broke into the home of William and Marion Watt, who lived there with their sixteen-year-old daughter Vivienne. William – a master baker who owned a number of shops in Glasgow – was on holiday at the time, so Marion's sister Margaret had moved in for the week. The bodies of Marion, Margaret and Vivienne, who had all been shot at close range, were found on 17 September by their cleaner, Helen Collison, who contacted the police. They were already investigating a break-in at another local house that had taken place that night, and felt that this might have been the work of Peter Manuel. Although nothing could be proven in either case, Manuel was soon sentenced to eighteen months for the break-in at the colliery. (Poor William Watt spent two months on remand on suspicion of his family's murder. After his release, he met Manuel on several occasions.)

On his release, Manuel visited Newcastle-upon-Tyne, where it is believed he shot and killed Sydney Dunn on 7 December 1957. Having returned to Scotland, he next murdered seventeen-year-old schoolgirl Isabelle Cooke, who had arranged to go to a dance with her boyfriend at Uddingston Grammar School on the night of 28 December. On New Year's Day 1958 Manuel broke into the home of Peter and Doris Smart, where he murdered them and their ten-year-old son Michael. Over the next few days he returned to the house several times to help himself to food. He also drove Peter's car – on one trip he gave a uniformed police officer a lift and advised him on the conduct of the investigation – and even fed the Smarts' cat.

Manuel was eventually caught because his sudden, inexplicable wealth was noticed in the bars he frequented. The police recovered some of the money he had spent and traced the notes back to Peter Smart, who had recently cashed a cheque in preparation for a holiday. Manuel was arrested and charged on 13 January 1958, when he confessed to the murders of the Smarts, the Watts and Annie Knielands. He took detectives to East Kilbride Golf Club to show them where he had buried her body and casually remarked, 'This is the place. In fact, I think I'm standing on her now.' With the type of misplaced arrogance displayed by many serial killers, Manuel defended himself in court. He was found guilty and hanged at HMP Barlinnie on 11 July 1958. His last words were 'Turn up the radio, and I'll go quietly.'

Like Haigh and Christie, Manuel used the opportunities that came his way to kill, although in his case those opportunities were created by other criminal activity, rather than war. As with Christie, all his victims – with the exception of Sydney

Dunn – were killed within a narrow geographical area, which in turn led to his arrest. Moreover, like both Haigh and Christie, Manuel became more careless and less organised as his murder count increased, as his offer of a lift to a police officer indicates.

Does this over-confidence reflect Manuel's arrogant belief in his own invincibility, or could it indicate his psychological unravelling as he lost touch with reality? The same question could be asked in respect to Christie's decision to leave three bodies in an alcove which he then merely papered over. Whatever the answer from the medico-psychological perspective of the serial killer, the reality is that all serial killers have to find suitable victims to murder, and the absence or inadequacy of formal and informal social controls allows them to achieve their objectives. This truism becomes all the more apparent as we move into the 1960s and beyond, when the numbers of both serial killers and their victims increase.

Chapter Six

'To kill undetected': gay men

> I think that you told the court that you had met Evans before. I am interested in the club which you claimed on Friday was frequented by homosexuals. You were a visitor there?
> **Brady:** I have been there about three times.
> What were you doing in that hive of homosexuals?
> **Brady**: Watching the antics of them.

This cross-examination took place during the trial of Ian Brady for the murder of five young people in the early 1960s. It refers specifically to Brady's final victim, seventeen-year-old Edward Evans, whom he implies that he had picked up in a gay club in Manchester on 6 October 1965. Brady then took Edward back to the house he shared with Myra Hindley and her grandmother in Wardle Brook Avenue, Hyde. Hindley's brother-in-law David Smith was also in the house that night. He remembered looking at some miniature wine bottles in the kitchen, then hearing Hindley shout, 'Help Ian!' He rushed into the sitting room to see Brady bringing an axe down on Edward's head, splitting it open.

Brady then continued to hack at the twisting and screaming Edward before finally pressing a cushion to his face and tying a cord around his throat. With Edward dead, Smith first helped clean up the sitting room and then carried the body upstairs with Brady. He also promised to return the following day with an old pram to assist in the disposal of the body. Instead, he went to the police and so brought the 'Moors Murders' to an end.

From hereon I will no longer follow a chronological narrative. Instead, the focus will be on themes related to the five main groups that have fallen victim to British serial killers over the past 120 years: gay men, prostitutes, babies and infants, 'runaways and throwaways', and the elderly. I have adopted this format because the numbers of both serial killers and their victims have increased dramatically since the 1950s. As a consequence, a straightforward chronological history would serve little purpose because several serial killers have often been active simultaneously, usually killing different groups of people. Furthermore, it makes sense to group together the victims of serial killers – almost 350 people since 1960 – because then they can tell us far more about the phenomenon than the killers themselves.

This chapter is about homophobia and how that has facilitated the murder of gay men by serial killers since 1960. Edward Evans, if he was in fact gay, was murdered at a time when homosexual activity was still illegal in Britain, and when condemnation of all gay people was widespread. The description of the club where Brady claims he met Edward – 'that hive of homosexuals' – gives an indication of the disgust and distaste that was prevalent at the time. Moreover, the questioning clearly attempts to trap Brady into admitting that he was a regular at the club, too. Such an admission would have seriously damaged his reputation in the eyes of the judge and jury, so instead Brady insists he was merely 'watching the antics of them' in a bid to distance himself from a group of people that most Britons found morally repugnant.

Given what he was being tried for, his attempt to display similar repugnance (albeit mixed with curiosity) is more than a little ironic.

The last acceptable prejudice

The term 'homophobia' was first used in the 1960s. The American academic Byrne Fone (2000) defines it as an 'antipathy towards [homosexuals] – and condemnation, loathing, fear, and proscription of homosexual behaviour'. He also labels it 'perhaps the last acceptable prejudice'. This prejudice is based on the perception that homosexuality disrupts 'natural law': it is seen as subverting the social, ethical, political, legal, moral and sexual order of society. Fone also notes that homophobia can be found within the gay community itself, which he suggests might be due to gay people internalising the prejudices of a homophobic society. It will be useful to remember this insight when we consider the cases of Peter Moore and Dennis Nilsen – both gay men.

As the twentieth century progressed, and especially once homosexuality was decriminalised, ever more gay people refused to conceal their sexuality. As a result, they became much more visible and therefore increasingly vulnerable to physical attack. The Australian academic Gail Mason (2002) suggests that gay people should produce 'safety maps', an ever changing, personalised, yet shared means of managing how they interact with the rest of society. Through these they can mitigate the threat of homophobic violence. However, there is a flipside. As Brady's cross-examination reveals, some serial killers learn all about these 'safety maps' and use them to gain access to – and the confidence of – their victims. Consequently, despite the precautions that gay men take, violence has continued to be perpetrated against them. And that violence has all too often led to murder.

Some everyday violence against gay men

David Morley was known to his friends as 'Sinders'. Originally from the West Midlands, he moved to London in the 1980s and found a series of bar jobs. By 2004 he had reached a managerial position within a brewery. On the night of 31 October, David was sitting on a bench with his friend Alistair Whiteside, near the Royal Festival Hall on the South Bank. The area is close to several gay entertainment venues, such as the Heaven nightclub, located just across the Thames, under Charing Cross Station. As they sat, the pair were approached by three young men and a fifteen-year-old girl who liked to be known by her graffiti tag, 'Zobbs'. As Zobbs moved towards David she said, 'We're doing a documentary on happy slapping. Pose for the camera.' This was the signal for all four to launch a sustained attack on David and Alistair, although David bore the brunt of the assault, sustaining forty-four impact injuries and a ruptured spleen. Alistair watched as Zobbs landed the final kicks to his friend's head: 'She kicked him like you would kick a football or rugby ball, just swinging her right foot back and kicking him really hard on the head. She did that two or three times, maybe more.'

David was rushed to hospital but he died from his injuries. The doctor who examined him said they were consistent with someone who had been in a car accident or had fallen from a great height. It is not absolutely certain that David and Alistair were attacked because of their sexuality – the gang had assaulted six other people in the previous hour – but it seems likely. Moreover, David was no stranger to homophobic violence. Five years earlier, he had been working as a barman at the Admiral Duncan in Old Compton Street, Soho. At about 6.30 p.m. on 30 April 1999 – with drinkers massing on the pavement outside to catch the last of the sun – David Copeland detonated a bomb that killed three people and injured over sixty others. Copeland was a racist and a member of the British National Party. A few weeks earlier he had planted bombs in Brixton and Brick Lane in the hope of starting a race war, but when that failed to materialise he turned his murderous attention on gay men and women. He would later claim that his actions were motivated purely by a desire to 'be famous'. That seems highly unlikely, though, given that his targets were so specific – well-known centres of London's black, Asian and gay communities, respectively. David Morley certainly did not believe his pub was targeted at random. He helped to distribute a poster that appeared throughout Soho in the wake of the bombing. On it was a simple message: 'They Can't Kill Us All'. Tragically, though, 'they' did kill him. Such was his standing in the gay community that over a thousand people turned out for his memorial service in St Anne's Church, Soho, there was a tribute from Mayor Ken Livingstone, and a busker sang the specially commissioned 'Sinders' Song'.

David Morley was not the victim of a British serial killer; and David Copeland was not a serial killer under the definition that I have chosen to use in this book. However, their stories reveal a great deal about the everyday violence that has been committed against gay people in this country. Even today, when we pride ourselves on being a more tolerant society, homophobia persists. And in the last half-century at least twenty-six gay men have died at the hands of five British serial killers – Dennis Nilsen, Peter Moore, Colin Ireland, Steven Grieveson and the first British serial killer of the 1960s, Michael Copeland. (Unfortunately, it is impossible to say how many lesbian women have died as a result of their sexuality.) This grim statistic is shocking enough, but it should be borne in mind that it is probably a considerable underestimate, given Britain's historic and continuing antipathy towards homosexuality.

Tops and bottoms

Peter Walker was an assistant director on the West End show *City of Angels* – a detective film-noir parody set in 1940s Los Angeles and winner of the Tony Award for Best Musical in 1990. He made no secret of the fact that he was gay and interested in sadomasochism, in which he preferred a submissive role. He was also a regular in the Coleherne pub, on the Brompton Road in West London, a place where he could meet like-minded people. On the night of 8 March 1993 Peter was in the Coleherne, as was Colin Ireland, although they did not know each other. Peter accidentally spilled a drink over Ireland, and then begged to be chastised. Ireland was happy to play along, posing as a 'top', the dominant partner in an S&M relationship, while a 'bottom' takes the submissive role. The two men returned to Peter's flat, where he was tied up and gagged with knotted condoms. Only then did Ireland's true intent become clear: he beat Peter with his fists, a dog lead and a belt, then produced a plastic bag which he placed over Peter's head to suffocate him. Once his victim was dead, Ireland burned Peter's pubic hair – he later told the police he was curious about how it would smell – and then looked through his things. In the course of this he discovered that Peter was HIV positive. This incensed Ireland, so he placed condoms in Peter's mouth and up his nostrils to humiliate him further. Finally, he arranged two teddy bears on the bed in a sexual position.

The manner in which Ireland located and was then able to kill his victim illustrates how 'safety maps' of gay clubs can be used against the gay community by someone with murderous intent. Under normal circumstances, the map can provide a degree of invisibility and privacy to a group of people who are routinely harassed by the rest of society, but that in itself has never guaranteed the safety of a gay man.

Ireland was an avid reader of true crime novels, FBI manuals and Robert Ressler's *Whoever Fights Monsters* (1992), a book about the tracking of serial killers. He fits the 'organised' serial killer stereotype perfectly, ensuring that he did not leave any forensic evidence in Peter's flat that might have connected him to the murder. It may be that he selected his victims carefully, so that he could 'become' a serial killer and thereby gain extra fame or notoriety. Whatever his motivation, he would kill again two months later. Again using the Coleherne as his base, he targeted thirty-seven-year-old librarian Christopher Dunn, who was also interested in S&M. The pair returned to Christopher's flat in Wealdstone, where Ireland tied up and beat his victim before suffocating him by stuffing pieces of cloth into his mouth. Christopher's body was discovered in the flat two days after his murder.

Just four days later Ireland was again in the Coleherne, picking up another victim, thirty-five-year-old Perry Bradley, the son of a US congressman, who was living in Kensington. Perry had never been interested in S&M, but somehow Ireland found an opportunity to tie him up and attach a noose to his neck. He then strangled him, and placed a doll on top of his dead body.

As so often happens with serial killers, the murders were coming in rapid succession now; and three days after he had killed Perry, Ireland struck again. Thirty-three-year-old Andrew Collier, a warden at a sheltered housing complex, took Ireland back to his flat in Dalston. Ireland strangled him with a noose, then rifled through his belongings, looking for items to steal. This followed the pattern he had established in the previous three murders. For the second time, he learned that his victim was HIV positive. Seemingly in retribution, Ireland burned parts of Andrew's body, just as he had done with Peter, and then strangled his cat. He later said he did not want Andrew to have any dignity in death, which explains why he placed the cat's mouth around his victim's condom-sheathed penis, and put the animal's tail, also wrapped in a condom, in Andrew's mouth.

With so many similarities between the two crimes, the police now connected the murders of Andrew and Peter. But it was Ireland himself who pointed them towards the full scale of his activities. On 12 June 1993 he contacted Kensington Police Station to tell them that he had already killed four men. Then he telephoned Battersea Police Station to ask: 'Are you still interested in the death of Peter Walker? Why have you stopped the investigation? Doesn't the death of a homosexual man mean anything? I will do another. I have always dreamed of doing the perfect murder.'

Ireland's final victim was Emanuel Spiteri, a forty-one-year-old Maltese chef who was living in Catford. Now the police attempted to reach out to the gay community, seeking their help in finding the killer. They issued an e-fit (electronic facial identification technique) image of a man seen catching a train from Charing Cross Station with Emanuel on the night he was murdered, in the hope that it might jog people's memories. However, the gay community seemed reluctant to help, maybe because they viewed the British establishment – with the police, of course, as an integral part – as far from sympathetic. In the very month that Ireland claimed his first victim – a gay man who enjoyed S&M – the House of Lords had ruled that consent was not a defence in sado-masochistic activities, and thus upheld the convictions of sixteen men in the so-called 'Spanner Case'. This concerned an investigation by Greater Manchester Police, which began in late 1987 after they anonymously received a videotape of a group of men beating each other. The beatings were so severe that the police concluded someone must have died, so they started to question some two hundred men they thought might have been involved. In September 1989 sixteen of those suspects were charged under the Offences Against the Person Act of 1861 with wounding and causing actual bodily harm. The men's defence rested on the fact that they all shared an interest in S&M and had all consented to the acts on the tape. However, this was rejected and several of the defendants were sentenced to various prison terms in December 1990. After various appeals to lower-level courts, the House of Lords decided by a majority of three to two that the convictions should stand. With the support of the civil rights group Liberty, three defendants then took their case to the European Court of Human Rights, but in February 1997 that court upheld the right of the British government to prosecute such activities in order to protect public health and morals.

In this climate, it is hardly surprising that gay men who were interested in S&M were reluctant to volunteer information to the police. After all, recent history indicated that they would end up in court and possibly even face a prison sentence if they revealed any details of their sex lives. Fortunately, despite the understandable silence from the gay community, Ireland did not take the opportunity to kill again, and several weeks after the murder of Emanuel Spiteri he gave himself up to the police. Eventually he confessed to all five murders.

We know relatively little about Colin Ireland's crimes because the tabloid press was far more muted when reporting his murders than it was in the cases of Peter Sutcliffe, the Wests and, to a lesser extent, Dennis Nilsen – all of which were greeted with near-hysteria. The few details that have been catalogued here emerged after Ireland was convicted, and he has never achieved the level of notoriety he craved. That is doubly ironic because, although he claimed fewer victims than Dennis Nilsen, Ireland is perhaps the most extreme example of a serial killer who targeted gay men through their own 'safety maps'. Perhaps editors simply felt they could not print details of the S&M scene in their 'family newspapers', so they gave the case scant attention. But a more unsettling possibility is that reporters and readers alike felt that anyone with an interest in such unconventional sex was 'asking for it'. Ireland's stepfather, for one, seemed to hold that opinion. After his stepson's conviction he commented: 'Colin wanted to rid the world of those sick perverts. He was sickened by what they get up to behind closed doors and decided that it was his mission to wipe them out. He did what he did and makes no apologies for it. It is the sado-masochists, the really sick ones, he cannot stand' (quoted in Gekoski, 1998). It is hard to imagine a similar comment being made by the relative of a serial killer who targeted the elderly or children.

It is interesting that Ireland eventually had to give himself up to the police in order to achieve at least a modicum of the fame he desired. He felt that the investigation was going nowhere because of official indifference resulting from the sexuality of his victims. As he asked on the phone: 'Doesn't the death of a homosexual man mean anything?' Gekoski (1998) suggests, 'one suspects that the murders of a handful of gay men were unlikely to cause the sort of public outrage and fascination as the murders of young women or children'. The fact that Ireland pleaded guilty at his trial also did not help in his quest for long-lasting fame. With no defence offered, the papers were unable to produce pages of salacious details over the course of many weeks. As a result, public awareness of Colin Ireland soon dwindled. Even so, we know more about him than about Michael Copeland and his victims, who are now all but forgotten.

'I hated things like that'

There are only a few newspaper accounts to remind us of the murders committed by Michael Copeland, although the story they tell is all too familiar. Copeland was a former soldier who murdered sixteen-year-old Gunther Helmbrecht in Verden, Germany, in November 1960; William Arthur Elliott, a sixty year-old estate clerk, in June 1960; and finally George Stobbs, a forty-eight-year-old industrial research scientist, in March 1961. The latter two victims lived in Derbyshire. At this time, homosexuality was still illegal, and it would not be decriminalised until the Sexual Offences Act of 1967 became law. Even then, homosexual activities were deemed legal only if they were undertaken in 'private'. ('Private' here is of course a form of invisibility.)

Copeland seems to have picked up both William and George in a pub in Chesterfield that was frequented by gay men (perhaps the Nag's Head). He then drove with his victims in their cars into the country, where he killed them by kicking or stamping on their heads. As he explained to Chief Inspector Bradshaw at Chesterfield Police Station: 'I killed Elliott and Stobbs and the German boy. I killed them because it was something that I hated. That is why I killed [them]. I hated things like that. I killed [them] because I hated what [they] stood for.' Speaking of George, he elaborated: 'I killed him because he belonged to something I hated most.' At his trial in 1965, his defence barrister quoted Copeland as saying, 'I hate such stuff, but I do not hate them more than most men. I have no obsession about them. My attitude is quite normal towards girls.' There is, then, no doubt about the depth of Copeland's hatred, although it is interesting to note he could not bring himself to name the 'thing' he despised so much, nor describe what George and William 'stood for'. Nevertheless, the jury would have been in no doubt what he meant.

By claiming that he did 'not hate them more than most men', Copeland was clearly attempting to tap into the general homophobia that was prevalent at the time. Of course, Brady attempted to do the same thing a little later by referring to the 'antics' of gay men. And Ireland's chief ally echoed these sentiments when he said his stepson 'did what he did and makes no apologies for it'. By 1993, homosexuality may no longer have been illegal, but the highest court in the land had still just ruled that some sexual behaviour – even when performed in private between consenting adults – was against the law. In effect, the House of Lords was 'sickened', just as Colin Ireland claimed to be, even though the men whose activities caused such revulsion made every effort to keep themselves as invisible as possible. However, the private spaces offered by the Coleherne in London, the pub in Chesterfield and the club in Manchester did not allow gay men to escape victimisation; their 'safety maps' provided no security. Instead, Brady, Ireland and Copeland learned enough about these spaces to enter them and gain access to their victims.

Both Ireland and Copeland denied that they were themselves gay, and any speculation about their sexuality would merely take us into the medico-psychological tradition of analysing serial killers. Of much greater interest is the fact that homosexuality has been marginalised and viewed as 'sick', and gay men have become 'hated' as a consequence. Pathologising gay men in this way – seeing them as 'sick' – was merely the first in a number of steps that led to them being victimised because of their sexuality. And this homophobia provides us with a helpful context when analysing the victims of Dennis Nilsen and Peter Moore.

Peter Moore and Dennis Nilsen – the 'fairy liquidators'

Dennis Nilsen and Peter Moore are two gay men who primarily targeted other gay men. In a typical example of jail humour, they have been dubbed the 'fairy liquidators' by other prisoners. There are several echoes of Copeland and Ireland in the crimes of Nilsen and Moore. Pubs and alcohol again feature regularly, as does S&M in the case of Moore. Homophobia, visibility and invisibility (to such an extent that several of Nilsen's victims remain unidentified to this day) and police incompetence are other common elements. For instance, Nilsen was caught largely because his fellow tenants could no longer flush their toilets. He had disposed of his victims' body parts down the drains, which had become blocked as a consequence. So it was the vigilance of a Dyno-Rod engineer rather than any great detective work that led to Nilsen's capture. The arresting officers merely expressed astonishment that someone had been able to kill repeatedly in a quiet London suburb without them knowing anything about it. Given that the crimes and arrest of Peter Sutcliffe should have been relatively fresh in the memory, especially of detectives, this seems a curious reaction. But perhaps it is suggestive of the largely anonymous lives of those men who were victimised by Nilsen, as described by Brian Masters (1986):

> [Nilsen's victims] all had the most slender connections with their origins. Some were in trouble with the police, some were drug addicts or 'punks', some (but not all) were

> homosexuals, many were homeless and jobless, and many drifted through the crowds of London without aim or purpose, their disappearance being such a regular event that their few acquaintances were neither surprised nor alarmed.

This goes some way to explaining why Nilsen was able to kill fifteen young men between 1978 and 1983. But before considering these victims, we shall look at the less well-known case of the first Welsh serial killer – Peter Moore – who murdered Henry Roberts, Edward Carthy, Keith Randles and Tony Davies in late 1995.

Moore lived at Darlington House in Kinmel Bay, North Wales. It was the most prominent house in the area, a home for Moore and his elderly mother but also a library and, on election days, a polling station. Moore was an entrepreneur who owned a chain of cinemas, and he was often to be seen and heard in the local media, promoting his business. As a result, he was very well known throughout North Wales, although he had managed to keep secret the fact that he was gay and interested in S&M. His neighbour Joan Marland would later comment, 'We didn't talk about being gay – we never gave it a thought.' Nevertheless, Moore visited various hidden places within the community where he could meet those who shared his interests. After the death of his mother in 1994, Darlington House itself increasingly became one of these hidden places.

Moore's first victim was Henry Roberts, a bachelor in his mid-fifties who lived alone in an isolated farmhouse and had an interest in Nazi memorabilia. Moore murdered him only two days after appearing on the local BBC news to talk about opening a new cinema, and only two weeks after being fined for possession of an offensive weapon. The weapon in question was a truncheon, found in the van he used to drive to and from his various cinemas. Henry was killed in what Detective Superintendent Peter Ackerley of North Wales Police described as a 'frenzied attack', sustaining forty-seven stab wounds to his torso, back and buttocks. His trousers had been pulled down during the attack. Henry's homosexuality was never doubted by the police, and there was some evidence of sexual activity prior to his death, but this information was not released to the public. However, David Sutcliffe – a BBC cameraman who was covering the story – noticed a pathologist's report mentioning all of these details while he was filming at police headquarters. He later claimed that an appeal to the gay community – of which he himself was a member – might have yielded Moore's name. Instead, the police remained tight-lipped about this aspect of the case, so Henry's sexuality remained invisible in a community that did not readily talk about 'being gay'.

Two weeks later, Moore murdered Edward Carthy, whom he had picked up in a bar in Liverpool. Like Henry, Edward was stabbed to death, then Moore buried his body in a forest close to the A5. Later, when he was interviewed by the police, Moore said Edward had asked him whether he was 'one of these ... "Nilsen type of fellows", apparently referring to one of the murderers who used to kill men'. Moore had replied, 'Yes.' Edward's body was found only when Moore himself directed the police to it after his arrest.

Moore's next victim, Keith Randles, was a father and grandfather who worked as a nightwatchman on a building site. He lived on-site, too, in a caravan. Again, he was stabbed repeatedly.

Tony Davies also had children. He was murdered by Moore on 17 December 1995 on Pensarn beach, between Rhyl and Colwyn Bay. Unknown even to most local people, the beach was a gay cruising area, which led the police finally to acknowledge that they might be dealing with a serial killer who was targeting gay men. Faced with a third murder in as many months (only Moore himself knew about Edward Carthy at this stage), an appeal was made to the gay community for information that might assist the police in their enquiries. Over fifty calls were received, and one led directly to Darlington House and Peter Moore. It is therefore tempting to conclude that the police were able to apprehend a serial killer only by making visible what had been invisible.

His 'tragic products'

Dennis Nilsen's first victim has no name. All we know is that he was young, Irish, had short, curly brown hair, and happened to be in the Cricklewood Arms – a rough Irish pub on the Cricklewood Broadway – on the night of 30 December 1978. He was drinking Guinness by himself when he was spotted by Nilsen. As the pub was about to close, he agreed to accompany Nilsen to 195 Melrose Avenue, where the pair drank until they were 'insensible'. Nilsen got into bed with the Irishman, although no sexual activity took place. Then, in the small hours of the morning, he first strangled the youth, then drowned him in a bucket of water. He hid the body under the floorboards until 11 August 1979, when he took it into his back garden and burned it on a bonfire. Then he pounded the ashes to powder and raked them into the ground. As a result, every trace of a young Irishman was destroyed by someone who knew nothing about him. It seems certain that we will never know who he was.

Brian McConnell and Douglas Bence – two *Daily Mirror* journalists who produced an account of the Nilsen murders in 1983 – claim that 7,177 people were missing in the United Kingdom in 1980, and that in subsequent years New Scotland Yard's 'active' missing persons index hovered around the 5,000 mark. Most of these 'derelicts', as McConnell and Bence label them, are attracted to London, where they can 'survive without identity, lost among the large anonymous section of the population ... without being identified, pilloried or punished'. This anonymity continues to draw people to the capital, so it is important to ask why so many of them do not want to be identified, and why they are afraid of being 'pilloried or punished'. Nilsen's first victim may well have been a 'derelict', although we have no way of knowing for sure. By contrast, there is no doubt about his final victim.

Stephen Sinclair was born in 1962 to an unmarried mother in Perth. Almost immediately he was taken into the care of the local authority, Perthshire County Council. At the time he did not even have a surname: on his birth certificate he was identified as 'Stephen Neil No Name' because his mother was not married. Fostered by Neil and Elizabeth Sinclair when he was fourteen months old, Stephen was legally adopted by them a few months later. The Sinclairs lived in a bungalow in Belbeggie, some six miles north of Perth. They already had three daughters and yearned for a son, although, as McConnell and Bence uncharitably put it, '[They] did not know that by nature Stephen was a misfit.' Stephen was an epileptic, and for a long time he had no control over his bladder or bowels. He spent long periods of time in the Royal Dundee Liff Hospital. When he was twelve, he was sent back home to the Sinclairs, who by this time had had another two daughters. Stephen proved difficult to handle, starting fires in the house and committing a variety of petty crimes. His early teenage years were spent in remand centres, 'special schools' and borstals, before he gradually drifted into a world of unskilled work.

As a young adult, Stephen attempted suicide, self-harmed, spent more time in custody, regularly used drugs, and on several occasions threatened his step-sisters. At their wits' end, the Sinclairs finally renounced him and stated that they wished to return him to the care of the council. Once again he would be 'Stephen Neil No Name'. He was eventually fostered again, but this proved to be no more stable than his time with the Sinclairs. Soon he gravitated towards the Norrie Miller Riverside Park in Perth, 'an open Mecca to drug pushers, from pot to marijuana to smack or junk', according to McConnell and Bence (1983). In effect, he was now a vagrant. He went through punk and skinhead phases and associated with drug addicts, drunks and male prostitutes. One of the Sinclair girls spotted him in a street in Perth in 1982, but soon after he made his way to London.

Stephen did not have much to offer by way of talent, education or skills. He seems to have survived as a male prostitute, and found accommodation in hostels run by the Salvation Army or the Scottish charity the Mungo Trust. He also registered with various social security offices and job centres, including the one in Kentish Town where Dennis Nilsen worked as a civil servant. By January 1983, Stephen was living in a hostel in Kentish Town, but he almost immediately ran into trouble there for stealing from a fellow resident. He was arrested and brought before magistrates at Highbury Corner, who remanded him on his own recognisances for a week. During this week he met Nilsen, although the pair probably knew each other by sight from the job centre. Stephen was never seen alive again, but Nilsen did not have time to dispose of his body. Consequently, the police were able to identify him through fingerprint records. At the time of his death he was just twenty years old.

Nilsen labels his victims his 'tragic products' (Masters 1986), implying that there was tragedy in their lives prior to meeting him. This is a very self-serving conclusion to draw. We might instead see the 'tragedy' beginning only when they met Nilsen, rather than in their childhoods and upbringings. Nevertheless, there is a recurring and depressing regularity about the backgrounds and circumstances of the men he murdered. (In so far as we are able to identify his victims. We have no details about at least seven of them, and Nilsen himself has been no help because he knew nothing about them either.) Graham Allan, originally from Newarthill in Glasgow, was an alcoholic and a drug addict. John Howlett (described by Nilsen as 'John the Guardsman'), from High Wycombe, worked on the travelling fairs and was on the run from the police. Martyn Duffey, from Merseyside, first travelled to London aged just fifteen and returned there two years later. He was constantly in trouble with the police and addicted to Valium. Malcolm Barlow, from Rotherham, was an epileptic. He first encountered Nilsen when he was having a fit. Nilsen called an ambulance, which took Malcolm to Willesden General Hospital. On his release, he visited Nilsen to offer his thanks and Nilsen killed him. Other 'tragic' young men were murdered and stored under Nilsen's floorboards before being burned or butchered, prior to being flushed down the toilet. Yet Nilsen also killed a Canadian tourist, Kenneth Ockendon, who did not fit the stereotype of his victims at all. Similarly, Paul Nobbs, whom Nilsen tried but failed to murder, was far from 'tragic'.

Paul was a twenty-one-year-old student at London University, where he was studying Polish. He met Nilsen at the Golden Lion in Dean Street, Soho, in November 1981, and the pair then visited Foyles bookshop. Later, they returned to Nilsen's new flat in Cranley Gardens, from where Paul twice phoned his mother. They both drank heavily, which ruled out any sexual activity, then went to bed together. Paul woke at about two in the morning with a dreadful headache and very bloodshot eyes. Nilsen said something to the effect of 'God, you look bloody awful,' but he was largely sympathetic, and the two men then returned to bed. The following day Paul was still feeling ill, so he went to University College Hospital and asked for a check-up. The duty doctor suggested that someone had tried to strangle him.

This episode is significant for two reasons. First, as was argued at Nilsen's trial, where Paul gave evidence for the prosecution, Nilsen's failure to see the murder through to its conclusion seems to have been calculated. After the phone calls to Paul's mother, Nilsen must have been aware that his target would have been missed. Of course, this could not be said about most of his victims. Furthermore, given their visit to Foyles, many people might have identified Nilsen as the last person to be seen with Paul. Second, Paul did not report the incident to the police because he believed they would not give much credence to his report on account of his homosexuality. There were good grounds for a gay man living in London in the early 1980s to feel that way.

Almost a year earlier, Nilsen had been in the Golden Lion, drinking and looking for a partner. There he met twenty-five-year-old Douglas Stewart, from Wick in the North of Scotland, who had come to London having trained as a chef at the Gleneagles Hotel in Auchterarder, Perthshire. Now he worked at the Holland Park Hotel in Ladbroke Terrace. His girlfriend, Dawn, was a chambermaid at the same hotel. Douglas liked the Golden Lion because he often met other Scots there – people like Nilsen, who himself had trained as a chef in the army. They both drank a great deal, and when the pub closed Nilsen invited Douglas back to his flat in Melrose Avenue, where he plied him with more alcohol. Douglas fell asleep in an armchair and when he woke up he realised it was very late, so he accepted Nilsen's offer to stay until the morning.

Nilsen also suggested that they should sleep together, but Douglas declined.

Some time later Douglas woke again. He was aching from sleeping in the armchair and tried to stretch, but he immediately realised that his ankles were tied to the leg of the chair. He then sensed that his tie was being loosened and knotted around his throat: Nilsen was throttling him. Douglas managed to aim a blow at Nilsen's face, and struggled out of the chair. He did not flee but stood his ground and accused Nilsen of trying to kill him. In the shouting match that followed Nilsen pointed out that if Douglas should go to the police, 'They'll never believe you. They're bound to take my word for it. Like I told you in the pub, I'm a respectable civil servant.' He then produced a knife, but Douglas somehow managed to calm the situation. Eventually Nilsen put away the knife before offering Douglas another drink. Unsurprisingly, this was declined, and Douglas finally decided to leave. By now, it was 3.30 a.m. He walked and then ran down Melrose Avenue until he found a telephone box, whereupon he dialled 999. When the police car arrived Douglas reported that Nilsen had tried to kill him and showed the two officers the red marks on his throat. One of the officers stayed with him while the other knocked on Nilsen's door. As Douglas would recall later, 'Nilsen denied everything I had told the police. He gave them the impression that we were going out together and it was just a lover's quarrel in a homosexual romance.' He claims that as soon as the word 'homosexual' was mentioned the police lost all interest, and he heard from them again only after Nilsen's arrest. By then, he was living in Thurso in the North of Scotland. As he says, 'The police made a bad mistake. They let him off when he attacked me. Now we don't know how many more he killed at Melrose Avenue after he took me back there. Or Cranley Gardens after that.' (Masters, 1986).

In fact, we know that Nilsen would go on to murder another ten young men and assault a further three.

The manner in which the police dealt with Douglas Stewart surely confirms that Paul Nobbs's assessment was justified: it would have been a waste of time for him to report Nilsen's assault. Nilsen – who in his time had been a policeman, soldier and civil servant – was used to dealing with authority figures and knew how to deflect their attention. And there was no better way of doing that than mentioning a homosexual lovers' tiff. Douglas, of course, was not gay and so did not possess the insight of either Nilsen or Paul. He was incensed by the attack that had been made against him and presumed he would be taken seriously. Given the evidence of the marks round his neck, he fully expected the police to arrest the man responsible. They failed to do so because they assumed Douglas was gay. His treatment is therefore indicative of the invisibility of gay men, and specifically of the violence to which they are so often subjected. If the police had arrested Nilsen, they would have publicised what had taken place 'behind closed doors', and so would have exposed a world that they wanted to remain hidden. In sum, they would have provided the same protection to gay men that they offered to the rest of society. Unfortunately, that was something they did not seem prepared to do at the time.

Cop culture and the policing of homophobic violence

Is it fair to conclude that the police do not take seriously violence perpetrated against gay men and women? Are these groups denied the protection of the state that is routinely offered to heterosexuals? To try to find answers to these questions, we must consider the issue of 'cop culture'.

Professor Robert Reiner of the London School of Economics

has been at the forefront of research into 'cop culture', investigating whether the police are guided by a set of beliefs and assumptions that influence their behaviour both on the streets and when conducting inquiries (Reiner, 1992). He asserts that 'an understanding of how police officers see the social world and their role in it . . . is crucial to an analysis of what they do, and their broader political function', which seems a fair assessment. On the basis of extensive interviews with police officers of various ranks, and in different areas, Reiner suggests that the main characteristics of British 'cop culture' are: mission–action–cynicism–pessimism; suspicion; isolation/solidarity; conservatism; machismo; prejudice; and pragmatism.

Of these, the sense of 'mission' is paramount: police officers do not see what they do as just another job, but one that has a worthwhile purpose of shielding the weak from the predatory. The police are an indispensable 'thin blue line' protecting society, and this inevitably means that they sometimes have to take action. However, some police officers might want to take more action than is necessary, and will pursue excitement and thrills, rather than repetitive, mundane and boring police tasks, such as filling in paperwork. Over time, Reiner suggests, officers become more cynical and pessimistic. They have 'seen it all before', and each new development in society is viewed in almost apocalyptic terms, with the potential to destroy the moral world that has shaped their sense of mission. Furthermore, the police are trained to be suspicious, but that can lead to stereotyping potential offenders, which in turn can skew crime figures. For example, a disproportionate number of young black men are stopped and searched in the street, which means a disproportionate number of young black men are arrested, which 'confirms' the stereotype that young black men are more likely to be offenders than young white men. But, of course, that 'confirmation' has no validity. Given that police officers are often socially isolated, there is little likelihood that they will encounter young black men who have similar values, interests and tastes to themselves. Similarly, the need to rely on one's colleagues in a tight spot means that there is a great deal of internal solidarity in the police, which exacerbates their isolation from other members of society. Reiner suggests that a consequence of this is that the police are hostile to and suspicious of black people (or at least they were when he carried out his research in Bristol in the 1970s). Unfortunately, the Macpherson Inquiry into the murder of the black teenager Stephen Lawrence in April 1993 seemed to indicate that little had changed over the next two decades. And more recent accusations of racism within the Metropolitan Police (sometimes from its own officers) have continued to plague the force.

Reiner also concludes that police officers tend to be politically and morally conservative, and so culturally distrust groups such as gay men and prostitutes that could be said to challenge conventional morality. This does not mean that 'cop culture' is puritanical; rather, it is characterised by 'old-fashioned machismo', in which there are high levels of stress, drinking and divorce. Finally, Reiner highlights pragmatism: police officers' simple desire to get through the day as easily as possible. Officers do not like fuss – especially paperwork – and would rather concentrate on the practical, no-nonsense aspects of the job. Reiner calls this 'conceptual conservatism', because it camouflages an aversion to research, innovation and change.

Pragmatic and conservative

Reiner's findings help explain why Paul Nobbs failed to report Nilsen's attack on him as well as what happened after Douglas

Stewart called the police. In Douglas's case, the two officers who responded to his 999 call were being pragmatic – they wanted to get to the end of their shift with the minimum of fuss and paperwork. Meanwhile, their moral conservatism about homosexuality meant they freely accepted Nilsen's explanation that the assault had merely been part of a lovers' tiff, something which they would rather remained behind closed doors. More broadly, analysing 'cop culture' allows us to see more clearly the quality of service that is provided not only to the gay community but to other people whose lifestyles might clash with moral conservatism.

Britain's most recent serial is Stephen Port, who is sometimes known by the press as the 'Grindr Killer', given his use of this gay dating app to attract his victims. On Grindr, Port pretended to have served in the Royal Navy and to have graduated from Oxford. He killed four young gay men – Anthony Walgate, a fashion student; Gabriel Kovari, who had moved to London from Slovenia; Daniel Whitworth, a chef; and, finally, Jack Taylor who worked as a fork-lift truck driver. Anthony's body was found outside the front door of Port's flat and the bodies of his other three victims were discovered in the nearby graveyard of the Church of St Margaret of Antioch in Barking – two of them found by the same woman walking her dog. Despite this connection to Port, the police never linked the first three deaths and nor were they seen at the time as 'suspicious'. Only consistent pressure from the families of the murdered men and the reporting of a number of gay newspapers led to a review of the cases and the unmasking of Port as a serial killer. However, the Independent Office of Police Conduct (IOPC) cleared the seventeen officers who worked on the case of any wrong-doing in July 2019 and so none were disciplined, although the IOPC did also suggest that there had been 'systematic failings' in the investigation. It is hard not to reflect that little seems to have changed since the days of Dennis Nilsen.

Of course, underlying all of this is homophobia. From pre-1967, when homosexuality was illegal, to the present day, with gay men and lesbians free to enter into marriage, antipathy towards the gay community has remained consistently virulent, if increasingly, although not exclusively, invisible. 'Invisible' because we often glimpse the reality of homophobia in its absences. Why, for example, are there no premier league football players willing to 'come out' as gay, in marked contrast to out lesbians in the women's game? Do gay football players fear a hostile reaction to their sexuality from fans on the terraces? For some – such as Michael Copeland – that antipathy can develop into personal hatred, loathing and murder. Others – such as Colin Ireland – utilise society's more latent antipathy to exploit the vulnerability of gay men. It is true that some gay men kill other gay men, but that should not disguise the fact that homophobia has created the circumstances that have allowed homosexuals to become prime targets of serial killers in this country. Small wonder, then, that many gay men still choose to remain secretive about their sexuality.

Chapter Seven

'It sounds a bit evil now': sex workers

> The fact that Sutcliffe managed to evade capture for five years was not due to his intelligence but rather to an astonishing lack of it on the part of the police ... [E]ven more amazing was the fact that detectives had questioned Sutcliffe at his home several times during the five-year hunt as, with his black beard, he fitted almost identically the police artist's portrait of the killer drawn from the descriptions of victims who survived. Why the police never thought to put him in a line-up for the surviving victims to identify defies comprehension.
>
> Ian Brady

On 30 October 2006 nineteen-year-old Tania Nicol left the house she shared with her mother Kerry and her younger brother Aaron. She was going to work in the small red-light area of Ipswich, clustered around Portman Road, the home of the local football team. It was the last time she was seen alive. Tania's mother claimed she did not know her daughter was involved in prostitution, while her friends preferred to remember her as a 'lovely girl who was always giggling at the back of the class' at the local comprehensive. After leaving school, Tania drifted into a variety of unskilled jobs, including working as a chambermaid in a local hotel, but soon her drug use meant she needed to earn more money, so she started to work in some of the town's massage parlours, including the one where her mother worked as a cleaner.

Tania's naked body was finally found on 8 December, in a stretch of Belstead Brook near the village of Copdock, six days after that of Gemma Adams had been discovered in the same stream. Like Tania, Gemma had been stripped naked. Her body was found over a mile from Tania's as the crow flies, near the village of Hintlesham. But it seems likely that their corpses were dumped together, with Tania's drifting downstream after several days of torrential rain. Gemma was twenty-five when she disappeared on 15 November, and was described by her father as a 'loving daughter' who was 'good company, bright and intelligent'. She had grown up in the village of Kesgrave, where she had enjoyed going to the Brownies, playing the piano, and riding horses. However, by the time of her death she had been using heroin for eight years, had lost contact with her family, and had become involved in sex work.

The discovery of the naked bodies of two young women in the space of a few days elevated this local story to one of national and eventually international interest. I was invited by Sky News to visit Copdock to see what I made of the locations where Gemma and Tania were found. It was immediately obvious that the killer must have had local knowledge of the roads, given that they were so isolated and almost hidden, and that he had been quite careful when disposing of the bodies. The disused roads near Hintlesham and Copdock gave him plenty of opportunity to park a vehicle containing two bodies; and because the area was so isolated, with no streetlights, there was very little chance that he would be disturbed. Moreover, by leaving the bodies in water, the killer significantly reduced the amount of forensic evidence that the police would be able to gather. He must also have been plausible as a 'punter' to persuade Tania and Gemma into his car.

This calculating murderer was clearly targeting sex workers, and the fear was that he would soon find the opportunity to kill again. But I could not help wondering if he had killed *before.* Five years earlier, another young woman, Natalie Pearman, had been murdered and her body had been dumped in a strikingly similar way. She had also lived in East Anglia – in Norwich – and had been involved in sex work. Her killer has never been found.

Over the next few days the bodies of three more young women would be discovered. Anneli Alderton, Paula Clennell and Annette Nichols were all sex workers and they all had serious drug habits. Anneli's body was found on 10 December, near the village of Nacton. Swingheaven.co.uk describes the location as a 'good dogging site – go through Nacton village, past the school, and then follow signs for the picnic area. The bottom two car parks are best for couples.' Anneli – who was three months pregnant when she died – was described by her friends as 'a bright soul [who] always made us laugh at school'. She had last been seen on the 5.53 p.m. train from Harwich to Colchester on 3 December. Because her body was left in woodland and was found relatively soon after her death, there was more opportunity for the police to gather forensic evidence. They also released CCTV footage of her last train journey to the public. After the discovery of her body, the police warned women in Ipswich to 'stay off the streets. If you are out alone at night, you are putting yourself at risk.' This caused the *Guardian* journalist Julie Bindel to comment, 'We could have been right back to 1977, when police effectively put a curfew on women during Sutcliffe's killing spree.' This might well have been the intention in Ipswich, too, because the investigation seemed to be going nowhere fast, and Anneli had been murdered after more police patrols had been deployed on the ground.

Paula's and Annette's bodies were found close together on waste ground, this time near the village of Levington. Paula was survived by her three young children. Annette, perhaps hoping to leave sex work behind her, had recently completed a four-year beautician's course at a local college.

Now the local drugs economy of Ipswich was opened up for public scrutiny: for instance, it was revealed that the price of a bag of heroin in Ipswich was fifteen pounds. Of course, drugs were at the heart of the local sex industry, whose workers had often displayed a determination to keep earning a living in spite of the risks they faced. When the local authority had ringed the red-light area with CCTV cameras in the hope that it would dissuade them from soliciting, they had instead used mobile phones to arrange meetings with their punters. Ironically, this was a far more dangerous way for the women to operate because it gave them less time to assess their clients – they simply arranged a meeting-place on the phone and jumped in the punter's car when he arrived. ASBOs, fines and 'zero-tolerance policing' had also done little to curb prostitution, and several of the women said being arrested was merely an 'occupational hazard'. They also talked of the tension that existed between themselves and the local police.

Then, suddenly, Steve Wright was arrested on 19 December 2006. In January 2008 his case finally went to court. He was found guilty of all five murders and sentenced to a 'whole-life' tariff in prison.

The Ipswich murders remind us once again of the persistent vulnerability of young women who are involved in sex work, whether in 1888 or in 2006. When working on the case, I was struck by how many people had theories on the identity of the killer and why he was targeting prostitutes. These ranged from suggestions of religious motives – the first two bodies had been left in water to 'cleanse their sins' – to more fanciful ideas that the murders had been ordered by the Russian mafia. Many of the theories had an Oedipal element, with the murderer assumed to be a middle-aged man living at home with his prudish mother and venting his sexual frustration in the only way he knew how. The medico-psychological tradition had clearly seeped deep into the public's consciousness! Of course, it is perfectly understandable that people wanted to help catch the killer, but amid all the suggestions of who he might be, no one thought to ask how he was finding it so easy to kill one woman after another. As ever, the answer lies in his choice of victims.

Between 1994 and 2004 over sixty women involved in sex work were murdered. The killer was convicted in only sixteen of these cases. Since 2011 sex workers have remained a persistent target of murderers, although the trend of late seems to have become for the woman to be killed indoors, whilst working alone, as opposed to being murdered when working out on the streets. Why do so many 'prostitute-killers' get away with murder? Is it simply easier for them to pick up vulnerable women? Is it harder to make evidence against them stick? Or is there a deeper problem resulting from our attitudes towards these women, attitudes that are shared by the police and the judicial system?

Two vulnerable young women and their killers

The campaigning journalist Nick Davies (1997) describes Natalie Pearman as a 'walking portrait of an ordinary girl'. She had four brothers and sisters and a cat named Lucy, and lived with her mother and stepfather in a neat council house on the edge of the village of Mundesley, half an hour's drive north of Norwich. Natalie took ballet lessons, liked to draw and had wanted to join the RAF. However, a part-time job in the village's takeaway burger bar propelled her into a very different world. Within a year of working there she was in care; within two – when she was just sixteen – she had changed her name to Maria, dyed her hair blonde and was working the streets in the 'Block' in Norwich. Her patch was outside the Ferry Boat pub, where she charged £15 for a hand-job, £20 for a blow-job, and £30 for straight sex. Her body was found dumped in a lay-by just outside the city's boundaries.

Nick Davies asks us to consider the slippery slope that saw Natalie's dreams of a career in the RAF disintegrate and what led her into prostitution. For Davies, the key is that the Pearmans were 'poor . . . they were trapped at the bottom of the financial cliff. They had enough to get by, but no more.' Natalie had no money for Brownies, or to go on school trips, and as one crisis after another hit the family the ballet lessons had to stop, too. Prostitution provided her with wealth she could barely imagine, and maybe even a way out of the poverty that was all she had ever known. Crucially, for Davies, she consciously chose this new life: 'She saw that she was trapped and when she looked at her future, it was even worse – getting pregnant, getting married, getting a house and stewing slowly in front of a television for forty years. What else was there?'

Irrespective of whether this is a true reflection of Natalie's life, it is undeniable that many young people drift from one place to another as they reach adolescence, and consequently become vulnerable in various ways. Some of them inevitably turn to prostitution as a 'survival strategy'. The government has recently calculated that of eighty thousand people currently involved in prostitution in Britain, fifty-six thousand began when they were children or young teenagers. Through his sympathetic, tragic portrayal of Natalie, Davies highlights the dangers faced by the thousands of women and girls who are just like her, as well as the ability of their attackers to escape justice.

One murderer who was caught was Paul Brumfitt, who killed Marcella Ann Davis in February 1999. Marcella was a nineteen-year-old single mother who earned her living as a prostitute in Wolverhampton. Brumfitt had previously served fifteen years of a discretionary life sentence for murdering two men in 1979. Given the time lapse between these two earlier murders and the killing of Marcella, I was initially reluctant to include Brumfitt in my list of British serial killers; twenty years is a very long gap in a 'series'. However, I did so as Marcella's story sheds light on the deaths of many other young women who worked as sex workers, and also offers a warning about the possibility that killers like Brumfitt can change.

Marcella had almost certainly turned to sex work to help support her nine-month-old daughter Dione. On the night of her murder, she left her daughter with a friend, promising to be back by 11 p.m., then took a taxi into Shakespeare Street. She phoned her friend six times during the evening to check on Dione; the last of these calls, presumably made just before she was picked up by Brumfitt, was at 9.11 p.m. Brumfitt, who would go on to rape two other sex workers before being caught, took Marcella back to his flat in Woodsetton, where he killed her. Then he took her body to a small yard he had rented in Cooper Street, where he dismembered and burned her remains. Marcella was identified only by her dental records and a small bunch of keys that were found in the ashes. Her story is typical of the life histories of many young women who turn to prostitution. They are young, have dependants and routinely face violence from punters. What makes Marcella's story unusual is not that she was murdered, but that her killer was caught before he could kill again.

The serial killer and the prostitute

Most people will not have heard of Natalie Pearman or Marcella Ann Davis, but they will surely be familiar with Peter Sutcliffe – the Yorkshire Ripper. Sutcliffe mainly targeted sex workers, although he killed and attacked other women, too. The crucial question is: why was he able to escape detection for so long?

In total, West Yorkshire detectives interviewed Sutcliffe on eleven occasions, nine of them during the formal investigation of a series of attacks and murders of women in the North of England between 1975 and 1981. Police incompetence therefore must be considered when analysing this case. Indeed, it was the subject of an investigation by Lawrence Byford, the former Chief Inspector of Constabulary. Byford presented his report to the House of Commons in January 1982, but it was suppressed by successive governments until June 2006, when its contents were finally released under the terms of the Freedom of Information Act.

As we have discussed in relation to the identification of Martha Tabram as a Jack the Ripper victim, one by-product of the Byford report was the establishment of the Home Office Large Major Enquiry System (HOLMES) in 1985. This information retrieval system helps senior investigating officers in complex cases to see if there are links between separate incidents within and between police force areas. It is also worth noting here that, seemingly 'inspired' by Sutcliffe, Steven Griffiths murdered Susan Rushworth, Shelley Armitage and Suzanne Blamires, all of whom sold sexual services, in Bradford between 2009 and 2010. Griffiths ensured maximum publicity for himself by giving his name when he first appeared at court charged with these murders as the 'crossbow cannibal'. He was enrolled at Bradford University on a doctoral programme related to homicide studies.

Sutcliffe was eventually convicted of murdering thirteen women, but he is suspected of killing more. As we have seen, many people believe Jack the Ripper killed more than the 'canonical five', too; and Thomas Neill Cream's list of victims would have been larger but for several lucky escapes. All of these men targeted prostitutes, and all of them literally got away with murder for long enough to find the opportunity to kill again. A similar killer may well have murdered eight sex workers in London in the 1950s and 1960s. Beginning with Elizabeth Figg in 1959 and ending with Bridget O'Hara in 1965, these murders have been attributed to one man – 'Jack the Stripper' – but the culprit has never been caught. Ironically, the murders started just months after the introduction of the new Street Offences Act of 1959, which made it an offence for a woman to loiter or solicit in a street or other public place for the purposes of prostitution. There was a ten-pound fine for a first offence, but subsequent convictions could result in a term of imprisonment. However, no matter how many women ended up in jail, the Act did not stop either the supply or the demand for women prepared to sell their bodies for sex.

For Elizabeth Figg and Bridget O'Hara read Marcella Ann Davis and Natalie Pearman, or any of the other women who appear in this chapter. As feminist commentators have argued with conviction, Britain is both a capitalist and a patriarchal society, which helps explain not only why so many women enter prostitution but why so many women – as opposed to men – fall victim to serial killers. Police incompetence and 'cop culture' go some way to explaining why Sutcliffe escaped detection for as long as he did; but he, his victims, their neighbours and the police all lived within a broader culture that valued one gender over another. Therefore, violence perpetrated against women generally, and against sex workers specifically, can be seen to reflect the patriarchal relations through which men maintain power. Recognising this inequality allows us to understand why serial killers so often murder women and children. Men possess power which they have used to dominate, oppress and, in some circumstances, kill.

The first victims of the Yorkshire Ripper

Peter William Sutcliffe first came to the attention of the police in 1969, after two incidents involving sex workers. Described by Lawrence Byford in 1981 as 'an otherwise unremarkable young man', Sutcliffe had become fascinated by women soliciting in Leeds and Bradford. For a while, he and his friend Trevor Birdsall were content to drive around the two cities' red-light districts in Birdsall's Reliant Robin, but soon Sutcliffe's fascination turned to violence. One summer night – leaving Birdsall in the car – Sutcliffe attacked a woman from behind with a cosh (a sock with a stone in it). He then returned to the car to boast of what he had done to his friend. However, his victim gave a statement to the police, which allowed them to trace Birdsall's car. Birdsall admitted he had given Sutcliffe a lift, and as a result Sutcliffe was questioned about the incident. In the interview he claimed he had assaulted the woman after a drunken argument, and 'the incident was written off as typical of the local culture of birds and booze'. He was merely given a caution. In other words Sutcliffe, rather than his victim, was given the protection of the state in a culture where violence towards women – and especially prostitutes – was the norm. A month later, on 29

September 1969, he was arrested in the red-light area of Bradford for possession of an offensive weapon: a hammer.

These two incidents offer chilling, early examples of Sutcliffe's modus operandi. There would be echoes of them in 1975, when he assaulted Anna Rogulskyj and Olive Smelt, and throughout his years of killing. He frequented red-light areas, targeted women involved in sex work, and attacked his victims from behind by hitting them over the head with a hammer. Later, Sutcliffe gained confidence as the police continued to fail to catch him. The frequency of his attacks increased and he would stay with his victims for longer periods, during which time he would repeatedly stab and mutilate them.

We can only speculate what might have happened if the two incidents in 1969 had been dealt with differently. As it was, they set in train a pattern of assaults, murders and police investigations that ran from 1975 until January 1981, when Sutcliffe was finally arrested. The table below lists the assaults and murders he committed in these years, and the dates when he was interviewed by the police.

Assaults and murders of Peter Sutcliffe

Name	Date	Murder or Assault	Interview
Anna Rogulskyj	5 July 1975	Assault	
OliveSmelt	15 August 1975	Assault	
Wilma McCann	30 October 1975	Murder	
Emily Jackson	20 January 1976	Murder	
Marcella Claxton	9 May 1976	Assault	
Irene Richardson	5/6 February 1977	Murder	

Name	Date	Murder or Assault	Interview
Patricia Atkinson	23 April 1977	Murder	
Jayne MacDonald	26 June 1977	Murder	
Maureen Long	10 July 1977	Assault	
Jean Jordan	1 October 1977	Murder	2 and 8 November 1977
Marilyn Moore	14 December 1977	Assault	
Yvonne Pearson	21 January 1978	Murder	
Helen Rytka	31 January 1978	Murder	
Vera Millward	16/17 May 1978	Murder	13 August and 23 November 1978
Josephine Whitaker	4/5 April 1979	Murder	29 July 1979
Barbara Leach	2 September 1979	Murder	23 October 1979, 13 and 30 January and 7 February 1980
Marguerite Walls	20/21 August 1980	Murder	
Upadya Bandara	24 September 1980	Assault	
Theresa Sykes	5 November 1980	Assault	
Jacqueline Hill	17 November 1980	Murder	

The complications of 'good-time girls'

The first woman Sutcliffe murdered was Wilma McCann. Born and brought up in Inverness, after school Wilma worked at the Gleneagles Hotel, near Perth. She was pregnant with her first child – Sonje – before she was out of her teens. Later, she met and married Gerald McCann, an Irish joiner, and they moved to Leeds, where they had three children of their own. However, the marriage failed after just six years, in 1974. Michael Bilton (2003) suggests that the couple divorced because Wilma 'couldn't settle, she hadn't the self-discipline to adapt to either marriage or motherhood. She liked her nights out. And she liked other men.' After Gerald left, Sonje – although she was only nine – assumed many of the responsibilities of bringing up her siblings. By this time, her mother was regularly out on the town to earn her living. On the morning that Wilma's body was found, Sonje and her brother were discovered freezing at the local bus stop, wearing their school coats over their pyjamas. They were hoping to meet their mother, who they thought might have caught an early bus home.

Wilma's personal circumstances were immediately apparent to Dennis Hoban, head of Leeds CID. As Bilton puts it: 'the fact that [Wilma] was a good-time girl would be a major complication'. Hoban needed witnesses to come forward so that he might establish Wilma's movements on the night she died, but he knew that he would not get far if he was completely open about the life she led. Quoting from interviews conducted with Hoban, Bilton explains: 'labelling a victim a prostitute in this situation was unhelpful. Experience showed the public were somehow not surprised at what happened to call girls.' Consequently, the police's media strategy was to concentrate attention on the children in a bid to evoke the public's sympathy. Every other effort was also made to catch the killer: at one stage, Hoban had 137 officers working on the case, who clocked up a total of 53,000 hours, calling at 5,000 houses and generating 538 witness statements. Even so, Sutcliffe was not apprehended. Then, less than three months later, the body of Emily Jackson was found.

Emily was murdered in a factory yard in Leeds. She had been hit over the head with a hammer, dragged to where her body was eventually found, then stabbed repeatedly with a Phillips screwdriver. Forensic evidence would show that this had been a frenzied attack: fifty-two stab wounds were found on her torso. Hoban linked the two murders immediately, and tried to build a picture of Emily's background in the hope that it might provide a clue to her killer. Through her husband Sydney – who was originally a suspect – Hoban learned that Emily had an 'insatiable sexual appetite'. Sydney would often even drive her to meet her clients. All of this again meant that Hoban felt compelled to be circumspect when dealing with the press. As Bilton puts it, the detective had to 'put the best possible gloss on the woman's private life'. Nevertheless, the investigation made little headway, and within a few months Marcella Claxton had been savagely attacked.

Marcella was a black, unemployed, twenty-year-old single mother of two children, with an IQ of just 50. Originally from the Caribbean island of St Kitts, at the time of her attack she was living in the Chapeltown area of Leeds and was three months pregnant. She insisted that she was not a sex worker, although Sutcliffe picked her up as she left a nightclub, and he may have thought she was soliciting. Clearly she was suspicious of him, because Marcella hid from Sutcliffe at some point later in the evening. After a few minutes – thinking he had gone – she emerged from her hiding-place, only to discover that Sutcliffe was still waiting. He then hit Marcella repeatedly on the back of the head with a hammer, which knocked her to the ground. She then 'played dead' while Sutcliffe masturbated over her. When he finally left, she half-crawled, half-dragged herself to a phone box and dialled 999. Sutcliffe then reappeared – maybe to ensure that she was dead; maybe to do further damage to her body – but he was unable to find Marcella, who continued to hide in the phone box. Eventually an ambulance arrived and took Marcella to Leeds General Infirmary, where fifty-two stitches were put into her head wounds. Unsurprisingly, she lost the baby that she had been carrying.

Despite her injuries, Marcella was able to give the police an excellent description of the man who had attacked her. However, the police insisted that she had been assaulted by a black man, rather than the white, bearded man she described. Bilton suggests: 'the simple truth was that West Yorkshire police did not believe what Marcella Claxton was telling them'. Moreover, they said the description she gave was 'hopelessly inadequate' when rejecting her claim for criminal injuries compensation in 1978. As a result of the police's attitude towards her, Marcella was included in the list of Sutcliffe's victims only after he himself admitted to the attack following his arrest.

A 'respectable local girl'

It is interesting to compare the manner in which the police dealt with the attacks on Wilma, Emily and Marcella with how they handled the murder of Josephine Whitaker, which took place on 4 April 1979. Josephine was born in 1959, the only daughter of Thelma and Trevor Whitaker. Her parents separated when she was a small child, so Josephine lived with her mother at her grandparents' house in Halifax. She was devoted to her grandparents, and continued to visit them on a regular basis after her mother remarried. Indeed, that was where she had been on the night she was murdered. As Josephine was returning home, Sutcliffe hit her twice on the back of the head, then stabbed her twenty-one times – nine on the front and twelve on the back. He also stabbed her several times through the vagina, and bit her breast. Sutcliffe himself would later describe the attack as follows:

I saw Josephine Whitaker walking up the street ... and I caught up with her after a couple of minutes. I realised that she was not a prostitute but at that time I wasn't bothered; I just wanted to kill a woman. When I caught up with her I started talking to her. I asked her if she had far to go. She said 'it's quite a walk' ... she started speaking to me about having just left her grandmother's and that she had considered staying there but had decided to walk home ... We were approaching an open grassland area. She told me she normally took a short cut across the field. I said you don't know who you can trust these days. It sounds a bit evil now there was I walking along with my hammer and a big Phillips screwdriver in my pocket ready to do the inevitable. We both started to walk diagonally across the grass field ... I asked her what time it was on the clock tower which was to our right. She looked at the clock and told me what time it was. I forget the time she said ... I lagged behind her pretending to look at the clock. I took my hammer out of my pocket and hit her on the back of the head twice ... she fell down and made a loud groaning sound. To my horror I saw a figure moving along the main road from my right. I took hold of her by the ankles and dragged her face down away from the road further into the field. She was still moaning as I did this ... I saw at least two figures walking along the path across the field [and] I forgot to mention that we passed a man walking a dog. We were within five feet of him. As these people were walking on the path she was still moaning loudly. I took my screwdriver. I remember I first pulled some of her clothing off. I was working like lightning and it [was] all a blur. I turned her over and stabbed her numerous times in the chest and stomach with the screwdriver. I was in a frenzy.

(Quoted in Bilton, 2003).

The murder of Josephine Whitaker should have been crucial in the police investigation. There were several eyewitnesses, one of whom had walked within five feet of Josephine and Sutcliffe, and others who had seen a man with a thick moustache parking his car in the vicinity. There were also new pieces of evidence in the form of the bite marks on Josephine's body and footprints left at the crime scene. It seems that even Sutcliffe was anxious about what the witnesses may have seen or heard. Furthermore, Josephine was an 'innocent woman' – or, as Byford described her, 'a respectable local girl' – rather than a sex worker. This had an impact on the investigation in two ways. First, there was an unprecedented public response to Josephine's murder: within a few days there had been over a thousand calls to the police from concerned members of the public who had information to share. Second, there was a change of attitude among the police themselves. As one female detective working on the case told Bilton, 'before that [murder] I just thought, well, he seems to be hanging around prostitutes, I'm OK, but after that one, I thought no one was safe'.

Unfortunately, though, the investigation still got nowhere. And it was thrown further off track in June 1979 – almost two months after Josephine had been murdered – when a tape was sent to the police by a man claiming to be 'Jack the Ripper'. Detectives were convinced the tape was genuine, but we now know that it was recorded by twenty-three-year-old John Humble. In March 2006 Humble admitted to four counts of perverting the course of justice by sending three letters and the tape to the police. As a result, he was sentenced to eight years' imprisonment. In court he was described as a 'hopeless alcoholic' who had led a 'spectacularly inadequate life'.

Certainly the tape was profoundly important in helping Sutcliffe to evade detection, but it is also instructive to look at how his victims were described by the police, and to assess how these descriptions affected the course of the investigation. Wilma, for example, was described as having no 'self-discipline' while liking her nights out and her men. Emily had an 'insatiable sexual appetite' and unconventional marital arrangements. While Marcella – who heroically survived a vicious attack and gave the police an accurate description of Sutcliffe – was simply not believed by detectives. It seems almost certain that Marcella's ethnicity, and possibly her low IQ, led the police to be less than sympathetic towards her. Similarly, the police had preconceived ideas about the sex workers, Wilma and Emily: they seem to have presumed that male violence was an occupational hazard which these women simply had to face. As a result, they felt the need to put a 'gloss' on Wilma's and Emily's private lives before appealing to the public for help. Otherwise, they feared the public reaction would be a lack of surprise and sympathy. These were 'bad women' who could be held morally responsible for what happened to them: it was their own fault that they had been murdered.

In contrast, Josephine was 'a respectable local girl'. Of course, 'respectable' instantly distances Josephine from Wilma, Emily and Marcella, but it is also interesting to note the use of the word 'local'. This implies that she belonged to the community: Josephine was one of 'us', not an alien 'other' like a prostitute, who, while she might reside within the community, could never be called part of it. Consequently, a blind eye could be turned both to prostitution itself and to the death of anyone involved in it. The same could not be done in 'respectable' Josephine Whitaker's case, which explains the massive public response to her murder. The police freely disclosed the number of officers, man-hours, houses that were visited, and witness statements that were taken in Wilma's case. All of these are very impressive and would seem to indicate a diligent police force trying to catch her murderer.

However, we do not know how many telephone calls the police received in response to their appeals for help from members of the public. One can only presume that this figure was nowhere near as impressive as it would be later when Josephine's murder was being investigated.

Not that any of this mattered to Sutcliffe. As he told his police interviewers, he knew that Josephine was not involved in prostitution, but by that stage he 'just wanted to kill a woman'. So he took Josephine's life in exactly the same manner as he had Wilma's and Emily's. He inhabited a world of 'birds and booze' where assaulting a woman was an everyday event. Consequently, he made no moral judgement when he chose to kill Josephine Whitaker: she was vulnerable simply because of her gender, and that allowed Sutcliffe to victimise her just as he had Wilma, Emily and Marcella.

By 1979, Sutcliffe was growing in confidence. Whereas previously he had gained access to his victims only because of their involvement in sex work, he was now self-assured enough as a killer to attack women like Josephine Whitaker. He had worked out how to incapacitate his victims and how to kill them, and must have started to think that he was never going to be caught, no matter whom he targeted. Indeed, none of his remaining victims was involved in sex work. In September 1979 he murdered Barbara Leach, a humanities and economics student at the University of Bradford; next to be killed, in August 1980, was Marguerite Walls, a civil servant from Leeds; Upadya Bandara, a doctor from Singapore, was attacked the following month but survived; as did Theresa Sykes, who was attacked in November; finally, Jacqueline Hill – Sutcliffe's last murder victim – was killed only days after Theresa had been assaulted. Jacqueline was a social worker and a Sunday school teacher. On the night that she was killed, she was returning home from a seminar organised by the Probation Service.

Many people have said that the police should have caught Peter Sutcliffe long before any of these crimes were committed. Perhaps they would have if his earlier victims had not been involved in prostitution. But is the criticism that is routinely levelled at the West Yorkshire Police justified? Did they not simply mirror the broader male-dominated culture in which they worked, a culture that used but did not value women in general, and certainly those involved in prostitution? That is certainly what the police themselves have argued: by stressing the effort that they put into the case in terms of man-hours, witness statements taken and so on, the implication is clearly that they did everything they could. In other words, it was not police incompetence or lack of commitment that allowed Peter Sutcliffe to attack women over a six-year period but reluctance among the public to become involved because of who his victims were. Keith Hellawell (2003) – who worked on the case – claims that officers 'worked eighteen hours a day for months on end. They did not take leave, for fear of missing some crucial piece of information. They became human databases.' He also says that the Yorkshire Ripper team were the 'finest detectives I ever worked with', and that finding Sutcliffe had been like looking for 'a needle in a haystack'.

However, there is another side to the story of the investigation. Much of the debate about police competence or otherwise has previously centred on office management and administration. Questions have been raised as to whether a computer would have helped; how the Major Incident Room was utilised; how records were stored and cross-referenced; and whether neighbouring police forces shared information as they should have done. However, no attempt has been made to assess the police handling of the Sutcliffe case by considering the number of times he was interviewed and whether these interviews were influenced by 'cop culture'. It should be recalled that over a decade later, when the police had all the advantages of numerous technological developments and were much more experienced in sharing information, they failed dismally when investigating the murder of Stephen Lawrence. And those failings were related directly to the police's 'institutional racism', rather than to administrative failures, or not having access to a computer.

Lost opportunities

Between 1975 and 1981, Peter Sutcliffe was interviewed nine times by the police, as is outlined in the table below.

Police interviews with Peter Sutcliffe

Number	Date	Reason	Interviewers	Decision
1	2 November 1977	£5 note	DC Howard	Further inquiries
2	8 November 1977	Follow-up	DCs L. Smith and Rayne	Filed; knew of 1
3	13 August 1978	Cross-area	DC P. Smith	Further inquiries; sightings; knew of 1 and 2
4	23 November 1978	Follow-up	DCs P. Smith and Bradshaw	Further inquiries; knew of 1, 2 and 3
5	29 July 1979	Triple-area sightings	DCs Laptew and Greenwood	Filed; did not know of 1, 2, 3 or 4

Number	Date	Reason	Interviewers	Decision
6	23 October 1979	Follow-up	DCs Vickerman and Eland	Filed; knew of 1, 2, 3 and 4
7	13 January 1980	£5 note	DS Boot and DC Bell	Further inquiries; knew of 1 and 2
8	30 January 1980	Follow-up	DCs McAlister and McCrone	Further inquiries; knew of 1, 2, 3, 4, 6 and 7
9	7 February 1980	Follow-up	DCs Jackson and Harrison	Filed; knew of 1, 2, 3, 4, 6, 7 and 8

As the table indicates, Sutcliffe was interviewed on average once every four and a half months in the last four years that he was active as a killer: twice in 1977, 1978 and 1979, and three times in 1980. In 1977 he was interviewed twice within the space of six days; and in 1980 twice within eight days. However, he was never detained as a result of these interviews or even taken to a police station for further questioning; and none of the interviews ultimately contributed to his arrest. (Sutcliffe's arrest on 2 January 1981 was as much a matter of luck as judgement. Having turned his attention once more to women involved in sex work, this time in Sheffield, he was arrested with a sex worker in his car. The police became suspicious when they realised that the car had false number plates and asked Sutcliffe to accompany them to the station. However, he was able to hide the hammer that he would have used to kill the woman, and this was not recovered until the following day.)

Sutcliffe was first interviewed about a five-pound note that was discovered in a secret compartment of Jean Jordan's handbag after she had been murdered on 1 October 1977. It was presumed – correctly – that this had been used by the killer in payment for sexual services. This was a significant find because it was one of a new batch of banknotes that the police learned had been delivered only to branches of the Midland Bank in Manningham, Shipley and Bingley. Some thirty-four local companies, employing six thousand people, used these branches to pay their staff's wages. Among them was a local firm of engineers called T. & W.H. Clark (Holdings), who at the time employed Sutcliffe. Furthermore, it seemed that Jean's killer knew the mistake he had made in leaving the note, because there was evidence that he had returned to the undiscovered body a week or so after the murder to try to retrieve it.

Sutcliffe was also interviewed as a result of 'cross-area' or 'triple-area' sightings, which some police dubbed the 'punter's index'. His car (which he changed regularly) had been spotted cruising the red-light areas of Leeds and Bradford, and later in the red-light area of Manchester, too. So, for example, between 19 June and 7 July 1978 his red Ford Corsair was spotted on seven occasions, six times in the red-light area of Bradford and once in the red-light area of Leeds. Between 26 June and 22 November 1978 his black Sunbeam Rapier was seen passing through Bradford's red-light area thirty-six times and Leeds's red-light area twice. Then, on 22 February 1979, it was also spotted in Moss Side, Manchester, by which time it had been seen on a further three occasions in Leeds and Bradford. All of this made Sutcliffe a potential, if not a prime, suspect for police hunting a killer of sex workers in Yorkshire.

The technique of using 'cross-area' and 'triple-area' sightings was developed because so many cars were being logged in each red-light district. In other words, there were so many men buying sexual services that the police could not keep track of the cars they were trying to record. In one night in Manchester, for example, four thousand cars were sighted and logged. One woman police sergeant recalled: 'It really hit me how many men were involved with prostitutes ... after a fortnight there were so many actions coming through I remember thinking: "Surely there cannot be that many men who need to go to a prostitute?" I couldn't believe the numbers of men doing it' (quoted in Bilton, 2003). This helps to contextualise the police's reaction to Sutcliffe's first assault on a woman in 1969, when 'the incident was written off as typical of the local culture of birds and booze'.

The first interview was conducted by DC Howard on 2 November 1977 at Sutcliffe's home in Bradford, which he shared with his wife Sonia. Sutcliffe was unable to produce any of the five-pound notes from his 29 September wage packet, which he had received two days before Jean Jordan was murdered. He did, though, tell DC Howard that he had been at home with Sonia on the night of 1 October, while on the 9th – when the killer had returned to Jean's body – he had been at a house-warming party. Sonia corroborated this version of events, and neglected to mention that her husband had driven some relatives home after the house-warming, and had been gone for some time. DC Howard also noted in his report that Sutcliffe did not own a car, which was not true.

Six days later DCs L. Smith and Rayne conducted a follow-up interview that only strengthened Sutcliffe's alibi for 9 October: his mother confirmed that they had all been at the house-warming party. The two detectives did learn that Sutcliffe owned a red Ford Corsair, but they did not bother to examine either the car or the garage. Lawrence Byford is especially critical of this interview, describing it as superficial, not at all probing, with the officers seemingly willing to accept every answer at face value. He concludes that if the officers had dug a little deeper, they would have broken Sutcliffe's alibi for 9

October; and if they had examined his car, they would have discovered that it had 'similar tyres to those which were left at the Richardson scene'. Irene Richardson had been murdered by Sutcliffe on 5 February 1977 on a playing field in Leeds. She had been struck over the head with a hammer, then her body had been exposed and slashed with a knife. Tyre marks were left at the scene of the crime, and a 'tracking inquiry' was mounted to identify the car. Fifty-one possible vehicle models were identified, with 53,000 registered owners in the West Yorkshire area, including Sutcliffe. Twenty thousand of these owners were then interviewed, but Sutcliffe was not one of them. Byford concludes that Smith and Rayne's attitudes were 'not as positive as [they] should have been'; that they 'failed to comply with their instructions' (they had been told to search Sutcliffe's car, if he had one); and that the interview was therefore a 'lost opportunity'.

Sutcliffe was next interviewed nine months later, after the punter's index had identified his Ford Corsair in the red-light areas of Bradford and Leeds. However, by then, he had already changed his car to a Sunbeam Rapier. This had also been sighted in the red-light area of Bradford, but DC Smith (not the same DC Smith who conducted the second interview), the interviewing officer, was unaware of the fact. When DC Smith arrived at the Sutcliffes' home on 13 August 1978 – three months after Vera Millward had been murdered in Manchester – he found Sutcliffe decorating the kitchen. Sutcliffe claimed not to remember what he had been doing on the night that Vera was murdered, but Sonia suggested that her husband 'would have come home from work and stayed with her all evening'. She then left the room to make some tea, whereupon DC Smith asked Sutcliffe if he used prostitutes. Sutcliffe strenuously denied the suggestion and seems to have convinced DC Smith that his car was logged merely because the red-light district was en route to his place of work. Once again Sutcliffe's home, garage and car were not searched, but this time Byford is more sympathetic to the interviewer, concluding: 'not unreasonably Constable Smith accepted that the Sutcliffes were a normal young couple who were anxious to improve their home and were putting most of their effort into doing so'. Three months later a follow-up interview was belatedly conducted, but this was 'treated as a matter of simple routine to the extent that Detective Constable Bradshaw who accompanied Detective Constable Smith on his visit to Sutcliffe's home did not even get out of the police vehicle'.

Sutcliffe's next interview took place on 29 July 1979, again because his car had been seen in the red-light areas of Bradford, Leeds and Manchester. It was conducted by DCs Laptew and Greenwood, who were unaware that Sutcliffe had previously been interviewed for similar and other reasons. This interview lasted over two hours, and Laptew and Greenwood were not satisfied with many of the answers that Sutcliffe gave: they felt that his explanation for the sightings in Bradford and Leeds lacked credibility and they were suspicious that he flatly denied the sighting of his car in Manchester. They also knew that Sutcliffe resembled some of the photofits that had been provided by survivors of his attacks, and that his shoe size matched footprints that had been found at the scene of Josephine Whitaker's murder three months earlier. Laptew and Greenwood did not arrest Sutcliffe, but they did submit a comprehensive report detailing their views to their commanding officer – Inspector Slocombe. However, Slocombe would later claim that he could not remember receiving this report. Byford – exhibiting great restraint – comments: 'Despite the most probing investigation it has not been possible to trace what happened to Constable Laptew's report after he submitted it . . . I cannot help concluding that one or other of the senior officers involved in these events is now loath to accept responsibility for what in effect was a serious error of judgement.' It is fairly safe to assume that Laptew's report was filed as requiring 'no further action'.

The remaining four interviews were simply follow-ups to the car-sighting interviews or the five-pound-note interviews. Several of the detectives involved were suspicious of Sutcliffe – thus ensuring that he was never ruled out of the inquiry – but these latter interviews were often perfunctory, with the last two being held at Sutcliffe's place of work. Overall, Byford concludes that Sutcliffe should have been arrested, and quotes Ian Fleming's *Goldfinger*: 'Once is happenstance. Twice is coincidence. The third time is enemy action.' He continues: 'If this concept had been applied to the record of Sutcliffe's association with the Ripper inquiry there were clearly grounds for him to be placed in the "suspect" category.' Byford criticises the interviewers for failing to take a positive line and not bothering to query Sutcliffe's lies. However, he rather lets them off the hook by saying that they were inadequately briefed and 'bogged down in routine paperwork', which meant they had little time to study the files relating to Sutcliffe before interviewing him.

This seems rather forgiving of those involved in the Yorkshire Ripper investigation, especially when one considers what West Yorkshire Police discovered about them. In September 1978 two detectives on the case were forced to resign, while thirteen others were subjected to internal disciplinary procedures after not completing the tasks assigned to them and making false statements that they had. Can such dereliction of duty be explained simply by the fact that these officers were 'bogged down in routine paperwork'? Bilton (2003) thinks not: 'even before the Ripper attacks, the attitude of the police in the 1970s towards violence against prostitutes was hugely ambivalent ...

police officers felt that it was hard enough keeping the peace and controlling crime at the best of times, without women putting themselves in harm's way by going with men with money and making themselves vulnerable.' Bilton does not develop this analysis. Nor does he seek to explain how 'vulnerability' is created by both the wider cultural climate of 'booze and birds' and by the failure of the police to provide adequate protection to women involved in sex work. Instead, he merely accepts that police ambivalence towards women involved in sex work exists, and implies that the prostitutes' vulnerability is their own responsibility.

But how widespread was this ambivalence at the time of the Yorkshire Ripper? In attempting to answer this question we need to reconsider the issue of 'cop culture' to determine whether – in the words of the Macpherson Inquiry into the murder of Stephen Lawrence – Sutcliffe's victims were given an 'appropriate and professional service'.

Cops displaying 'cop culture'

To reiterate, Professor Robert Reiner (1992) says 'cop culture' is dominated by seven factors: mission–action–cynicism–pessimism; suspicion; isolation/solidarity; conservatism; machismo; prejudice; and pragmatism. It is important to assess the extent to which these characteristics were visible during the nine interviews with Peter Sutcliffe undertaken as part of the Yorkshire Ripper inquiry. (It should be remembered at this point that not one of these interviews led to Sutcliffe being arrested or even being viewed as a prime suspect.) Some of the interviews were certainly perfunctory, and Byford has drawn attention to the failure of several officers to carry out their enquiries in a way that was 'positive'. They also consistently failed to search

Sutcliffe's house, garage or car. The first officer to interview Sutcliffe incorrectly thought he did not even own a car. Another officer left the interviewing entirely to his partner, remaining in their squad car throughout.

We might see this as indicative of the final element Reiner identifies: pragmatism. These officers seemingly wanted to get through the day as easily as possible, with the minimum of fuss and the minimum of paperwork. The interviews they conducted were routine, mundane and repetitive. We should also remember that some officers viewed their interviewing and administrative responsibilities with such disdain that they fraudulently claimed to have completed them when they had not, and that two detectives were forced to resign as a consequence. The failure of senior officers to act upon the Laptew report is also significant, prompting the sternest criticism Byford was able to muster. In sum, there was a 'failure of leadership of senior officers', just as there would be over a decade later in the Stephen Lawrence investigation.

However, there was another element to the Yorkshire Ripper investigation, and particularly to the inquiry into it. Byford claims to have conducted the 'most probing investigation', but he constantly faced another aspect of 'cop culture': solidarity in the face of adversity. The officers involved in the Ripper investigation supported each other throughout the inquiry and refused to give evidence against their colleagues. Consequently, even the Chief Inspector of Constabulary could not get to the bottom of how Laptew's report came to be ignored, nor who might have been responsible. One is tempted to conclude that if Byford was unable to pierce this solidarity, no one else would have succeeded in doing so.

Perhaps the most obvious expression of 'cop culture' within the interviewing process can be found in the attitudes and opinions that several officers formed about Sutcliffe and his wife.

These are prime examples of what Bilton calls police 'ambivalence' when they investigate violence towards women involved in prostitution. Reiner's fourth characteristic of 'cop culture' – conservatism – can also be glimpsed in DC Smith's conclusion that the Sutcliffes were a 'normal young couple who were anxious to improve their house and were putting most of their effort into doing so' after Smith had discovered Sutcliffe decorating his kitchen. The adjective 'normal' is important here, as it suggests that Smith saw something of himself, and his own moral order, in the Sutcliffes. They came across as just like him and his friends, so how could one of them be a serial killer? Nevertheless, Smith is there to interview Sutcliffe, so when Sonia is out of the room – making the tea (a 'woman's responsibility') – Smith asks Sutcliffe 'man-to-man' if he has ever 'used' prostitutes. When this is denied the denial is immediately accepted, even though Sutcliffe's car had been repeatedly spotted cruising through red-light districts where women had been murdered.

It is interesting to speculate what officers such as Smith viewed as 'normal' behaviour for men, and for women. Was it normal for men to use women involved in sex work? Conversely, was it abnormal for women to be prostitutes? One way of answering these questions is to look again at how Josephine Whitaker was described after her murder: she was an 'innocent ... respectable local girl', in marked contrast to Sutcliffe's previous victims, who were viewed as 'good-time girls' with 'insatiable sexual appetites', 'lacking in self-discipline'. These descriptions leave little doubt as to what West Yorkshire Police detectives conceived as normal, and what they saw as abnormal.

Finally, another of Reiner's 'cop culture' characteristics – machismo – crops up in the perfunctory investigation into his very first assault, which was dismissed as typical of a 'local culture of birds and booze'.

All of this is important. For if the interviews had been conducted in a more professional, 'positive' manner, Sutcliffe would almost certainly have been viewed as a strong suspect, and his alibis might well have been exposed as lies. The interviews reveal that vulnerability can be created by the police failing to provide an 'appropriate and professional service' to people, on this occasion to women involved in sex work. That vulnerability was not self-created by the women putting themselves in harm's way, as Bilton would have it, but was the responsibility of the police. They failed to carry out their duties appropriately and collectively failed to deliver a service to one group within the community because of how the members of that group lived their lives. Consequently, they failed to provide the protection of the state to many women. The assumption was that violence, and even murder, went hand-in-hand with prostitution, so no one – least of all the police – found the fact that sex workers were being brutally attacked unusual or out of the ordinary.

We cannot be certain what Sutcliffe thought of the nine interviews, as he was never officially asked about them following his arrest. However, as we saw in the epigraph that opens this chapter, Ian Brady – who befriended Sutcliffe in prison and discussed the interviews with him – could not understand why Sutcliffe was not arrested earlier. In an insightful assessment, Brady felt that the investigation displayed an 'astonishing lack of [intelligence]' on the part of the police. It is fair to conclude that, by escaping capture for as long as he did, Sutcliffe was able to perfect the way that he killed, and gained the confidence that he needed to kill again. Indeed, Sutcliffe told Keith Hellawell (2003) that he grew in confidence each time he was stopped by the police but not arrested: he interpreted their inaction as a sign that God was on his side. Perhaps it is not too fanciful to suggest that if Sutcliffe had been arrested after the first or second interview, several women would still be alive today.

There have been many attempts over the past hundred or so years to change attitudes towards women involved in sex work. In particular, there has recently been a move to view sex workers, especially young sex workers, as victims, and to offer them protection, support and a way out of the life they are leading, rather than simply to prosecute them. Increasingly, there has been recognition that Britain's social policy needs to alleviate the circumstances that make young people vulnerable to exploitation and coercion into sex work. Many of those who end up working on the streets suffer physical and sexual abuse within their families, homelessness, poor school attendance and problematic drug use, so it seems clear that tackling these issues must be the first step on the road to combating prostitution.

However, some elements of sex work remain the same as ever. Many women are driven to it by simple economic necessity, with the knowledge that they can earn money because of the seemingly insatiable demand for sexual services. Furthermore, society in general continues to be ambivalent towards women involved in sex work, a fact that is revealed most starkly when they are victimised, and especially when they are murdered.

Chapter Eight

'I read what you sead about me': runaways

> The police are going to knock on my door and they've found a young girl. 'Can you come and identify the body?' It's so horrible. It's a horrible feeling inside.
>
> Mother of Laura

In the week before Christmas 2007 the BBC broadcast a documentary called *Runaway*. Its subject was fifteen-year-old Laura, who had run away from home over 150 times. The documentary followed her for a few months, trying to piece together what drove her to such extreme behaviour and giving a glimpse into what it is like to be young and homeless in Britain today. Often Laura would disappear for days – sometimes weeks – before returning home with black eyes, scars, bruises and scratches. Once she was picked up by a man who drove her to Manchester. She explained that she was not afraid of getting into cars with strangers, and refused to believe that such people might be a danger to her. Her mother was less trusting of those who tried to lure young women with promises of drink and drugs, as the quote at the start of this chapter indicates.

Laura's mother is right to be afraid for her daughter, because several serial killers have targeted the homeless, young, addicted, poor and desperate. In *Dark Heart* (1997), Nick Davies describes the children he encountered on the streets of 'hidden Britain'. One of these was Emma in Nottingham: 'she is homeless, she is a crack addict, she is a child prostitute, she has been raped, robbed, strangled and whipped, and yet she makes no protest'. We do not know what became of Emma, but homelessness, addiction, rape, robbery and strangulation were all still prevalent in Nottingham in 2004 and 2005, when Mark Martin fulfilled his desire to become the city's first serial killer. As he boasted to a fellow prisoner while on remand at HMP Nottingham, 'If you kill one, you might as well kill twenty-one' (see 'Drifter Craved to be a Killer', *The Times*, 17 January 2006).

Martin was a 'homeless drifter' who committed some of his crimes in the company of another homeless man called John Ashley. He first murdered eighteen-year-old Katie Baxter, whom her father remembered as 'a lovely, happy girl with her whole life ahead of her', in a derelict building in the city. Next he lured twenty-six-year-old Zoe Pennick, a homeless heroin addict who had been sleeping rough, to the same building on the promise of giving her cigarettes, clothes and a stolen credit card. Finally, Martin killed twenty-five-year-old Ellen Firth after a drink- and drug-fuelled afternoon at the property he used as a squat following an argument about money to buy drugs. He then set light to the squat in an effort to conceal Ellen's body. All three women were strangled.

The families of Katie, Zoe and Ellen all denied that the women had been homeless, but all three were certainly sleeping rough when they were killed. Some measure of Zoe's circumstances can also be gleaned from the fact that her father's claim for £11,000 criminal injuries compensation was turned down on the grounds that Zoe had a number of criminal convictions.

The focus of this chapter is homelessness resulting from young people running away, deliberately choosing to stay away, or being thrown out of their homes by their families or carers. It concentrates on the nine victims of Fred and Rosemary West whose bodies were found in the cellar and garden of 25 Cromwell Street, Gloucester. Eight of those nine victims – the exception is Lucy Partington – provide an insight into the phenomenon of young people moving away from home and thereby becoming vulnerable to serial killers. There is no analysis of the other murders known to have been committed by West, including those of his first wife Rena, their eldest child Charmaine, and Ann McFall, a young Scottish nanny who was West's lover. Rena's and Ann's remains were found in a field in Much Marcle, where West had grown up in the 1950s; Charmaine's at 25 Midland Road, Gloucester, where the Wests had once lived. West is suspected of having committed more murders, too: David Canter (2003) believes that he may have killed another twenty young women. Again, though, these will not be analysed here.

This focus on the Wests is inevitable, because 25 Cromwell Street was a house that attracted runaways, and the Wests generally targeted young women who were, or had recently been, homeless. The house became well known as a place where young people could find a bed for the night, and West himself called it a 'bloody communial [*sic*] centre' (quoted in Burn, 1998). Howard Sounes (1995), one of the first West biographers, describes it as 'almost open house to every waif and stray looking for shelter . . . these visitors were not the sort who would be inclined to go to the authorities. In many cases they were in trouble with the police themselves, or runaways from institutions which they feared and loathed.' Gordon Burn (1998) notes that the house attracted 'floaters and drifters. Floating and drifting. [The Wests] were like a magnet for these kind of people.' In 1994 the police investigation discovered that over 150 people had spent some time at 25 Cromwell Street over the years. Detective Superintendent John Bennett said 'runaways from local children's homes or absconders' gathered there, which gave the house a 'reputation that made it attractive to rebellious teenagers' (Bennett and Gardner, 2005).

DS Bennett, like so many police officers we have encountered, is exhibiting classic 'cop culture' here. He assumes that the young people at Cromwell Street must have been 'rebellious', but such a supposition flies in the face of studies that have explored why teenagers run away from home. They can be motivated by myriad different reasons, although family instability, violence, conflict, neglect, rejection, problems at school, and sexual and physical abuse are often cited as root causes. Indeed, fewer than half of the Wests' victims were even reported as missing to the police, which gives some indication of their domestic circumstances and the complexity of what we term 'homelessness'.

Runaways and throwaways

The Children's Society has conducted extensive research with young people aged sixteen and under who have left home for one reason or another. It was also the driving force behind the first refuge for child runaways – the Central London Teenage Project – which opened in 1985. The charity makes a useful distinction between those young people who choose to leave home – runaways – and those who are forced (or feel that they have been forced) to leave – throwaways. Some young people do not feel that they have run away, preferring to describe themselves as 'staying away' from home. There are also important distinctions to be made between those who have run away and those who are reported as missing: many runaways are simply ignored by their families or carers and their disappearance is not reported to the police; but, equally, many of those who are reported as missing have not in fact run away at all. Notwithstanding these problems of definition and reporting, though, a good estimate is that about a hundred thousand children under the age of eighteen run away from home each year in Britain.

Research undertaken by the Children's Society in 1999 and 2005 makes for depressing reading. The charity calculated that at least 66,000 first-time runaways had stayed away from home for one night or more in England and Wales in 2005. The majority of these were aged between thirteen and fifteen. In total, 7.5 per cent of fourteen- or fifteen-year-olds had run away, while ten per cent of runaways were under eleven. Girls were more likely to leave home than boys, and those with moderate learning difficulties or who characterised themselves as gay ran away more than other children. Most runaways were white or of mixed race.

Once it had gathered this evidence, the Children's Society tried to determine if there was a link between teenagers' family structure and the likelihood of them running away. It concluded that young people living in single-parent families were roughly twice as likely to run away as those living with both parents, while those with a step-parent were almost three times as likely. Unsurprisingly, those who ran away from home usually expressed a negative opinion of their relationship with their parent or carer, which suggests a general unhappiness at home or at school. A third of young runaways admitted having problems with school attendance, while those who had been excluded from school were three times more likely than most children to run away.

Poverty was also a significant factor. The Children's Society questionnaire asked how many adults in the household had a paid job, and whether the young person was entitled to free school meals. Of the children who answered 'yes' to the latter question, 13.4 per cent had run away, compared to just under ten per cent of those who answered 'no'. Even more revealingly, 15.6 per cent of runaways came from families with no adults in paid employment, compared to just under ten per cent from households where at least one adult was in work.

Most of the young people who were interviewed gave 'problems at home' as the primary reason for their running away. This encompassed general conflict with parents and other family members in addition to physical, sexual and emotional abuse and neglect. The words 'slapped', 'beaten', 'hurt' and 'hit' occurred frequently in the runaways' responses to questions. Understandably, therefore, many of them did not view 'home' as a safe environment. Consequently, many suffered from depression, which led almost inevitably to self-harm and even attempts at suicide.

Survival strategies

One of the runaways interviewed by the Children's Society was Debbie, who left home when she was fourteen. She had been living with her mother, stepfather, brother and two stepsisters. As Debbie explains, her stepfather's behaviour towards her and her brother was very different to his treatment of his biological daughters:

> I didn't get on with my stepdad. It was because he fetched us up differently from the others. He used to give us real hidings, too. I used to be scared to go in the house, and people used to say 'he's not your real dad anyway', and that would do my head in because my mum would never tell us who our real dad was. I ran away at 14 to stay with my friends and wouldn't go to school. My mum didn't even bother to look for me. I don't have any contact with her now. At first I slept at friends' houses and once I had to sleep in a shed for three nights.
> (Quoted in Rees, 2001)

Debbie shoplifted to support herself, but often she still had to sleep rough. Eventually, with no better options available, she reluctantly moved in with a drugs pusher:

> I went and stayed with this lad who was a smack dealer. I didn't know anything about heroin until then. I didn't want to stay with him but I had nowhere else to go and the police were after us. I didn't even like him. Then I started taking it because he was taking it. I've been on it for four years now. I've lived in seven houses with this lad but we were never settled because he was a dealer.
> (Quoted in Rees, 2001)

Debbie's story provides a glimpse of what life is like for a young person who has run away from home. While the majority of those surveyed by the Children's Society were away for only one night, some ten per cent of the sample – including Debbie – had been away for more than a month. During that time most usually slept at friends' houses, but one in six of those surveyed – mainly boys – slept rough or with someone they had just met. This was one of the 'survival strategies' identified by the research, as were shoplifting, begging and stealing. Some of the interviewees – about one in twelve – also admitted to having been hurt while they were away from home, especially if they had been sleeping rough. Nevertheless, very few of the runaways sought help from any voluntary or statutory agency, and a staggering two-thirds stated that their parents or carers did not even report them as missing to the police. Of course, such ambivalence gives a good indication of why they felt compelled to leave in the first place.

While Debbie started using heroin after moving in with a dealer, other children in similar circumstances were groomed to provide sexual services. The Children's Society found a strong link between young people running away from home and thereafter being sexually exploited. In effect, runaways were recruited into prostitution once they had become detached from their families, and usually from social services and the care system, too.

Overall, the Children's Society survey paints a picture of a vulnerable group of young people who leave home and are then forced to sleep rough, beg, steal or sell sexual services in order to survive. Moreover, the members of this group rarely ask for assistance from the authorities or from charities that might be in a position to help them. Consequently, they often suffer harm.

But who are these young people, living lives with no stability or direction, doing anything they can merely to survive? Their stories are rarely told, although Alexander Masters has written an extraordinary account of the life of Stuart Shorter (2005), which articulates how sexual abuse can force a young man to leave home. And Nick Davies (1997) brought the reality of teenage homelessness vividly to life by telling the story of 'two small boys in the middle of an English city in the 1990s'. Davies first encountered Jamie and Luke – aged eleven and thirteen, respectively – selling sex outside a toilet in Nottingham. Over a cup of tea and some food, Jamie described his life as best he could. He told Davies that he was one of nine children, that he had three 'dads', and that 'the third one ... got rid of me and my brother and sister, got me put in care'. While in care he was beaten up and then sexually abused by another boy. That boy was reported to staff, but others took his place and forced Jamie into prostitution. Luke was from Mansfield and had a fairly conventional upbringing by comparison, at least until the age of six, when his father died. Within a year, he and his sister and brother had been taken into care. By nine, he was sexually active and experimenting with drugs. Soon, like Jamie, he turned to the streets to sell his body. As Davies puts it: 'they described lives that had become one long sequence of misery and pain'.

Thereafter, Jamie and Luke – 'symbols of ruined childhoods, guards at the door of darkness' – acted as Davies's guides and gave him a tour of the city he thought he knew. They led him to Lisa, whose story resonates with those of most of the young women who met their end in 25 Cromwell Street. She had been put in care when she was ten, after her parents had gone their separate ways. She was regularly bullied, and as a consequence she ran away – to London, Scotland, Birmingham and Manchester – but she was always found and brought back to Nottingham by social workers. Eventually, she stopped running and simply hid from the authorities in the underbelly of the city itself. One day she met a prostitute who encouraged her to sell herself. She was eleven at the time. By the time Davies met her she was fourteen, earning eight hundred pounds a week, and claimed to have had sex with three thousand different men over the previous three years. She would 'never forget' one of those clients:

> This man had picked her up and said that he wanted to go back to the flat that she rented for business. So she had taken him there, and she'd just got undressed and laid down on the bed when he turned around and put a knife to her throat. He had kept her there for nine hours, mucking about with her, pleasing himself. He had used the knife on her, on her thighs, teasing her and tormenting her and occasionally splitting the skin to show her he meant business, and then he had broken off a chair leg and started shoving that into her. She had thought that he'd never stop, but eventually he had given up and got dressed and driven away in his car, leaving her all on her own . . . it was just before her thirteenth birthday.

Jamie, Luke and Lisa were only the tip of the iceberg that Davies encountered in Nottingham, but their stories are indicative of the lives that children are forced to lead when they run away from home. A life of prostitution might be at the extreme end of runaways' experiences, but all children and young people are extremely vulnerable when their families or carers do not provide the love and support they need.

25 Cromwell Street: 'a bloody communial centre'

Caroline Raine was the first woman to be attacked by the Wests after they moved into 25 Cromwell Street in August 1972. She was relatively lucky, though, because she survived. However, her story tells us something of how the Wests operated as serial killers, and the tactics they used when targeting vulnerable young women.

Caroline was born in 1955 and lived for the first five years of her life in the Forest of Dean, some twelve miles from Gloucester. Her mother Betty, a pub cleaner, was married to a gay merchant seaman called Albert Raine. Caroline's biological father – and the father of her brother Phillip (whom she hated) – was an Irish roadman called Michael Mahoney. By 1960, Betty had divorced Albert and married a miner called Alf Harris. Betty, Caroline and Phillip all then moved into Alf's home in Cinderford. It seems that this was little more than a marriage of convenience: Betty needed a home, while Alf needed someone to look after him and his four children. Nevertheless, Betty soon gave birth to another daughter, Suzanne, and later to twins. Unsurprisingly, there was a great deal of domestic rivalry, noise and tension in this large family of siblings and half-brothers and -sisters. In addition to Phillip, Caroline did not get on with her eldest half-brother, Raymond. Furthermore, she was sexually abused by an elderly neighbour at the age of eight, and when she was ten. Later, she would describe herself as a 'wild child': she had numerous sexual liaisons before relocating to Portsmouth, a move that might be characterised as staying away from home, rather than running away or being thrown out. Eventually, though, she returned to Cinderford and started to see a boy called Tony Coates.

Caroline used to hitch-hike to and from Gloucester to visit Tony, as even the bus fare seems to have been beyond her means. In August 1972 she accepted a lift from the Wests. In the course of the journey they asked her to become a nanny for their three children – Anna-Marie (eight), Heather (two) and May (four months). As many people would later testify, Fred West was a smooth-talker, and no doubt he made this sound like an attractive opportunity for a young girl. Caroline was just coming up to her seventeenth birthday and she was keen to escape from an overcrowded home and establish a degree of independence for herself. Burn (1998) also suggests that 25 Cromwell Street itself must have appealed to Caroline: 'There was a sense of solidness and space. It wasn't prefabricated or fast built. It was old. You sensed the depth of its foundations and the weight of its thick walls.' Space was a luxury that Caroline had never been able to enjoy. And the same could be said of most of the women whose lives would be cut short by Fred West. They had often spent time in care or in foster homes, so the privacy of a suburban house must have seemed like a dream. Furthermore, the old house, with its thick walls and deep foundations, suggested a level of respectability and belonging in the community that had previously appeared out of reach. It surely came as no surprise to Caroline that this house's owners needed a nanny, rather than, say, a child-minder or a baby-sitter. Given the impressive exterior, the shabbiness of the interior and the lack of furniture must have come as a disappointment; and the absence of locks on the toilet and bathroom doors probably disconcerted several of the Wests' future victims. Nevertheless, the appeal of 25 Cromwell Street itself is crucial to understanding why so many vulnerable women overcame their misgivings and moved in with Fred and Rose West.

Having accepted the job as nanny, Caroline soon grew tired of West's relentless sexual innuendoes, his bullying of Rose (who was only two years older than Caroline), and his boasts that he had performed 'operations' and 'abortions' on women. Consequently, she moved out after only six weeks. In that short time West had already revealed that eight-year-old Anna Marie was not a virgin, with the implication (which we now know to be true) that he was having an incestuous relationship with his daughter. Caroline reported this to the authorities, but it seems that no investigation was launched.

Once she had left Cromwell Street, Caroline's life returned to normal, and she soon resumed hitch-hiking to Gloucester to see Tony. On 6 December 1972 the Wests were waiting for her.

Rose got out of their car and said, 'Oh, we really miss you. The children really miss you.' Charmed by the flattery, Caroline again accepted their offer of a lift. Rose got into the back with her, while Fred started making sexual suggestions. Then Rose began to assault Caroline sexually, and as soon as Fred found an opportunity to stop the car he knocked her out. They took her back to 25 Cromwell Street, bound and gagged her, and subjected her to an appalling sexual assault that lasted all night. Finally, West raped her. When it was over West started to cry and asked Caroline not to tell Rose what had happened. In fear of her life, Caroline agreed to keep quiet about the rape and said she would return to her job as the children's nanny. She even helped with the housework the following morning. Then, with the children sent off to school, the Wests went to the laundry, which allowed Caroline to escape. She went straight to the police and reported her ordeal.

Obviously, Caroline was traumatised by what had just taken place, and her anxiety was not eased by PC Kevan Price, who interviewed her. At one point Price asked, 'You like your sex, don't you? Don't tell me you weren't loving it.' In spite of this unsympathetic questioning, the Wests appeared in Gloucester Magistrates' Court on 12 January 1973, although neither was charged with rape. They both pleaded guilty to indecent assault and causing actual bodily harm, and were fined a total of one hundred pounds. They were also advised, but not compelled, to seek psychiatric help.

After the trial Caroline tried to get on with her life. She became Miss Forest of Dean in 1977, which led to some glamour modelling, and the awful events in 25 Cromwell Street started to fade in her memory, at least until 1994. Tragically, the Wests were allowed to return to their lives, too, and just three months after the trial, in April 1973, they murdered Lynda Gough.

Over the next two years they would kill another four young women: Lucy Partington, Carol Cooper, Juanita Mott and Shirley Hubbard.

Having been tried for the sexual assault on Caroline, it seems that the Wests decided that they could no longer afford to let their victims go free once they had abused them. Imagining that Caroline would want to return to their home as the children's nanny reveals some very twisted thinking, but thereafter the Wests were more logical, if no less depraved.

Allowing her to escape had led only to arrest, a trial, conviction and exposure. They were determined not to make the same mistake again.

I have deliberately not dwelt on the details of Caroline's ordeal. Suffice to say that it resembled what Lisa, the young girl in Nottingham, was forced to endure. She too experienced a horrific sexual assault and feared for her life over a significant period of time. These two events, separated by two decades, reveal the persistence of misogyny in British society, as well as the vulnerability of young women and girls when they are raised in poverty and see little hope of escape. Lisa did not report her rape to the police. However, had she done so, can we really be sure that her interviewer would have been more sympathetic than PC Price?

The attack on Caroline sheds more light on the future activities of the Wests because of the central role played by Rose. It was she who persuaded Caroline to get in the car and it was she who initiated the sexual assault. This is important, because some people have argued that Rose did not receive a fair trial and that there was no solid evidence to tie her to any of the murders. She has also never confessed. Brian Masters (1996) has even suggested that 'there was nothing in Rosemary's past to indicate criminal tendencies'. However, the attack on Caroline clearly indicates what Rose West was capable of when the opportunity arose.

Lucy Partington and the Wests – when good met evil

On the night of 27 December 1973 Lucy Partington was abducted and then murdered by Fred West in or near Gloucester. We know very little about how Lucy, a twenty-one-year-old student, met her end. However, we do know that she had been visiting a disabled friend in Cheltenham, Helen Render, and that they had discussed applying to the Courtauld Institute in London, where Lucy thought she might like to continue her studies after completing her undergraduate degree at Exeter University. According to a compelling biography written by her cousin Martin Amis (2001), Lucy was serious, artistic, musical, religious and resolute. She left Helen's house with a completed application form in her hand, and walked the short distance to the bus stop to return home. But she never posted the application and she never boarded the bus. It would be another twenty-one years before the Partington family finally discovered her fate.

Lucy's body was found in 1994 in the cellar of 25 Cromwell Street. She had been decapitated and dismembered, and her remains had been crammed into a shaft between leaking sewerage pipes, along with a knife, a rope, some masking tape and two hair grips. The bodies of other victims lay close by. West scandalously told the police that he had been in a relationship with 'Juicy Lucy', and that she wanted to move in with him after becoming pregnant. When he refused, she threatened to tell Rose, so he strangled her and buried her in the cellar. This is a total fabrication: Lucy died because she was simply in the wrong place at the wrong time. Martin Amis uses something he knows well – literature – to illustrate how far apart Fred West and Lucy Partington were culturally and intellectually, and therefore how unlikely it was that they were ever involved in a relationship. Below are a letter written by West to his daughter May, then a poem composed by Lucy.

> Hi May it is your Dad Writeing to you. Or lette me have your telephone number . . . or Write to me as soon as you can, please may I have to sort out watt Mr Ogden did to me, my new solicitors are Brillaint I Read What you sead about me in News of the that was loylty you read what Scott canavan sead he had –

> *Things are as big as you make them –*
> *I can fill a whole body,*
> *A whole day of life*
> *With worry*
> *About a few words*
> *On one scrap of paper;*
> *Yet, the same evening,*
> *looking up,*
> *can frame my fingers*
> *to fit the sky*
> *in my cupped hands.*

The 'Mr Ogden' mentioned in West's letter is his solicitor, Howard Ogden, whom he had just sacked out of fear that Ogden was about to sell his story. West himself wrote 111 pages of autobiography after his arrest and prior to his suicide. David Canter (2003) notes that it contains no mention of his crimes, nor of the deaths of his victims, but rather is a rambling, 'Mills & Boon'-type account of West's life as a hardworking, loving father who was regularly persecuted by others. Canter suggests that West's aim was to deceive by presenting only those things that he wanted to be revealed. So while the language, spelling, missing words and poor grammar reveal a man with an IQ of just 84, Canter nevertheless describes West as having 'inherent savvy'. Moreover, he calls West 'a clever killer who developed a well-articulated, deviant philosophy, using his intellect to tie investigators in knots. He survived for so long because of the world he created for himself.' West's ridiculous suggestion that Lucy was pregnant with his child is one indication of the fantasy world in which he lived. Others occur in his autobiography, where, among other things, he claims to have fathered forty-two children. Canter finds this obsession with fatherhood 'most curious'. However, now is a good point to move away from trying to determine what was going on in Fred West's mind and instead concentrate on what allowed him to murder young women for so long.

It is important to look beyond West's 'inherent savvy' and his creation of a world that he could control and where he could commit murder at 25 Cromwell Street. As has been stressed throughout this book, it is much more illuminating to study the victims who were first controlled and then murdered in these circumstances; and, specifically in the Wests' case, to ask why these women willingly entered the world of a 'bumbling yokel, devoted to a happy family life' (Burn, 1998). After all, at least on the surface, the Wests had a stable home where they had lived for many years. And, as Howard Sounes (1995) points out, they also had 'a mortgage which they worked hard to pay off, and a large family. They were the people next door, who waved a cheery hello to neighbours as they walked down the street.' Many 'respectable' people were taken in by this façade, so it should come as no surprise that a succession of 'runaways and throwaways', with very little to look forward to, or indeed back at, were lured into Fred West's fantasy world.

The abducted and the abandoned

The Wests' victims fall into two distinct groups: the abducted and the seduced. In the first category are: Lucy Partington, Carol Cooper, Shirley Hubbard, Juanita Mott and Therese Siegenthaler. In the second group are: Lynda Gough, Shirley Robinson and Alison Chambers, as well as 'Sandra Johnson' (not her real name), who survived an attack by the Wests. Sandra's story, like that of Caroline Raine, echoes those of the young women who did not escape.

In 1975 thirteen-year-old Sandra started a relationship with Rose West's brother, Graham Letts, who was eighteen. Two years later, following her parents' separation, she was living in care at Jordan's Brook House in Gloucester, a former approved school that cared for 'delinquent girls, most of whom had already been expelled from other homes. They were vulner able adolescents, often from deeply troubled families and easily corrupted by people like the Wests' (Sounes, 1995). Indeed, West's van was often seen parked outside the gates of the home. Gordon Burn (1998) notes that it held 'twenty-three of the most difficult and disturbed girls in the country'. Sandra was certainly disturbed, and may even have been schizophrenic. She had been raped by her father and had suffered further sexual assaults by her brother. Eventually, she made her way to 25 Cromwell Street, having absconded from Jordan's Brook House and spending one night sleeping rough. This indicates the pull of the address on vulnerable girls in Gloucester, because it seems Sandra was unaware that Graham Letts was Rose West's brother. As ever, Rose was charm itself when the new arrival showed up, offering a shoulder to cry on and listening to Sandra's problems over 'orange squash and biscuits'.

Throughout the summer Sandra was a regular visitor, even after returning to Jordan's Brook House. One day, though, Rose led her upstairs and subjected her to a serious sexual assault, which culminated in Sandra being raped by Fred West. When it was over she ran out of the house and wondered whom she should tell about her ordeal. However, she came to the conclusion that 'there was nobody now. Because you were in care you were bad. There was nobody' (Burn, 1998). A few weeks later she returned to 25 Cromwell Street with a can of petrol, fully intending to pour some through the letterbox and set the place alight. But she could not bring herself to do it.

Sandra's failure to carry out this act of revenge would seem to indicate a despair that there was no point even trying to change her lot in life, let alone reporting her abusers to the authorities. In her mind she was 'nobody', written off by the rest of society because she was in care. Most of the Wests' victims probably felt exactly the same way. They, too, tended to come from very damaged backgrounds and had spent significant periods of time in care.

Shirley Robinson, for example, was a seventeen-year-old who came from a broken home and had been in care in Wolverhampton since the age of fourteen. She was so badly nourished that the Wests nicknamed her 'Bones'. Gordon Burn describes her as a 'friendless and homeless lemon to take home and put with Rose'. Just like Sandra, Shirley must have felt she had no one to turn to in a time of crisis. The Wests stepped in to fill that void for their own sordid reasons. Eventually, Shirley fell pregnant with West's child, which is probably why he killed her in May 1978. When her body was discovered in 1994 her unborn baby was found buried with her.

Alison Chambers was another resident of Jordan's Brook House, and has been described as 'the most tragic girl to visit Cromwell Street' (Sounes, 1995). She was very insecure, and had run away from various homes in South Wales after her parents' divorce. She had also previously absconded from Jordan's Brook House, reaching Paddington Station before being found and brought back. Alison told staff that she wanted to go 'on the game', and she wasn't popular with the other girls, who bullied her regularly. Yet again, then, this was a friendless 'nobody' who ultimately found her way to 25 Cromwell Street, the home of the man who often sat outside her care home in his Transit van.

Burn imagines West in his van, all 'jokes and banter. Rollups and offers of rides. Lightly, lightly. If it takes a year, it takes a year. He could be tirelessly patient.' When this patience is added to West's 'inherent savvy' you have a very dangerous individual indeed. West told Alison that he owned a farm in the country, and said when she was eighteen he would let her ride his horses and walk in his fields all day long. Rose reinforced the lie by giving Alison a picture of the farmhouse they claimed to own: in reality, it was a photo from an estate agent's brochure. This is another version of the routine the Wests first used on Caroline Raine, tailored to meet the needs of the specific victim that they had targeted. Caroline was offered security and a good job in a quiet house; Alison was offered a rural idyll she could only imagine. At one stage she wrote her mother a long letter, in which she described her new life with a 'homely family ... I look after their five children and do some of their housework. They have a child the same age as me who accepts me as a big sister and we get on great ... the family own flats and I share with the oldest sister.' This gives some indication of how the Wests must have been viewed by most, if not all, of the young women who entered 25 Cromwell Street. Many of them had never been part of a 'homely family', so they had been denied the status that comes with being a member of a stable household. Perhaps for the first time in her life, Alison was able to play the role of big sister: finally she was someone, rather than nobody. Moreover, the Wests' lies clearly extended beyond the fantasy of the fictitious farm. Alison was under the impression that they also owned flats, which must have suggested the wealth and entrepreneurship of the upwardly mobile. In all likelihood her mention of this was designed to impress her mother, and to convince her that Alison was staying with people of substance and probity.

Alison had been reported as missing after absconding from Jordan's Brook House just four weeks before her eighteenth birthday. However, because of the letter to her mother, no further action was taken to contact her. In 1994 her decapitated and dismembered body was found buried in the garden, next to a wall of the bathroom extension. A plastic belt was found strapped under her chin, and another had been looped around her head to clamp her mouth shut, to stop her screaming.

Carol Cooper – known as 'Caz' – was not seduced by the Wests, but her background was similar to those of Sandra, Alison and Shirley. Her parents divorced when she was four and her mother died when she was eight. Thereafter she lived with her father for a time, but when this did not work out she was placed in a succession of children's homes. Since the age of thirteen she had been living at the Pines Children's Home in Worcester. Caz was pretty, intelligent, tall and strong, but she did not like any of the homes, including the Pines, so she regularly absconded, slept rough and survived by shoplifting. By late 1973, now aged fifteen, she had a boyfriend called Andrew Jones. On Saturday 10 November they went to the local Odeon, had fish and chips, then went to a pub where Caz had a soft drink. Afterwards,

Andrew walked Caz to the bus stop, gave her the fare back to the Pines, and waited with her for the bus to arrive. It was the last time he ever saw his girlfriend alive. Six weeks later, West snatched Lucy Partington.

Shirley Hubbard was also last seen boarding a bus in Worcester. She had lived in children's homes from the age of two, but was eventually fostered by Jim and Linda Hubbard, who lived in Droitwich in the Midlands. At fifteen Shirley ran away from home and was found sleeping rough with a soldier in a field some five miles outside Worcester. Around this time she also tattooed 'Shirl' on her forearm. However, she was not totally out of control: for instance, she did some work experience in Debenhams. At the time of her death she was seeing a boy called Dan Davies. On 14 November 1974 she and Dan spent the afternoon walking around Worcester until he put her on the bus to Droitwich. She never returned home. When her decapitated body was discovered in 1994, her skull was still encased in a hood mask. The mask had two holes through which had been inserted plastic tubes. Clearly this had been designed to keep her alive for as long as possible, but John Bennett believes Shirley nevertheless died of 'suffocation or strangulation' (Bennett and Gardner, 2005).

Juanita Mott's father was a US serviceman who returned to Texas without his wife or daughter. Juanita was dark and fiery, and her mother found her difficult to handle. As a result she was taken into care on a number of occasions, and when she reached fifteen she left home and found herself a flat in Stroud Road, Gloucester. The following year she suffered an ectopic pregnancy and moved to a new flat in Cromwell Street. Soon, though, she was found guilty of stealing a pension book and sent to Pucklechurch Remand Centre in Gloucester. At her trial she received a sentence of two years' probation, but this did not stop her finding a job in a local bottling factory. By 1975, she was living with a friend of her mother in Newent, but she would hitch-hike into Gloucester to socialise. Nineteen years later her remains were found in the cellar of 25 Cromwell Street.

Therese Siegenthaler was born and raised in Switzerland, but by 1974, at the age of twenty-one, she was studying sociology at Woolwich College and living in digs in Deptford. In April she set out to hitch-hike to Holyhead in order to catch the ferry to Ireland and meet up with a friend. We do not know where she was picked up by West, but her body was found in the cellar of 25 Cromwell Street, next to that of fellow-student Lucy Partington.

Lynda Gough was another of the Wests' victims who did not fit into their normal pattern of targeting 'runaways and throwaways': she lived at home with her mother and father in Gloucester and worked as a seamstress at the Co-op. However, she befriended some of the male lodgers who lived at 25 Cromwell Street and over time became a regular visitor to the house. When she did not return home after several days her mother went looking for her. Eventually, her search led her to the Wests' home. The Wests denied ever having met Lynda, but Mrs Gough noticed that Rose West was wearing her daughter's slippers, and that more of Lynda's clothes were hanging on the washing line. Once she pointed this out, the couple suddenly remembered that they had seen Lynda, but she had since left and gone to Weston-Super-Mare. The Goughs tried to reach her there, but by then she was dead and buried below the ground-floor bathroom. Surprisingly, the Goughs never reported Lynda's disappearance to the police.

The Wests' final victim was their own daughter, Heather. Her death eventually brought their murderous world to an end because her siblings did everything they could to find out what had happened to her. Heather disappeared four months before her seventeenth birthday. In her awful childhood she suffered gross sexual abuse by her father and uncle; was forced to sleep in the cellar where the bodies of the young women who had been murdered were buried; and was routinely strapped into her bed at night to stop her running away. She and her elder sister would stand guard outside the bathroom while the other was showering, so that they would know in advance if their father was on his way to abuse them. Despite all this, Heather did well at school and earned eight GCSEs, then landed a job cleaning chalets at a holiday camp in Devon. (Like Alison Chambers, she dreamed of living in the countryside.) The job fell through, but the rest of the family was told that Heather had gone to Devon, and they never saw her again. It seems that West killed her simply because he could not risk her going to the authorities and telling them about her life at 25 Cromwell Street. As he had learned all those years ago with Caroline Raine, he and Rose were in control within the house, but once their victims escaped to the wider world, anything might happen.

Heather's yearning to leave behind an appalling childhood was shared by many of the young women who were murdered by her father and mother. Like them, she suffered terrible abuse but hoped for a better life. Tragically, Fred and Rose West denied her that chance.

At the end of the road

Gloucester responded to what happened at 25 Cromwell Street in several ways, most famously by demolishing the house where the murders were committed and replacing it with a quiet walkway. The city also set up the ASTRA Project. 'ASTRA' stands for 'Alternative Solutions To Running Away', and the project aims to reduce the numbers of children and young people who abscond from family, foster or care homes. As its website (www.astraproject.org.uk) explains, 'few young people run away because they really want to. In the majority of cases a young person runs away because they feel that adults don't care, don't listen, or don't understand.' The project has conducted interviews with many runaways in and around Gloucester and has passed on its findings to those contemplating doing the same. In response to the question 'What dangers could young people face if they run away?' one interviewee answered:

> Loads! People could leave you hurt and no one would know where you are. People might offer you somewhere to stay, but you wouldn't know if they could be trusted. You might have to steal, beg or even sell your own body to get money for food – this could get you into trouble with the police. You could even be abducted and murdered – it DOES HAPPEN!

Perhaps Laura, whom we met at the start of this chapter, will see and heed that warning from one of her fellow runaways.

But that is far from certain. Since the Wests' atrocities were uncovered in 1994, Britain has done very little to tackle the issue of young people who run away from, stay away from, or are thrown out of their homes. As the Children's Society discovered, tens of thousands of young people still run away from home each year. Many of them have nowhere to go and are forced to sleep rough. They then rapidly develop survival strategies that involve stealing, begging and even prostitution. Consequently, they expose themselves to a level of danger that men like Mark Martin are only too happy to exploit.

The phenomenon of teenage runaways is not only a story of the rebellion of young people against their parents or carers.

Rather, time and again we find evidence of physical and sexual abuse, the inadequacies of the care system, and grinding poverty. Many runaways' lives have been blighted by one or all of these issues. Who can blame them for trying to escape?

Chapter Nine

'A public scare': children

Sooner murder an infant in its cradle than nurse unacted desires.

William Blake, *The Marriage of Heaven and Hell* (1793)

With *The Story of Childhood: Growing up in Modern Britain* (2006), the journalist Libby Brooks produced what she called 'a travel book about a state of being'. Through the course of her interviews with children and their parents – and remembering herself what it had been like to be a child – she uncovered a 'deep ambivalence' about children and childhood in Britain. This manifests itself in parents being overly protective towards their own children, less concerned about other people's, and more demanding of those children's severe punishment if they transgress. Brooks talks to many children who are merely 'enduring and surviving' childhood, rather than learning and growing in a stress-free environment. She points out that they are the only members of British society who can, by law, be hit and that a 'defendant not old enough to buy a hamster legally can be tried in an adult court and named and shamed in newspapers, in direct contravention of their internationally recognised human rights'. In 2005 over 70 per cent of children in England and Wales were subject to curfew orders, which allowed the police to send home anyone under the age of sixteen if they were on the streets without a supervising adult after 9 p.m.

Brooks surely would have found enthusiastic support for her case from Alvaro Gils-Robles, the European Commissioner for Human Rights. Speaking in November 2004, Gils-Robles condemned the British government's record on children's issues. He admitted he was 'surprised to learn' that the age of criminal responsibility was just ten in England and Wales, and even lower – eight – in Scotland. And he found Anti-Social Behaviour Orders (ASBOs) 'particularly problematic', concluding that there had been an 'ASBO-mania' in Britain in the misguided belief that they would prove to be a 'miracle cure for urban nuisance'. Gils-Robles argued that they had merely led to intolerable levels of child detention.

The four children's commissioners of the United Kingdom, who in 2008 reported to the UN Committee on the Rights of the Child, echoed these sentiments: too many children were being criminalised and brought into the youth justice system at a young age; the age of criminal responsibility was too low; and there was a widely held fear of young people, fuelled by a consistently negative portrayal of them in the media, where they were represented as antisocial, selfish, uncaring and criminal.

This chapter is concerned with those serial killers who have targeted children, and the 'deep ambivalence' that Libby Brooks uncovered helps us to understand why and when they become vulnerable. 'Childhood' is not fixed; rather, it should be seen as a social construction that changes over time in response to various pressures. One of those pressures has been the recent 'discovery' of the scale of child sexual abuse, which in turn has helped to shape how all children experience childhood, irrespective of whether they are likely to be sexually abused, or indeed are at risk of being murdered by a serial killer.

The usual suspects?

Most British people – when asked about serial killers who have targeted children – will instantly come up with just two names: Ian Brady and Myra Hindley. They killed five children (two girls and three boys) between the ages of ten and seventeen in the early 1960s and were dubbed the 'Moors Murderers' because they hid the bodies on Saddleworth Moor, near Oldham. Brady and especially Hindley have become emblematic of serial killing in Britain: their story and images are virtually omnipresent within the true crime genre and popular media reporting about serial killing. More than thirty years after their trial, Hindley's police photograph – reworked as a series of child's handprints by the artist Marcus Harvey – caused controversy at the 'Sensation' exhibition at the Royal Academy of Art in 1997. Windows at the Royal Academy were smashed, and two demonstrators hurled ink and eggs at the picture, requiring it to be temporarily removed and repaired before being re-exhibited behind Perspex and guarded by security men. The pressure group Mothers Against Murder and Aggression also picketed the picture alongside Winnie Johnson, the mother of one of Brady and Hindley's victims. Despite the outcry – or perhaps because of it – the exhibition attracted some three hundred thousand visitors between September and December, and then went on an international tour. Twelve years later, Harvey says his painting was only a work in progress, and he did not even expect it to make it into the exhibition. Moreover, he still claims to be mystified by the outrage it caused ('Myra, Margaret and Me', *Guardian*, 21 February 2009).

Such a comment is either naïve or disingenuous. Harvey must be aware that Britain persists in recalling a mythical 'golden age' before the Moors Murderers, when parents had no fears for their children's safety out on the streets, after school, in the evenings and at the weekend. Irrespective of the accuracy of this rose-tinted image, many people continue to believe in it and feel that Brady and Hindley not only destroyed it but replaced it with a type of fear that has come to be known as 'stranger danger'. However, this type of thinking confuses where and at whose hands children have been most at risk, even in the 'golden age' of childhood. The number of children placed on the Child Protection Register after 1965, for example, continued to increase because of the risks they faced from their own parents or carers rather than from the attention of serial killers. There has been a similar increase in the number of children taken into care. These figures indicate that it is overwhelmingly the home, not the street, that is unsafe for children. The one serial killer who did target children on the streets, Robert Black, snatched his three young victims as they played or walked to and from their homes between 1982 and 1986. However, few people remember him or are able to describe the circumstances in which he came to kill. Meanwhile, the Moors Murders continue to exercise a hold on our collective imagination. The most obvious reason for this enduring obsession would seem to be that one of the murderers was a woman. Yet I suspect few people would be able to name another female serial killer who murdered four young children, and attempted to kill nine others, in 1991, over a quarter of a century after Brady and Hindley had been exposed. She is Beverly Allitt, and unlike the other two British female serial killers – Hindley and Rose West – she acted alone.

Allitt worked for the National Health Service, one of the cornerstones of social policy in the post-war period, when, as we have seen, 'people mattered'. Yet, just forty years later, Allitt was able to kill her charges with relative ease. Obviously, the relative physical weakness of children, coupled with their inability or reluctance to question an adult, helped Allitt to commit her crimes. However, I would suggest that British society's deep ambivalence towards children also makes them more vulnerable than they should be, and that the organisation, management and lack of resources within the NHS created the context in which Allitt could murder repeatedly. For instance, by the time that she came to attack her last victim, it was already abundantly clear that there was a killer on the ward.

This chapter looks beyond the personal responsibility of people like Allitt in the deaths of children who have fallen victim to serial killers, and proposes that childhood vulnerability is created in society generally.

Brady, Hindley and Black

Given the extensive coverage that the Moors Murders have received in both popular and academic literature, this chapter will not dwell too long on the victims of Ian Brady and Myra Hindley. In contrast, the convicted paedophile Robert Black and his victims have received little attention, so I shall focus on how Black came to kill, and what his crimes – committed two decades after those of Brady and Hindley – reveal about the changing nature of childhood in Britain. I shall then consider the victims of Beverly Allitt.

Brady and Hindley were indiscriminate serial killers in that they killed both boys and girls and did not seem particularly concerned about the ages of their victims. Their first victim was sixteen-year-old Pauline Reade, killed on 12 July 1963 after being enticed into Hindley's car as she walked to a dance at the Railway Workers' Social Club in Manchester. Their last was seventeen-year-old Edward Evans, murdered on 6 October 1965. In between, Brady and Hindley killed twelve-year-old John Kilbride, twelve-year-old Keith Bennett and ten-year-old Lesley Ann Downey.

Lesley Ann's murder – on Boxing Day 1964 – was particularly awful, although at the time her disappearance did not provoke much police interest. Her body was finally found buried in a shallow grave on Saddleworth Moor on 10 October 1965, after David Smith had alerted the police to Brady and Hindley's activities following the murder of Edward Evans. The police also discovered two suitcases in a locker at Manchester Central Station containing pornographic photographs of Lesley Ann, and a harrowing tape-recording of her begging for her life.

Based on comments that Hindley made during a TV documentary in the 1980s, Colin Wilson (2001) suggests that Brady preferred to kill younger children because Pauline Reade had been hard to subdue. The fact that their next victims were two twelve-year-olds and a ten-year-old would seem to support this idea. So, while Brady and Hindley were indiscriminate killers, they were pragmatic when choosing most of their victims. The murder of Edward Evans was not well organised, which explains why he does not fit into the pattern of their later victims.

Robert Black was much more discriminating than Brady and Hindley: he was interested only in young girls. He killed eleven-year-old Susan Maxwell in 1982, five-year-old Caroline Hogg in 1983 and eleven-year-old Sarah Harper in 1986. Black was not tried and convicted of their murders until several years later, in 1994, and he is suspected of having killed many more girls. Certainly the therapist Ray Wyre, who interviewed Black at some length, believes that he molested 'hundreds' of young girls, abducted 'dozens' and that 'at least eight may have died' (Wyre and Tate, 1995).

Like the Wests, Brady and Hindley seem to have lured their victims into a car on the promise of a lift. And just as Rose West's presence in the car reassured the Wests' victims, Hindley's surely eased the reservations of her and Brady's targets. Hindley also concocted stories to make the subsequent journey more plausible: for example, she asked John Kilbride to help her move some boxes, and Pauline Read to help her find a glove lost on Saddleworth Moor. When they arrived at the moor Brady was waiting, having ridden there on his motorbike. By then, it is likely that the children trusted Hindley completely. Brady established similar trust with Edward Evans, meeting him several times in a gay club in Manchester before the tragic final occasion when he murdered him. By contrast, Black did not know any of his victims: he simply snatched them as they walked or played in the streets then bundled them into his van.

A glimpse of Black's modus operandi is provided by the testimony of Teresa Ann Thornhill, who narrowly avoided abduction by him on 28 April 1988. Teresa was fifteen at the time – older than Black's normal target range – but she was slight and small, and looked much younger than her age. She was walking back to her house in Nottingham when a blue Transit van passed her.

> I saw the driver get out and open the bonnet of the engine. As I walked level with the van the man shouted 'oi' to me. I looked towards him to make sure he was talking to me. I couldn't see anybody else about. I ignored him, looked away and carried on walking. Then he shouted 'Can you fix engines?' I replied 'No, I can't' . . . I suddenly felt the man grab me from behind. I screamed and tried to struggle free.

> He picked me up and carried me across the road to the big blue van. I was still screaming and fighting to get away . . . he then put his big hand over my mouth, covering my nose. With his hand over my face I felt as if I was going to pass out, so I bit him on his hand. This forced him to release his hand from my face. I then bit him on the arm and screamed again . . . I think that it was at this point that I knocked his glasses off. As he held me he opened the driver's door of the van and tried to bundle me inside. I fought with all my strength and used . . . my feet to push backwards and stop him from getting me inside. I think he said something like 'Get in, you bitch,' as we were struggling.
>
> (Quoted in Wyre and Tate, 1995)

This statement provides some graphic evidence of how difficult it must have been for Brady to have subdued Pauline Reade, who was slightly older than Teresa and probably fought just as tenaciously. Furthermore, it suggests that Black planned his attacks – in other words, he was organised – and developed a method for overcoming his potential victims. However, he made two mistakes with Teresa: he thought she was younger than she was, and he believed she was alone. These errors were revealed when Teresa put up more resistance than Black had expected and, crucially, when her boyfriend heard her screams and came to her aid. Black also asked Teresa for help (a technique similarly employed by Hindley), although of course this was merely an excuse to get her close to the van so that he could bundle her inside.

More than anything else, though, the passage reveals the bravery of Teresa and her strategy for overcoming an assailant. She screamed, she bit, she knocked off Black's glasses, and she did everything in her power to delay being bundled into the van.

Black's response to her vigorous defence – 'Get in, you bitch' – reveals his frustration at his inability to overcome Teresa and achieve his objective. It is also worth noting that when someone finally responded to her screams and came to her aid, it was another child – Teresa's boyfriend – rather than an adult.

Black's final intended victim was much more typical of the children he targeted: six-year-old girl Mandy Wilson. He attempted to abduct her on 14 July 1990 from the village of Stow, on the border between Scotland and England, as she walked to a friend's house to play. The attack was witnessed by Mandy's neighbour, David Herkes, as he cut his grass: 'All I could see were her little feet standing next to the man's. Suddenly they vanished and I saw him making movements as if he was trying to stuff something under the dashboard. He got into the van, reversed up the driveway that the child had just come from and sped off towards Edinburgh' (Wyre and Tate, 1995). Herkes noted down the van's registration number and immediately called the police, who were on the scene in a few minutes. In an amazing coincidence, one of the officers was Mandy's father. While Herkes was giving his statement, Black's van suddenly reappeared and Herkes shouted, 'That's him.' Mandy's father stepped into the road, which caused Black to swerve and come to a halt. Mandy was saved, although she had already been sexually assaulted. Black was given a life sentence for her abduction and assault in August 1990. While serving time for those offences, in May 1994, he was charged and convicted over the attempted abduction of Teresa, and the murders of Susan, Caroline and Sarah.

Commentators have pointed out that it took eight years from the death of Susan for the police finally to apprehend Black, three years longer than it had taken them to catch Peter Sutcliffe. In the interim, various police computer packages – such as

HOLMES – had been developed which were supposed to be of assistance in investigations of this kind. Yet Black was able to continue to murder and abduct young girls until a piece of great good fortune and the unusual vigilance of a member of the public led to his arrest. Wyre scathingly suggests that 'Black's life, and, with it, his career as a sex offender illustrated an almost complete failure by every part of the investigative and penal system in Britain' (Wyre and Tate, 1995). The penal system had failed to stop Black from offending, and the police had failed to catch him when he did.

Unlike Brady and Hindley, Black was a geographically transient serial killer, and this undoubtedly helped him to escape detection. He committed his crimes all over the country, crossing from one police jurisdiction into another. This mobility was possible because of his job as a delivery man, and he utilised his time on the road to locate both suitable victims and sites where he could dispose of their bodies. His deliveries took him through the Midlands and the North of England to the Scottish border, Edinburgh, Glasgow and as far north as Dundee. In July 1982 – the month when Susan Maxwell disappeared while walking back to her home in Cornhill-on-Tweed after a tennis match – Black was on the Scottish run, delivering posters. No doubt Susan was abducted using much the same method that Black later employed against Teresa and Mandy. Her body was discovered on 13 August 1982 in a shallow ditch beside a lay-by on the edge of the A518 at Loxley, two miles outside of Uttoxeter, and some 250 miles away from her home.

Caroline Hogg was murdered on 8 July 1983. She lived in the seaside resort of Portobello, on the outskirts of Edinburgh. On the day in question she had been to a friend's house for a birthday party. Returning home at around 7 p.m., she asked her mother Annette if she could have five minutes to play on the swings in the park. When Annette agreed, Caroline slipped off her party shoes, put on her pink trainers and left the house. Less than fifteen minutes later, Annette went in search of her daughter. Thirty minutes after that she called the police station in Portobello High Street. Caroline's body was found ten days later, again dumped on the edge of a lay-by, this time near Twycross in Leicestershire.

Sarah Harper lived in Morley, Leeds, with her mother Jacki, her nine-year-old sister Claire and her five-year-old brother David. On the evening of 26 March 1986, just as *Coronation Street* was starting, Jacki asked Sarah to fetch a loaf of bread from the corner shop, which was about a hundred yards from their home. On her way out of the door Sarah grabbed two empty lemonade bottles so she could claim the twenty-pence refund. She reached the shop, bought the bread and cashed in the bottles, but she never returned home. Her body was found in the River Trent at Wilford on the outskirts of Nottingham on 19 April. She had been sexually assaulted, bound and gagged. She had also been alive when she was thrown into the river, so the cause of her death was recorded as drowning.

These three horrific murders are revealing because they indicate that, contrary to the general assumption, the nature of childhood did not change in Britain as a result of the Moors Murders. Rather, the way children behave – and are allowed to behave – has changed much more recently, probably in response to widespread moral panic about paedophiles. In the mid-1980s, twenty years after Brady and Hindley had been locked up, young girls still ran errands for their parents; they walked alone to the tennis courts; they went to birthday parties and then ran out of the house in the evening to play on the swings. While doing all of these things they were out of the sight of their parents. This does not indicate that parents cared little for their children's welfare, nor even that they calculated that the chances of abduction and murder by a stranger were extremely small. Instead, it shows that they appreciated and understood the normal process of their children gaining independence, taking responsibility and growing up. Some of that appreciation and understanding has now been lost, but our response to these awful murders should not be to place even more control and greater surveillance on children. Childhood should not be regulated by adults who believe that children are constantly at risk of attack. Rather, we should ask why Robert Black started to kill, and why it took so long for society to stop him.

Black first came to the attention of the courts when he was just seventeen, as a result of an assault on a young girl in Scotland in the summer of 1963. In this attack Black enticed the girl to accompany him to a disused building on the promise of showing her some kittens. Once inside he held her by the throat – almost strangling her – and sexually assaulted her. The girl was later found walking the streets bleeding, confused and crying. Black duly appeared at Greenock Juvenile Court, where he was charged with lewd and libidinous behaviour against a seven-year-old girl. He was found guilty but given nothing more than an admonishment – in effect a warning that he should behave himself in the future. He walked away from court a free man, and not a single paragraph about the case was reported in any newspaper.

Thereafter, Black continued to molest young girls. As a result of another sexual assault, this time on a six-year-old girl, he was sent to Borstal in 1967. On his release, he relocated from Scotland to England, probably in the hope that he would be able to resume his abuse of young girls where he was not known to the local community. He increased his chances of doing so when he started working for the PDS delivery company in 1976. Ray

Wyre is in no doubt that Black did indeed continue to offend at this time, and that he became an obsessive collector of child pornography. The therapist imagines Black 'slip[ping] through the gratings of the urban streets in which he existed: another grimy worker in a part of the city crumbling away, a loner, a man with no girlfriend, wife, or family and no apparent prospects of finding any one of them' (Wyre and Tate, 1995). This evokes Black's anonymity while he worked for the PDS, delivering posters to sites on the outskirts of towns and cities, but also his isolation from other people and normal family life. However, we should note that two of his victims – Caroline Hogg and Sarah Harper – lived in urban areas that were 'crumbling away'. It is also worth reflecting on the fact that Black managed to slip through the 'gratings' of the criminal justice system, too.

Indeed, we might view that system itself as 'crumbling'. Black had been offending for decades before he was caught with Mandy Wilson in the back of his van, he had been convicted of at least two offences against young girls, and he had served a prison sentence for the sexual assault of a child. At no point in all of these contacts with the criminal justice system was he offered or compelled to undergo counselling or treatment for his compulsion to abuse young girls. Once he had served his time he was simply released back into the community, in all probability a more dangerous man than when he had been sentenced. His name did not appear on any police database, which explains why he was never a suspect in any of the three murders for which he was eventually convicted. Consequently, without a great deal of luck, Robert Black might never have been caught.

Thankfully, though, he was caught, albeit far too late. Nevertheless, the murders he committed can be used to assess the circumstances that allow serial killers to victimise children.

Changing childhoods

It is interesting to view the social construction of childhood in light of the recent moral panic about paedophilia. Professor Jenny Kitzinger (1997) suggests that the sexual abuse of children is not an anomaly or an aberration, but rather part of the structural oppression of children. She then argues that the only way to overcome that oppression is through fundamentally altering how we conceive of childhood, because childhood is 'an institution that makes children "vulnerable"'. Instead of assuming children need adult 'protection' on account of their 'vulnerability', we should talk openly about power, and think conceptually about 'liberation' and 'oppression'. Far from viewing children as 'defenceless' in relation to sexual abuse, we should build on their 'existing sense of self-protection and their ability to kick, yell and run'. Of course, we have already seen how effective Kitzinger's approach can be in Teresa Thornhill's repulse of Robert Black's assault. Nevertheless, largely because adults continue to focus on their sons' and especially their daughters' 'vulnerability', 'children's successful defences rarely come to public/adult attention'. Such defences include children sleeping with the family dog by their bed; deliberately making themselves look unattractive by refusing to bathe or wear make-up; and establishing relationships with other young people in order to 'gain comfort, information, and assistance from each other rather than from adults'.

The 'discovery' of paedophilia and child sexual abuse has been crucial in changing the nature of childhood. This so-called discovery has little to do with any increase in the scale of sexual abuse of children by adults, but rather seems to be related to how adults have come to view childhood because of other changes in society. Children and childhood have become a way of interpreting the world in a deeply paradoxical way: adults recall their own childhoods with great nostalgia, yet they see some children as threatening and their own children as potentially at the mercy of myriad dangers and difficulties.

Adding to the paradox is the fact that the 'discovery' of paedophilia in modern Britain has occurred at a time when young people and their bodies have increasingly been coveted, fetishised and marketed. The music, fashion and cosmetics industries all now use young – often very young – people in sexual ways. In the wake of the adolescent British pop group S Club 7 came the pre-pubescent S Club Juniors. The seventeen-year-old Britney Spears dressed as a junior schoolgirl in the video for her first worldwide hit, while real schoolgirls dressed like adult women, blurring the line between 'child' and 'adult'.

The adulteration of the child in crime and punishment In the Middle Ages there was no collective perception of children being different from adults. As soon as a child was physically able, he or she would go to work with adults and become part of the adult world. Constructions and reconstructions of childhood are thus relatively recent phenomena, and so far there has been little agreement on what the ideal should be. The debate has often been prompted and shaped by two contrasting perspectives on children and their behaviour: the 'Dionysian' and the 'Apollonian'. In the former, the child is viewed as a wilful, impish force, capable of evil and thus needing adult control and surveillance. In the latter, the child is seen as essentially angelic, innocent and unpolluted by the world, and thus needing adult protection, facilitation and encouragement. Of course, irrespective of which perspective is taken, power remains in the hands of adults, who are also able to dispense with the concept of childhood altogether, should they wish to do so. Some would even argue that we are currently witnessing the wholesale disappearance of childhood, but I feel that this goes too far, given recent legal attempts to establish precise boundaries for how the criminal justice system should treat children. Nevertheless, the debate is far from resolved.

Two recurring issues in the criminal justice system are how to prevent young people from committing crimes, and how to respond to them once they have done so. The criminologists John Muncie and Gordon Hughes (2002) have argued that Britain has a 'history of conflict, contradictions, ambiguity and compromise' with respect to youth crime, alternating between viewing 'youth as a special deserving case and youth as fully responsible for their own actions'. The end result has been that the youth justice system has steadily expanded its remit in terms of both its sentencing powers and its system reach. In other words, it is interested not only in those who offend but in those who are 'at risk' of offending, resulting in childhood becoming 'increasingly tightly defined and regulated'. Consequently, children are now intensively governed by adults who enforce discipline through a variety of means, including prison.

The general acceptance of prison as an appropriate punishment for children is best illustrated by the case of the murder of James Bulger in 1993. The two ten-year-old boys who carried out this murder, and many other young people who have since committed lesser offences, have become the human equivalents of dangerous dogs, viewed as deserving the full weight of policing, sentencing and custodial initiatives. New Labour has been at the forefront of this development, and it is significant that Tony Blair was Shadow Home Secretary at the time of James Bulger's death. As the nation struggled to make sense of the murder, Blair abandoned the Labour Party's traditional emphasis on the social and economic causes of crime in favour of a new stress on moral values and the importance of individual responsibility and duty. He demanded that children be taught 'the value of what is right and what is wrong', and continued to repeat the mantra once he became Prime Minister in 1997. Once New Labour were in power the youth justice landscape started to change, with Muncie and Hughes characterising the process as 'adulteration'. This took several forms. For example, in 1998 the ancient legal presumption of *doli incapax* was abolished. Previously applied to children between the ages of ten and thirteen, this had presumed that they did not know the difference between right and wrong, and therefore could not commit a crime because they lacked the necessary criminal intent. Anti-Social Behaviour Orders (ASBOs) were introduced in the same year, and can be applied to children as young as ten – the age of criminal responsibility in England and Wales. While the Home Office did not initially view young people as the primary targets for ASBOs, strong lobbying by local councils saw to it that they were soon seen as central to the 'anti-social paradigm'. In addition, children – irrespective of whether they have committed an offence – are now routinely subjected to curfews, while adults can be slapped with Parental Responsibility Orders if their sons or daughters play truant, are excluded from school or get into trouble with the police. Meanwhile, Child Safety Orders have increasingly been used to 'protect vulnerable' children. Children and their families have therefore become the focus for New Labour's criminal justice policies, all of which seem to be based on conceptions of what 'normal' children and families should be like. (It should be recalled at this point how crucial ideas of 'normality' and 'abnormality' were to our discussions of serial killers who target gay men and sex workers.)

The murder of James Bulger was a defining moment in public consciousness because it stirred a host of fears that Britain in the 1990s was a menacing, violent, crime-ridden society. Fundamental questions were posed about why the country had changed from being a benchmark of common decency founded on the rule of law to a moral wasteland that produced children who could not understand the difference between right and wrong. Wider social anxieties started to be viewed through the lens of childhood, and consequently children were scrutinised by adults as never before, whether in terms of their protection and empowerment, or with a view to their control and regulation. This reconstruction is still ongoing, with the boundary between childhood and adulthood becoming ever less defined, all to achieve an outcome that suits adult needs and desires. In the youth justice system the blurring of the boundary gives the illusion of control: the authorities can claim that 'something is being done' about youth crime when young people are treated as if they are adults and are sentenced accordingly. More broadly, new markets and commercial opportunities have evolved as the line between 'child' and 'adult' has all but disappeared, while adult sexual fantasies have been facilitated by the same process. It is ironic that all of this has occurred at a time when so much effort has gone into proclaiming childhood as precious and worth protecting, especially when society confronts a high-profile crime involving the murder of a child or children.

'Quick, quick, she's gone blue again'

Claire Peck was admitted to Ward Four of Grantham and Kesteven General Hospital on 22 April 1991. Over the previous two months, the hearts or lungs of several children on the ward had mysteriously stopped on twenty-four separate occasions. For several weeks, no one could explain why this was happening, nor indeed why three of the children had died. Then, on 12 April, Dr Nelson Porter, one of the ward's two consultant paediatricians, learned that a boy called Paul Crampton had a large quantity of exogenous insulin in his bloodstream. The logical, albeit alarming, conclusion should have been that someone on the ward was injecting the children with insulin in order to kill them. However, nobody at the hospital – not Dr Porter, nor his fellow consultant Dr Charith Nanayakkara, nor any administrator – called in the police to investigate. Worse still, no new security procedures were introduced to monitor the issuing of drugs, and there was no review of recent cases that resembled Paul's. Sick children like Claire continued to be admitted on to the ward as if it were a safe place in which they could recover.

Claire was suffering from a bad asthma attack and was wheezing badly when she arrived at the hospital. She was fifteen months old, was learning to walk, and had a 'cheeky way of blinking both eyes when she laughed' (Davies, 1993). She was also no stranger to the staff, as she had been in and out of the hospital since her birth. Her worried parents, Sue and David, accompanied her, unaware of the ward's recent history, and continued to believe that the hospital staff would do everything they could to help their little girl.

Dr Porter arrived at the Treatment Room to assess Claire's condition at 5.10 p.m. He ordered some X-rays, then decided to give her an injection of aminophylline by intravenous drip. This is a delicate procedure and has to be done slowly over fifteen to twenty minutes to avoid damaging the patient's heart. Dr Porter left the Treatment Room to calculate the correct dosage while a nurse went to find David and Sue – who were waiting in the Parents' Room – to let them know what was happening. That meant Claire was left alone in the Treatment Room with the other nurse who had been attending her, Beverly Allitt. A few minutes later another nurse entered the room to find that Claire's face had turned dark blue, her back had arched up off the bed, and she had stopped breathing. She was immediately given oxygen through a face mask, Dr Porter injected some of the aminophylline, and Claire quickly recovered and started to breathe normally. With the crisis apparently over, Dr Porter left the room again to speak to David and Sue.

The Allitt Inquiry – chaired by Sir Cecil Clothier (1994) – takes up the story at this point:

> [A]n hour later Allitt raised the alarm again. Claire was dark blue and not breathing. The other nurses and the consultant, Dr Porter, returned to the room just as her heart stopped beating. The team made vigorous attempts to resuscitate her. They were successful in restoring circulation and oxygen saturation of the blood, but her heart would still not restart. Claire was declared dead later that evening.

This may be factually correct but it hardly captures the appalling drama that unfolded that evening and the dreadful situation that Claire's parents had to face. The inquiry's version ignores the fact that Dr Porter returned to the Treatment Room with David, Sue and Sue's parents, and that they had all responded to Allitt's cries of: 'Quick, quick, she's gone blue again.' It must have been obvious that Claire was dead as soon as they entered the room. Nevertheless, Dr Porter and his team tried to resuscitate her for an hour and a half. Throughout that time, Sue and David leaned over Claire, touching her arms and legs, stroking her wavy blonde hair, and cradling her in their arms before finally kissing her goodbye. Claire was pronounced dead at 8.25 p.m. – just over four hours after being admitted to the ward (Davies, 1993). (Although Nick Davies's *Murder on Ward Four* (1993) provides much of the detail that is missing from the official inquiry report, the latter had little time for the former. A footnote on page 88 of the report dismissively mentions 'a journalist's account of the matter' and then states, 'there seems no need to deal any further with the rest of the book'.)

It is abundantly clear that Claire Peck did not need to die. Ward Four should have been shut down at least two weeks earlier, when conclusive evidence emerged that there was a killer active on it. But even after Claire's death the hospital waited a further eight days before calling in the police. Between 12 and 30 April, Allitt attacked four children: Claire, Patrick Elstone, Christopher Peasgood and Christopher King.

Thankfully, Patrick and the two Christophers survived.

As might be expected, Davies and the Allitt Inquiry are not in agreement over why these attacks occurred. Davies concludes: 'Ward Four was trapped by habit and lack of supervision, by low morale and lack of funds, staked out and helpless, the perfect victim. The problems which the Health Service inflicted on the hospital conspired together to set the scene for Nurse Allitt's crimes and then enabled her to get away with them.' A year later, the inquiry concluded: 'The main lesson from our Inquiry and our principal recommendation is that the Grantham disaster should serve to heighten awareness in all those caring for children of the possibility of malevolent intervention as a cause of unexplained clinical events.'

To find a balance between these contrasting conclusions we must look more closely at how Allitt came to be employed on Ward Four and how she was supervised. We also need to assess how various people responded as events unfolded between February and April 1991. In particular, we should explore which steps were taken – or rather not taken – after 12 April, when Dr Porter was advised about Paul Crampton's blood sample.

Training, supervision and 12 April

As a result of her age and insufficient qualifications, Allitt attended Grantham College to complete a two-year prenursing course. She experienced some difficulties with the course during the first twelve months, but more pressing problems started to emerge in the second year. Allitt claimed to be suffering from a number of illnesses and injuries, and she would show these to her tutors as a way of drawing attention to herself. In fact, she was suffering from Munchausen's syndrome, a condition first identified in the 1950s in which sufferers become addicted to hospitals and injure themselves to gain admission. In 1977 Professor Roy Meadow identified an even more disturbing variant of this mental illness – Munchausen's syndrome by proxy – in which the sufferer injures others, usually a child. About a quarter of those diagnosed with Munchausen's syndrome by proxy also have Munchausen's syndrome. In total, Allitt missed 52 days out of a possible 180 in her second year. Even so, she applied to South Lincolnshire School of Nursing to train for a further two years as a pupil nurse. She did not name anyone from Grantham College as a referee on her application form.

During Allitt's pupil-nurse training there were some unexplained incidents – such as mysterious fires at the nurses' home where she lived – but of greater concern was her continuing sick record: she missed a total of 126 days' training during her 110-week course. The official inquiry noted simply, 'Such a high level of sickness was unusual.' In her time on the course, Allitt attended the Accident and Emergency Department of Grantham General Hospital on at least ten occasions, but the School of Nursing was never informed of any of these incidents. At the end of her two-year training, Allitt passed her exams to become an enrolled nurse, but her regular absences meant she had not recorded the required number of days on a ward, so she was obliged to complete a further placement before qualifying. She undertook that placement on Ward Four.

Allitt was interviewed in the general recruitment round for nurses at Grantham General Hospital in December 1990, but she failed to impress the interviewers and was not offered a job. Two months later she had nearly completed her practical experience, and her formal training was due to end on 18 February. She had no job to go to, but Mrs Moira Onions, the Clinical Service Manager, made enquiries on Allitt's behalf about training courses that would lead to her becoming a Registered Sick Children's Nurse (RSCN). Such a course was available at Pilgrim Hospital in Boston, but once again Allitt failed to impress at the interview and did not manage to secure a place.

At that point Grantham General Hospital made a fateful decision. The hospital was short of RSCNs – two had left Ward Four in December 1990 – so Mrs Onions created an enrolled nurse post on Ward Four and told Allitt she was welcome to apply. Allitt was interviewed by Mrs Onions and Sister Barbara Barker – the Ward Manager – on 15 February, and was offered a six-month contract on the ward. She began work in this new post four days later, even though she had undergone no satisfactory health screening nor the required police check. The official inquiry was moved to conclude: 'Virtually none of the procedures in the hospital's recruitment policy was followed when Allitt was appointed.' On 24 February Allitt killed her first victim – seven-week-old Liam Taylor.

To sum up, two factors were crucial in Allitt being appointed to a position of responsibility on a children's ward. First, none of the hospital's normal recruitment procedures were followed. Second, the managers on the ward would appear to have been in a hurry to recruit a newly qualified nurse with an appalling sickness record who had recently been turned down for a post in the hospital's normal recruitment round. Was this just a case of Mrs Onions feeling sympathy for a student nurse with no job to go to, or were there other forces at work?

In February 1991 Ward Four was supposed to have 10.66 whole-time equivalents (WTEs). In other words, the total number of nurses employed – whether full time or part time – should have added up to 10.66 nurses working full time. But Ward Four did not get close to this figure: between February and April there were only three full-time nurses and one part time nurse who held the RSCN qualification – 3.53 WTEs. This serious understaffing meant the ward regularly had to turn to 'bank' nurses to make up the shortfall, only one of whom was an RSCN. Consequently, there was often no RSCN on duty on Ward Four, and, as the official inquiry rather obliquely notes, 'On some shifts an enrolled nurse was left in charge of the ward.' Of course, after 19 February, one of those enrolled nurses was Beverly Allitt. She therefore had responsibilities and power that she would not normally have been given in light of her inexperience and lack of qualifications. This meant, for example, that she had access to the drugs cabinet. Moreover, when she was the only qualified nurse on duty, she was expected to 'special' a sick child – in effect give that patient her undivided attention – which often entailed being left alone with them.

However, as a recently qualified nurse, Allitt should have been subject to regular supervision by more senior colleagues. Sister Barbara Barker, the Ward Manager, was the most experienced nurse at the hospital, and she held the RSCN qualification. Under normal circumstances, someone in her position would be expected to oversee the work of a very junior nurse, such as Allitt. However, as the official inquiry puts it, 'We have heard evidence that Sister Barker did not function well in her role as leader ... [and] did not take an interest in the training of learners.' In other words, Allitt was left to her own devices, with little supervision, guidance or questioning about what was happening to the children in her care, even when they suffered inexplicable heart or lung failure, and even when they died as a result.

Paul Crampton was five months old and had a history of wheezing. He was admitted on to Ward Four on Wednesday, 20 March 1991, and was diagnosed as suffering from either a moderate chest infection or mild asthma. However, when nurses – including Allitt – came to give Paul his medication three days later they noticed that he was cold and clammy. He was also showing signs of low blood sugar, even though he was not diabetic. Paul was put on a glucose drip and soon recovered. The next morning the drip was removed, but it was reinserted later, when Paul's father again found him cold and clammy. A blood sample indicated that Paul's blood glucose was low. After more treatment he was fine for the next three days, but then he had a further attack on 28 March, the day when Allitt returned to the ward after three days' leave. Following this episode Paul was transferred to the Queen's Medical Centre in Nottingham, where he gradually recovered.

Dr Porter could not understand why Paul's blood sugar had dropped so dramatically during his time on Ward Four, so he sent blood samples to a laboratory in Cardiff for analysis. It was after analysing these samples that the lab told Dr Porter on 12 April about the high levels of exogenous insulin in Paul's bloodstream. Dr Porter phoned the Queen's Medical Centre in Nottingham to discuss the lab's findings, but it seems they had little to say on the matter. He also talked through the results with colleagues on Ward Four, but just three days later he and Dr Nanayakkara left the ward to attend the annual conference of the British Paediatric Association, which would seem to indicate that they did not think the situation was particularly serious. The same could be said of the decisions not to phone the police, not to implement new procedures for access to the drugs cabinet, and not to review the cases of children who had exhibited similar symptoms to Paul's.

Davies (1993) has suggested that if the lab results had been taken seriously, the ward would have had to close, at least temporarily, which would have been catastrophic for the hospital. He notes that Grantham General Hospital was £200,000 overspent. Although this was 'a tiny fraction of the budget ... the money had to be found and the hospital could not afford to go creating a public panic, driving valuable patients away'. He goes on to suggest that if Ward Four closed, the hospital would not have the funding to pay the two consultants, so the Grantham's special Baby Care Unit would have to shut. Consequently, the Maternity Ward would have to close, too. 'If they lost that, they would have lost one of their "core services" and they would then lose their status as a District General Hospital. In other words, in the brave new world of the NHS market, if they created a public scare when none was necessary, they could lose the hospital' (Davies, 1993).

What Davies is arguing is that there was therefore a great deal of pressure on hospital staff to play down what was happening on Ward Four. Nevertheless, two weeks after the results had been obtained from Cardiff, the situation could be ignored no longer, and Martin Gibson – the hospital's Manager – finally decided to call in the police.

Where does responsibility lie?

Beverly Allitt's story is central to the argument at the heart of this book. To what extent were the murders of four children, and the attempted murder of nine others, her personal responsibility? Was she solely responsible for the deaths of the children in her care or should we also look elsewhere when apportioning blame? Specifically, were Allitt's recruitment, training and (lack of) supervision factors in these children's deaths? And, if they were, should we then look towards the organisation, financing and management of the NHS in order to understand why so many children suffered at Allitt's hands? Furthermore, should responsibility for the serial murder of the other children in this chapter be laid solely at the doors of Hindley, Brady and Black. Or should we also take into account how childhood has been socially constructed, often predicated upon children's 'weakness' and 'vulnerability', and the failings of the criminal justice system, which allowed a paedophile to walk free from court with only an admonishment? In trying to answer these questions we need to remember that all serial killers need to gain access to suitable victims in order to kill without being detected, and they tend to find these within weak social arrangements, where people do not look out for each other.

Opportunities to kill arise for many reasons. In Allitt's case there was a lack of vigilance and supervision, but equally crucial was the failure of anyone to act when it became clear that someone on Ward Four was trying to kill patients. That failure was due to many factors, and according to Davies's investigation, one of them could have been financial: given the 'house-of-cards' nature of the hospital's funding, closure of the ward was seen by everybody as a last resort.

It seems fair to conclude that the system was also responsible for the murder of her four victims. If she had been recruited into a robust clinical environment with an appropriate level of senior staff who were prepared to act upon a series of unexplained medical emergencies, she would surely have been prevented from injuring and killing as many children as she did. If any of this had been in place, the life of Claire Peck certainly would have been spared. And if Allitt had been adequately supervised, several earlier victims might never have suffered at her hands, either.

In Robert Black's case, the failures of the police and the penal system allowed him to gain access to victims long after he should have been behind bars, which meant he could repeatedly abuse and kill young girls. But there is another factor that we should consider, too: the social context in which he committed his crimes. Black's defining characteristic, the facet of his personality that has motivated the vast majority of his actions in his adult life, has been his paedophilia. From the early 1960s, when Black first came to the attention of the courts as a seventeen-year-old, he has lived in a society that has increasingly fetishised young people's bodies. By the 1980s, when Black committed the murders for which he was ultimately convicted, the music, fashion and entertainment industries were all routinely sexualising children and young people. Of course, Black took this sexualisation to an obscene level by abducting and abusing young girls, but his paedophiliac tendencies were not at odds with what was happening in the rest of British society; rather, they were an extreme manifestation of it. Who could doubt that Black used this fact first to facilitate and later to justify his behaviour?

Broadening the responsibility for the murders committed by Hindley and Brady is much more difficult, not least because they have come to epitomise 'pure evil' in the British collective memory. Yet, even in their case, the manner in which we conceptualise 'childhood' helped create the conditions in which they could operate. In the 1960s, and some would argue even more so now, many children are not valued or taken seriously by the adults they know. Consequently, they look elsewhere for support and protection, and sometimes they inevitably make mistakes when deciding whom to trust. This is not meant to imply that the victims of Hindley and Brady were not valued or loved by their parents, nor that they turned to Brady and Hindley for protection. Far from it: those children were loved, and Brady and Hindley simply exploited their willingness to trust adults who asked for help. Rather, what is being suggested is that children face difficulties during childhood that have usually been created, and can be exploited, by adults. Negotiating and overcoming these difficulties is part of what it means to 'grow up'. As Libby Brooks puts it, childhood is about 'enduring and surviving'.

Recently, ever-greater restrictions have been placed on children's freedom – for instance, a child is now much more likely to be driven to school than to walk – but we should remember that similar controls existed when Brady and Hindley were looking for victims. It is a moot point whether those controls have ever been effective or appropriate. What is much more important is to acknowledge that childhood 'vulnerability' is both created and maintained by adults who define what it is to be 'a child', and then keep children powerless by dictating how the space we call 'childhood' must be occupied and experienced. This deep ambivalence has then been exploited by serial killers such as Brady and Hindley to target, abduct and murder their young victims.

Chapter Ten

'Grave turn for the worse': the elderly

> Hyde, like many of its population, is now in its twilight years and living on a lower income than it did when it was younger. But that doesn't mean it is tired of life. The market has recently had a makeover with brightly coloured canopies and there's plenty of new building and renovation work going on. In other words, Hyde, like its elderly population, still has plenty of energy and a future to look forward to.
>
> Carole Peters, *Harold Shipman: Mind Set on Murder* (2005)

At Northampton Crown Court in November 1999, Souren Ramdoo was convicted under an obscure section of the Mental Health Act of 1983 over the ill-treatment and wilful neglect of a mentally ill patient the previous year. He was sentenced to nine months' imprisonment, and was struck off the Community Care Register.

The patient in question was eighty-nine-year-old Alec Taylor, who had dementia. Alec should have been cared for in the

£315-a-week Oathurst Residential Care Home, near Oxford, but he was known to staff as 'the body in the attic', and for the last four months of his life he saw no one but Ramdoo. Far from looking after Alec, Ramdoo would often attempt to clean the elderly man's chronic bed-sores by hacking at the skin around them with a pair of office scissors, then ripping out the rotting flesh while wearing gloves that he had just used to wipe faeces off the sheets. It was only when Oathurst employed Andrew Barnes as its new office manager that this cycle of abuse came to an end. Barnes blew the whistle on Ramdoo, who was suspended, and Alec was moved to a local hospital, where he later died of pneumonia.

An estimated three million people currently live in England and Wales's 25,000 residential and nursing homes. Tragically, Alec's story is by no means unusual. Action on Elder Abuse suggests that abusive treatment of elderly residents in these homes is rife and that neglect is systematic. In December 2007 the charity was busy lobbying Parliament, because in its view the current system 'lacked [the] resources and drive to ensure comprehensive protection'. Undoubtedly people like Alec die from neglect much more frequently than they should, but others die as a result of more direct action.

Parkfields Residential Home in Butleigh, Somerset, could house sixteen elderly people in its two-storey main building, and nine others in bungalows dotted around its grounds. The main building, as might be expected in a home catering for 'elderly frail people', had a stair lift. Parkfields was described as having a 'friendly atmosphere', and several of the residents had lived there for a number of years. In 2006 it passed an unannounced inspection by the Commission for Social Care Inspection (CSCI), the independent inspectorate which has had responsibility for overseeing all social care services in England since

April 2004. So Parkfields was officially doing well. Moreover, the home's owners were held in high regard by the villagers of Butleigh.

All of that changed after the death of ninety-seven-year-old Lucy Cox on New Year's Day 2007. This in turn led the police to become suspicious about the deaths of several other residents at the home: eighty-nine-year-old Nellie Pickford, a keen singer and actress; seventy-nine-year-old Marion Alder, a former company secretary and grandmother to four children; and eighty-one-year-old former crane-driver Fred Green. (There was also a fifth, unidentified resident whose death came under scrutiny.) By March 2007, Parkfields had been closed. The police and the Crime Prosecution Service are still investigating what took place.

Since 1960, some 241 elderly people (mostly women) have been killed in Britain by serial killers. The most prolific British serial killer – Harold Shipman, a general practitioner – specifically targeted the elderly, and his story and the issues it raises dominate this chapter. However, four other British serial killers – Patrick Mackay, Kenneth Erskine, Colin Norris and Stephen Akinmurele – also murdered older people, and aspects of their stories afford further insight into the Shipman case. Mackay killed his final victim, Father Anthony Crean, a sixty-four-year-old Catholic priest who had befriended him, four days after Shipman murdered for the first time.

Hyde, in the Tameside borough of Greater Manchester, is coincidentally where Brady and Hindley were arrested. The town – just like Todmorden, where Shipman began his clinical practice – first grew as a result of the success of its cotton mills. To me, the epigraph that opens this chapter paints a picture of two realities of life in Hyde in the 1980s and 1990s: the town's changing social and economic structure; and the sense that those who lived there had seen life pass them by and were, as a consequence, not worth bothering about. Of course, this impression is the exact opposite of what Carole Peters intends to convey: she specifically says that Hyde is not 'tired of life'; it has 'plenty of energy' and a bright future. But she draws these conclusions only after viewing the town's recently erected 'brightly coloured canopies' and other examples of urban renewal. Consequently, her optimism seems rather forced, and by emphasising the positive she underplays the continuing vulnerability of the elderly in British culture, a culture which has come to value production and consumption above everything else. As the journalist A. A. Gill put it, 'Most people in this country die weepingly lonely, left in no doubt that they have overstayed their welcome. This is the greatest shame and horror of our age' ('No Country for Old Men or Women', *Sunday Times Magazine*, 29 March 2009). So Hyde, 'living on a lower income than it did when it was younger' gives a clue to the value of the town within the wider economy, and the value of its ageing population. Given these circumstances, we should scarcely be surprised that virtually no one noticed or cared when large numbers of Hyde's elderly inhabitants started to disappear.

It is important to remember that most elderly people who have been murdered by a British serial killer were victims of a medical practitioner: either Shipman or Colin Norris, the 'Angel of Death', a male nurse who was convicted of killing four elderly patients at Leeds General Infirmary and St James's Hospital in 2002, although it should be noted that doubts about this conviction regularly surface. In other words, they were usually ill at the time of their death, and so cannot be considered a representative sample of Britain's elderly people as a whole. But then it is difficult to say what would be a representative sample, given the problems in defining 'old age' and the disparities of wealth within the retired population, a sizeable number of whom would be considered rich at any age. That said, according to the National Pensioners Convention, in 2005, 2.2 million older people were living below the poverty line in the UK, and around 1.5 million were either malnourished or at serious risk of it. Furthermore, as the case of Alec Taylor graphically illustrates, we should not assume that the three million elderly people in residential and care homes are any better off. By 2016 almost twenty per cent of the UK's population were sixty-five or older – nearly 12 million people

In this chapter I shall not offer a detailed explanation of how vulnerability and dependency are created in our society, nor of why the elderly are especially vulnerable and dependent as a result of employment practices, pension arrangements and healthcare policies. Rather, I shall focus on how that vulnerability and dependency are experienced in order to gain an understanding of why so many elderly people have fallen victim to serial killers. This group has been victimised more than any other, so looking at their circumstances gives us the best sense of what it means to be excluded, marginalised and powerless – three factors which tend to lead to someone's sudden death being greeted with silence, rather than questioning or surprise.

Harold Frederick Shipman

Before his death, the sociologist Keith Soothill lamented that his discipline has been remarkably loath to engage with the phenomenon of serial killing generally, never mind Harold Shipman specifically. Moreover, this reluctance to discuss Shipman has been mirrored in other disciplines, such as psychiatry and psychology, whose practitioners have historically been much more willing to comment at length on serial killers. As far as Shipman is concerned, though, all we have had are some vague notions related to his desire to possess 'power over life and death' and the usual platitudes about a 'difficult childhood' and the murderer's arrogance. Nobody has addressed the most pressing question: why was Harold Shipman able to kill *repeatedly*?

Initially, this reluctance to discuss Shipman might have been due to the Secretary of State for Health's announcement of an independent (and private) inquiry, to be chaired by Lord Laming, following Shipman's conviction in early 2000. Reasonably enough, many people preferred to wait and see what the inquiry concluded before making any comment. After a great deal of pressure it was announced in September 2000 that the inquiry would become public, and thereafter it was chaired by Dame Janet Smith. She began work the following February but her final report was not published until January 2005. The inquiry was formally decommissioned a few months later.

The inquiry had a fourfold brief: to enquire into the actions of the statutory bodies, authorities, other organisations and responsible individuals concerned in the procedures and investigations that followed the deaths of Shipman's patients who died in unlawful or suspicious circumstances; after receiving and hearing the existing evidence, to consider the extent of Shipman's unlawful activities; to enquire into the performance of statutory bodies, authorities, other organisations and individuals with responsibility for monitoring primary-care provision and the use of controlled drugs; and, following those enquiries, to recommend any steps that should be taken to protect patients in the future. Without doubt, this final component of the inquiry's brief is the most important.

Another reason for the relative silence over the Shipman case may well have been the general assumption that he was simply 'evil'. With virtually everyone in agreement about Shipman's personality, there seemed little to debate. There was also a widespread belief that he was such a freak of nature that someone similar would be very unlikely to strike in the future. In other words, Shipman was viewed as a lone, rogue predator who was too bizarre to be analysed.

However, the Smith Inquiry did not support this popular interpretation of Harold Shipman. Dame Janet's first report, *Death Disguised* (July 2002), reminds readers that: 'The Inquiry's Terms of Reference require me to consider the extent of Shipman's unlawful activities. They do not expressly require me to consider the motives behind Shipman's crimes, or the psychological factors that underlay them. However, I decided that I ought to consider and report on those matters, as well as I am able.' And consider them she did. With a group of forensic psychiatrists – including Professors John Gunn and Pamela Taylor and Drs Clive Meux and Alec Buchanan – to support her, Dame Janet raised hopes and expectations that an authoritative explanation of Shipman's motivation might emerge. However, those expectations were dashed almost immediately, as Shipman refused to have anything to do with either the inquiry or Dame Janet's team of psychiatrists. Without being able to interview him, the psychiatrists were forced to rely at best on second-hand information. Dame Janet admits that her team could not 'gain any real insight into Shipman's character', and so was 'unable to reach any conclusions'. Therefore, 'in the end I have been unable to attempt any detailed explanation of the psychological factors underlying Shipman's conduct'.

As is obvious from this candid admission, plenty was left unresolved after the inquiry had completed its investigation. Yet the media, usually so keen to boost circulation and advertising revenue with a serial killer story, still seemed reluctant to discuss Shipman. One of the few programmes to try was ITV's *To Kill and Kill Again*, broadcast on 1 March 2005, but it offered little in the way of explanation as to why Shipman killed, despite a plethora of 'experts' (mostly forensic psychologists) offering opinions. Carole Peters – the producer/director of *To Kill and Kill Again* – attempted to probe deeper in her subsequent book, *Harold Shipman: Mind Set on Murder*. But all she could conclude was that Shipman became a serial killer because 'he enjoyed what he did'.

I am sure everyone will share the hope that Shipman was indeed a freak of nature and that we shall never see his like again. Viewing him in this way makes us feel better about our own elderly relatives and friends, whose care we may have entrusted to residential home-owners, local GPs and community nurses while we get on with the rest of our lives. However, deep down, we all know that Shipman is unlikely to be the last serial killer of his type. Certainly the government believed that a new Shipman could be waiting in the wings, which is why part of the inquiry's brief was to look into how vulnerable patients could be protected in the future. Of course, an inquiry can also be used by the authorities to dampen down speculation and generate a conspiracy of silence. No one is keen to second guess its findings for fear of looking foolish when it finally publishes its conclusions. But if an inquiry takes as long as Dame Janet's did to issue its final report, serious interest in the topic will have all but disappeared, and the media agenda will have moved elsewhere.

Perhaps we have all colluded in the conspiracy of silence about Britain's worst serial killer because Shipman's story is simply too difficult to confront. It upsets us by demanding that we acknowledge issues we would prefer to ignore, deny or not discuss, such as the fate of Alec Taylor, 'the body in the attic'. Alec personifies all those elderly people who are no longer seen as living human beings with hopes, fears and desires but simply as bodies, which makes it so much easier to ignore them when they disappear or die. This is why it is crucial to understand the circumstances that allowed Shipman to murder so many elderly people, because only then will we be in a position to stop others following in his footsteps. However, before considering these issues, we need to examine what Shipman did and whom he murdered.

Eva Lyons to Kathleen Grundy: 215 other 'bodies in the attic'

The sheer amount of information generated by the Smith Inquiry is astounding. Over 2,500 witness statements were taken and the inquiry's database runs to approximately 270,000 pages. It is impossible to generalise about so many victims, and there is not the space here to analyse a representative sample (should such a thing exist), so instead I have decided to focus on Shipman's first and last victims, to give an indication of how he operated and whom he targeted.

Eva Lyons was the first woman to be murdered by Harold Shipman. She was born, raised, married and had a child in Todmorden – and that was where she died. Like most of her contemporaries, when Eva left school she started to work as a weaver in one of the cotton mills that dominated the town and were the source of its prosperity. Now the mills have long since disappeared, and Todmorden mostly serves as a commuter town for people working in Manchester, Leeds, Bradford and Huddersfield. When Eva was twenty-eight years old she met her husband Dick, a shuttle-maker at another factory, and soon they had a baby girl whom they named Norma. By early 1975 Eva was ill with cancer, although a new drug regime at Halifax Royal Infirmary seemed to be helping with her condition: her hair had started to grow back and she was eating again. Even so, on the night of 17 March she was in some discomfort, so Dick called their local GP. He soon arrived at the house and told Dick that he was going to give Eva something to 'ease the pain'. He took a syringe from his bag and inserted the needle into Eva's hand, all the time maintaining a normal conversation with Dick. Five minutes later, Eva was dead.

Eva's doctor would eventually be convicted at Preston Crown Court on 31 January 2000 of murdering fifteen of his patients while working as a GP in Hyde. He was also found guilty of one count of forging a will. Harold Shipman was sentenced to life imprisonment, but he took his own life at HMP Wakefield in January 2004. Following his training at the University of Leeds Medical School, Shipman had acted as a pre-registration house officer at Pontefract General Infirmary before joining the Abraham Ormerod Medical Practice in Todmorden in 1974. Perhaps during his student days, and certainly by the time he was at Todmorden, he had developed an addiction to pethidine. He appeared before Halifax Magistrates' Court in 1976 and pleaded guilty to three counts of obtaining the drug by deception, three counts of unlawfully possessing it and two counts of forging prescriptions. He also asked for seventy-four further offences to be taken into consideration. The court fined him six hundred pounds. Thereafter, Shipman moved to Newton Aycliffe Health Centre, where he worked as a clinical medical officer, before relocating to Hyde in 1978.

In Hyde, Shipman worked at the Donneybrook Practice for fourteen years prior to setting up his solo practice in Market Street in 1992. He rapidly gained a reputation as a particularly good, 'old-fashioned' doctor, especially with elderly people, whom he was prepared to visit in their own homes. A measure of the esteem in which he was held in the Hyde community can be gleaned from the fact that there was a 'Shipman's Patient Fund', which raised money to buy medical equipment for his practice. When allegations about the murders started to circulate, one group of incredulous patients formed a support group for their GP. At the time of his arrest, over three thousand patients were registered with his practice, a considerable number for a sole practitioner.

Shipman was caught largely because of a bungled attempt to forge the will of his last victim – Kathleen Grundy – whom he murdered on 24 June 1998. Kathleen's daughter, Angela Woodruff, was a lawyer, and she had suspicions about the document from the moment she saw it. Two conclusions have been drawn from Shipman's forgery of the will: there might have been a financial motive to all of his murders; and, in light of the fact that the document was so poorly faked, by this stage he wanted to be caught. The second of these conclusions certainly seems to be borne out by Shipman's reckless behaviour. By the time of Kathleen's murder, he was killing at the rate of once every ten days, and the Smith Inquiry concluded that he was 'no longer in touch with reality'.

Over twenty-three years, starting with Eva and ending with Kathleen, it has been calculated that Shipman killed 215 people: 171 women and forty-four men. The Smith Inquiry also harboured suspicions about the deaths of another forty-five of his former patients, making a total of some 260 people whom he may have killed.

These killings came to an end because the authorities treated Angela Woodruff's suspicions with the respect they deserved. But many others in the Hyde community had previously harboured suspicions about Shipman and had tried to make those in authority listen to their concerns. Once again, therefore, we need to consider who has a voice in British society and, more significantly, who goes unheeded.

Ordinary voices

John Shaw, a former policeman, started K Cabs in Hyde in 1988, having spotted a gap in the market. Thereafter, he drove elderly clients around the town in his blue Volvo. His business prospered largely because the older ladies of Hyde grew to trust him. They came to be on first-name terms with John, who would also sometimes do odd jobs for them. He was therefore in a prime position to notice that significant numbers of his clients were dying in very similar circumstances: always at home and 'posed' in an easy chair. He also started to realise that they were all Shipman's patients. From the death of Monica Sparkes in October 1992, John started to compile a list of his clients' seemingly untimely deaths, and he would periodically try to voice his concerns. However, few people were prepared to listen. For instance, one early police investigation into Shipman, conducted by Detective Inspector Smith of Greater Manchester Police, completely ignored John's list. Ann Alexander – the solicitor who would eventually represent the families of Shipman's victims – commented on this investigation:

> I had always believed that it was a policeman's job to go out and ask questions. And in this particular case Smith didn't ask any questions. He sat and waited for information to be given to him. He just completely failed to get to the bottom of it, failed to make any notes, and because of the way in which he approached the whole thing it was inevitable that he wasn't going to get anything that would have given rise to an earlier arrest.
>
> (Peters, 2005)

Of course, this echoes the failures of the police in the Sutcliffe case. Tragically, John and his concerns were taken seriously only after the awful truth about Shipman had begun to emerge. In other words, he was silenced until those with more powerful voices made a complaint that was given credence by those in positions of authority.

Another element of the silence in the Shipman case relates to the class of most of his victims, the vast majority of whom were working-class people. Perhaps more than other sectors of society, they had been socialised into trusting and respecting doctors. Their very 'ordinariness' can be contrasted with Shipman's final victim, Kathleen Grundy, a former Mayor of Hyde and a local councillor who owned property in both the town and the Lake District and possessed a considerable investment portfolio. Moreover, her well-educated solicitor daughter was used to dealing with the police, coroners and magistrates, which meant she had the confidence to press the authorities to look into Shipman's activities. Even so, Mrs Woodruff and her husband were initially obliged to investigate the forged will themselves, before handing over their findings to the police. So Shipman was brought to justice because of a forged legal document and concerns over inheritance that were voiced by professionals who knew how to make their anxieties known. By contrast, a taxi driver who recognised that a surprisingly high number of the local GP's patients were suddenly dying for no apparent reason was ignored. This conclusion is not intended to be disrespectful to Mr or Mrs Woodruff, whose persistence was vital in stopping the terrible activities of Harold Shipman. Rather, it is designed to encourage reflection on who has the power to complain and demand action, and who has to shut up and make do.

Could lightning strike twice in the same place? The Smith Inquiry made strenuous efforts to deal with any issues that could be definitively 'proven' one way or another, where evidence could be evaluated and a decision reached. The first of Dame

Janet's reports concentrated simply on the number of patients who had been murdered; the second on the conduct of the police investigation; the third on the conduct of coroners and the issuing of death certificates; the fourth on the regulation of controlled drugs in the community; the fifth on suggestions for how patients might be protected in the future; and the sixth and last on Shipman's career as a junior doctor in Pontefract. Speaking in 2009 in a documentary on BBC Radio 4 called *Shipman: Could it Happen Again?*, Dame Janet expressed her worry that the authorities had been slow to take action to ensure that someone like Shipman could not strike again. She focused especially on the status of medical examiners: 'It is said that he or she will be independent, but I fear that that will be very difficult.' More ominously, she added that Shipman's name drew no response at all when she spoke to junior doctors about his case. All this seems to indicate that Shipman is being treated as a freak of nature, a one-off.

However, Shipman was not the first doctor to be accused of killing his patients, and Colin Norris and Beverly Allitt also used their positions within the medical profession to murder those in their charge. There is an interesting and seemingly parallel case to Shipman's involving Dr John Bodkin Adams, who, despite being acquitted of murder in the 1950s, features in Keith Simpson's *Forty Years of Murder* (1978). Bodkin Adams worked as a GP in Eastbourne, and was favoured over a hundred times in the wills of his elderly patients. In 1957 he was tried over the murders of two of them, Edith Morrell and Gertrude Hullett. At the time, the trial was the longest for murder in English criminal history. Bodkin Adams was eventually acquitted unanimously by the jury, which perhaps explains why he is not even mentioned in the Smith Inquiry reports. In another echo of the Shipman case, he was later convicted under the Drugs Act on a minor charge of 'loose' prescribing of hard drugs, which led to him being struck off the Medical Register. However, his name was later restored to the register, so 'he was free to continue to treat rich elderly widows with such quantities of morphia and heroin as he considered appropriate' (Simpson, 1978).

Simpson continues:

> Doctors are in a particularly good position to commit murder and escape detection. Their patients, sometimes their own fading wives, more often mere ageing nuisances, are in their sole hands. 'Dangerous drugs' and powerful poisons lie in their professional bags or in the surgery. No one is watching or questioning them, and a change in symptoms, a sudden 'grave turn for the worse' or even death is for them to interpret. They can authorize the disposal of a dead body by passing the necessary death certificate to the Registrar of Deaths, who has no power to interfere unless there is some statutory shortcoming in the way the certificate is filled out, or death appears due to accident or violence of some kind, or the wording is so vague or unintelligible that the Registrar has to seek the help of the Coroner . . .
>
> Are there many doctor murderers? . . . No one can know, but if doctors do take the law into their own hands, the facts are only likely to emerge by chance, through whisperings of suspicion or, rarely, through carelessness in disposal of the dead body, as when Dr Buck Ruxton threw the remains of his wife and her maid Mary Rogerson in an open ravine at Moffat in Dumfriesshire.

This should remind us of some earlier cases, notably that of Dr Thomas Neill Cream, who unwisely wrote a series of letters relating to the deaths of his prostitute victims. There was also the famous Dr Hawley Crippen, who stupidly lied about his wife's 'disappearance' before dashing to America in 1910. A less well-known case concerned a certain Dr Lawson, who walked into a private school to poison his crippled brother-in-law with a piece of cake laced with aconite. He was caught after the chemist who supplied the poison read an account of the murder. Simpson notes: 'There are 70,000 doctors in England and Wales alone, so a mere handful of professional murders in fifty years speaks generally very highly of their moral fibre, *or the ease with which they can conceal crime*' (emphasis added).

The Bodkin Adams case is again instructive here. At the time of his trial he was a portly, bespectacled Irishman of sixty who had practised medicine in Eastbourne for many years. The crux of the case was whether this elderly doctor occasionally got his sums wrong and mistakenly gave a little too much sedative to one of his frail patients, or whether he was deliberately murdering them and profiting from their wills as a result. The whispers about what had been happening to Bodkin Adams's wealthy old ladies were widespread, but the trial focused on the death of just one of them, Edith Morrell. Simpson – who acted on behalf of the Medical Defence Union, which organised Bodkin Adams's defence – still seemed to be on the doctor's side over twenty years later:

> On the face of it the case looked hard to prove. There was no body (an obvious handicap in a case of alleged poisoning) as Mrs Morrell had been cremated, at her own request. She had died six years before. She was eighty-one, and half paralysed by a stroke, after which she had been given from six to twelve months to live, only to survive another two and a half years under the care of the doctor now charged with her murder. She had left an estate of £157,000, out of which the doctor

received an elderly Rolls-Royce and a chest containing silver valued at £275 . . . Hardly a rich legacy.

The prosecution's case ultimately collapsed because of the unreliability of and conflicts in the medical and nursing evidence. Nevertheless, as Simpson admits, 'one mystery remained. The defence had proved that the amount of morphine and heroin prescribed (and supplied by the chemist) greatly exceeded the amount administered to Mrs Morrell: what had happened to the rest?'

Since that case in the late 1950s, concern about serial killers and theorising about them have both grown enormously. Whereas fifty years ago few people seemed able to see past pecuniary gain as being the only plausible motive for killing a rich old lady, now we know that serial killers murder for myriad other reasons, too. So the fact that Bodkin Adams did not secure a 'rich legacy' from Mrs Morrell's death would scarcely aid his defence today. Nevertheless, the possibility of financial gain cannot be dismissed entirely as a motive: the forensic psychologist Paul Britton suggests that Shipman may have forged Kathleen Grundy's will in order to secure funds that would have enabled him to move to a new location (Bennett and Gardner, 2005).

There are more definitive links between the Bodkin Adams and Shipman cases, too: for instance, their long experience as doctors in tight-knit local communities with ageing populations. However, there is also one highly significant difference: Bodkin Adams was acquitted in court, while Shipman was found guilty, and nobody seems to harbour any doubts about that verdict. So how should we explain his behaviour?

Individual and social explanations

The first place to look for an explanation of how Shipman was able to kill so many people is in the work of the medical sociologist Eliot Freidson (1970). Forty years ago, Freidson suggested that analysis of the work of the professional classes is problematic because professionals – including medical professionals – have secured freedom from control by outsiders. He further emphasised that a solo medical practice – such as Shipman's – is the most likely setting for professional abuse. In a solo practice the burden of control over performance rests almost entirely on individual motivation and capacity. Freidson pointed out that physicians routinely create an informal structure of relatively segregated, small circles of practitioners, the extremes of which are so isolated from each other that mutual influence on behaviour is absent. This creates opportunities for malicious doctors to gain access to vulnerable people, as well as the opportunity to do them harm.

Even so, in his Foreword to *Harold Shipman's Clinical Practice 1974–1998* (2001), Professor Sir Liam Donaldson – the Chief Medical Officer at the Department of Health – maintains that 'everything points to the fact that a doctor with the sinister and macabre motivation of Harold Shipman is a once in a lifetime occurrence'. This indicates that the common conception of Shipman as a lone, rogue practitioner is shared by the highest echelons of the British medical and political establishment. Unfortunately, though, neither Donaldson nor anyone else can offer evidence to support this conclusion. Donaldson attempts 'to describe factually the circumstances applying to the deaths of Shipman's patients ... [but] cannot explain how or why the events came to happen'. He also admits that the 'why' question would remain unknown until Shipman agreed to cooperate. As we now know, that was something Shipman was never prepared to do. But even the assumption that he would have shed light on his motivation if he had talked is seriously flawed. As I stressed at the start of this book, it is always unwise to rely on the testimony of serial killers. Nevertheless, in this instance, I am reminded of an observation made by Ian Brady (2001) about Peter Sutcliffe:

> It is yet once more paradoxical that, on the one hand, the serial killer often wishes to demonstrate his contempt for society, yet still feels compelled to maintain his good name, as it were . . . the inner knowledge that he is a house divided slowly corrodes the artificial boundary the killer has tried to build within his two separate selves, his dual personality. The inevitable collapse of this edifice will almost certainly result in psychotic chaos.

Leaving aside for a moment the depth of Brady's psychological or psychiatric understanding of dual personalities, his notion that a serial killer displays contempt for society by repeatedly murdering while at the same time maintaining a 'good name' seems to fit Shipman perfectly. After all, Shipman was both a respected, hardworking GP who was prepared to visit his patients in their homes and this country's most prolific serial killer. He was truly a 'house divided', even if we do not know – or much care – how he prevented this duality from collapsing into 'psychotic chaos'. Brady comes close to describing the need that many serial killers have for attention, control and power (which is precisely why he wanted to write his book). He also gives an insight into how, if they are allowed the access and the opportunity, they exploit that power to murder time after time.

This brings us back to the structural tradition, the social explanations that help to identify the groups that are more vulnerable to attack than others. As Chris Grover and Keith Soothill (1999) argue:

> The victims of modern British serial killers are *not* from the relatively powerful middle classes, but are from relatively powerless and vulnerable groups – children and young adults; gay men; women (particularly those vulnerable through their work in the sex industry or on account of the breakdown of familial relations); and pensioners. In fact, the general *absence* of persons from relatively powerful positions is especially noticeable.

Shipman overwhelmingly chose victims who were poor, elderly and female, and therefore vulnerable on three counts. Peters (2005) suggests that he may have targeted them because 'the elderly or infirm would go first because they simply ceased to be as valuable as human beings and so there was no reason to keep them'. In this way they could be perceived as living outside the moral order of a competitive capitalist society. They were not seen as an asset to the community but as a socioeconomic burden.

As the stories of the victims described in this chapter have made abundantly clear, a great many elderly people are marginalised and isolated in modern British society. Shipman gave himself the perfect cover for his murderous activities by becoming a respected local GP. He gained the trust of his patients because of his 'old-fashioned' demeanour and his willingness to visit them in their homes. That provided him with easy access and the opportunity to kill as he pleased, while his 'good name' generally ensured neighbours', friends' and relatives' silence, in spite of any suspicions they might have held. But that silence was even more pervasive because so many of his victims had lost touch with their immediate families and the rest of society.

This structural explanation of why Shipman was able to continue killing for over two decades might not satisfy everyone, but let us look for a moment at the alternative. If we adopted the medico-psychological tradition and attempted to probe Shipman's psyche, we would, in all likelihood, simply find a mass of contradictions. It is doubtful that we would uncover the evil man so beloved of tabloid headline writers. Rather, we would find someone who is still viewed as a good doctor by many of his former patients. He may also be described as arrogant, which perhaps leads us to an understanding of his contempt for the law. But surely most people would expect their doctor to be at least confident and self-assured, if not exactly arrogant. And this was certainly part of what made Shipman a good doctor in the eyes of so many of his patients throughout the 1980s and 1990s. Other doctors who have come before the courts have been similarly lauded by their patients: for example, several of Bodkin Adams's patients were keen to come forward and give glowing character references at his trial in 1957. However, the social context in Britain changed dramatically over the next few decades, and that background made it much easier for Shipman to kill repeatedly.

Over Shipman's lifetime, changes in British culture and society provided the context for his crimes. In many respects the dominant economic development was the move from production to consumption, which left in its wake large numbers of poor people who were no longer deemed 'useful' because their labour was now unimportant. Nor could they consume to the same extent as those who had money, or as they themselves had done previously, which is why they came to be viewed as a burden. Britain also became a more secular society, so the sanctity of life is now less maintained by religious conviction. In contrast, doctors have increasingly become the moral arbiters of life and death. Shipman simply demonstrated this power in an outrageous way. We will never know *why* he wanted to demonstrate his power in this manner. But two other aspects of his case are much clearer. Society totally failed to control and monitor his activities as a medical professional. And it offered wholly inadequate protection to the poor and vulnerable, specifically poor and vulnerable pensioners, to whom Shipman had unrestricted access that gave him the opportunity to murder over two hundred times.

The more recent case of sixty-nine-year-old Peter Farquhar, who was murdered by his younger male companion Ben Field in Maids Moreton near Buckingham in 2015, offers up another example of how those who want to kill can gain access to the elderly. Field, who had enrolled on a PhD in English Literature at Buckingham University, was the son of a Baptist Minister, a Church Warden at Stowe Parish Church and was going through the process of ordination at the time that he committed the murder. He also volunteered at a local nursing home and, after he was arrested, the police discovered that he had a list of a hundred other people – many of whom were elderly – that he thought would be 'useful' to him. Indeed Field would have got away with his murder of Peter, had he then not targeted another elderly and devout neighbour which aroused suspicions. It is hard to escape the conclusion that whilst Shipman had used medicine to target his elderly victims, and his status as a doctor to ensure silence about what he was doing, Field was going to use religion and his place within the Church.

Patrick Mackay and Kenneth Erskine

Patrick Mackay and Kenneth Erskine also repeatedly targeted the elderly. Mackay, in particular, had what might be called the 'classic' background of a serial killer who is analysed in the medico-psychological tradition. His father was a violent alcoholic and beat him as a child. Mackay, in turn, seems to have found some solace in torturing animals and bullying other children. He was a loner, attended school only intermittently, and got into trouble with the police for a series of increasingly serious offences. At the age of fifteen he was already being described as a 'cold psychopathic killer' by a psychiatrist who visited him in Moss Side Secure Hospital, where he had been sent under Section 60 of the Mental Health Act of 1959. Another spell in the hospital would follow before he was released in August 1972. Like Ian Brady, Mackay was fascinated by Nazism; and, like his father, he became addicted to alcohol.

On 14 February 1974 Mackay knocked on the door of Isabella Griffiths, an eighty-four-year-old widow who lived alone at 19 Cheyne Walk. She answered the door with the security chain attached, but Mackay broke through it with ease. Isabella backed into the hallway, and it was there that Mackay strangled her. He then dragged her body into the kitchen before wandering around the rest of the house. He would later claim that during this walk he had a 'strong compulsion to kill her outright' (Clark and Penycate, 1976). Consequently, he returned to the body and stabbed Isabella with a kitchen knife while listening to Edward Heath on the radio talking about the Common Market referendum. Isabella's body lay undiscovered for twelve days, and the crime remained unsolved for over a year, by which time Mackay had significantly added to his tally of victims.

In July 1974 Mackay was sentenced to four months' imprisonment for theft. While at HMP Wormwood Scrubs, he 'planned the campaign of terror and violence that he was to wage when he was released'. This entailed robbing elderly women, something that he had done off and on for years, whenever he had needed money. 'Mackay never forgot how vulnerable and defenceless old ladies were as potential victims of robbery . . . in the winter of 1974–75 this became a planned and systematic reign of terror.' Over the next few months he attacked eighty-year-old Jane Comfort, an actress who was appearing in Agatha Christie's *The Mousetrap*, Lady Belcher and two other unnamed elderly women, but did not kill any of them. Then, on 29 January 1975, he 'descended on an old ladies' hostel, Murray House in Vandon Street, Westminster, within a stone's throw of New Scotland Yard.

He snatched a handbag containing £5 from Mrs Evelyn Grahame. He made a mental note of the fact that many elderly ladies seemed to live in the hostel. Easy pickings' (Clark and Penycate, 1976). He killed again on 10 March 1975, having gained entry to the flat of eighty-nine-year-old Mrs Adele Price by asking for a glass of water. He then strangled Mrs Price and left her face-down on her bedroom carpet. Finally, eleven days later, he travelled to Gravesend, where he killed Father Crean.

These final two murders reveal significant differences between the modi operandi of Shipman and Mackay. Shipman gained access to his victims by securing their trust and respect, whereas Mackay used a combination of guile, trickery and brute force. Shipman liked to pose the bodies of his victims before he left them, because he wanted to give the impression that they had peacefully 'slipped away'. Mackay had no such interest in generating a good impression. Finally, while Shipman's victims were killed with a syringe of morphine, Mackay murdered through strangulation, stabbing or, in the case of Father Crean, with an axe. Mackay himself relates how he barged down the bathroom door to gain access to the fearful priest and what happened next:

> He tumbled and half fell into the bath. He then started to annoy me even more, and I kept striking at his nose with my arm and the side of my hand. I then pulled out my knife from my coat pocket and repeatedly plunged it into his neck. I then got a little more excitable and stuck it into the side of his head, and then tried to plunge it into the top of his head. This bent the knife. I grabbed for the axe and with this repeatedly lashed out with it at his head. He sank into the bath. He had been in the sitting-up position with the knife but when I first hit him with the axe he sank down into the bath. I then got increasingly more annoyed, and lashed at him with the axe.
>
> (Quoted in Clark and Penycate, 1976)

It is impossible to comprehend how Father Crean could have made Mackay 'increasingly more annoyed'. After all, by this stage, the priest was absolutely at the mercy of his attacker, having been stabbed repeatedly in the head. Of more relevance is the fact that the deaths of Mrs Price and especially Father Crean were sufficiently violent to be deemed worthy of intensive investigation by the authorities. There could be no silence in the aftermath of such brutal killings. Rather, they generated questioning and surprise. Who could have done such a thing? How could he be stopped? Who was a likely suspect? In contrast, Shipman's tactics of posing his victims and especially of encouraging their families to cremate the bodies – thus destroying vital forensic evidence – ensured that he was able to continue to kill for decades. Shipman was also helped by his status: a doctor was above suspicion, whereas a young man who had been labelled a 'cold psychopathic killer' could not escape detection for long and Mackay was swiftly arrested after Father Crean's murder. He was tried and sentenced in November 1975. Finally, as will be recalled from our earlier discussion of 'organised' and 'disorganised' serial killers, the latter – like Mackay – are much easier to catch than the former.

Kenneth Erskine – dubbed the 'Stockwell Strangler' – was another disorganised serial killer who targeted elderly men and women. He robbed, sodomised, then killed a succession of pensioners over the summer of 1986. His first victim was seventy-eight-year-old Nancy Elms, whom he sexually assaulted and then strangled in her flat in Wandsworth. In June similar fates befell sixty-seven-year-old Jane Cockett, eighty-four-year-old Valentine Gleim and ninety-four-year-old Zbigniew Strabawa. The following month Erskine strangled and sexually assaulted eighty-two-year-old William Carmen, seventy-four-year-old William Downes and his final victim, eighty-year-old Florence Tisdall. Writing in *The Times* on the day of Erskine's arrest, 28 July 1986, Marcel Berlins attempted to paint a 'portrait of a serial killer' and quoted from a consultant psychologist, Edmund Hervey-Smith, in a bid to identify a motive for the murders. Dr Hervey-Smith suggested, 'it is possible ... that his preoccupation with old people stems from something that has happened to him. Perhaps his mother died after a lot of suffering and as a result he feels sorry for old people. If he is a schizophrenic he may genuinely believe that he is putting his victims out of their misery.' Whatever Erskine's motivation, Martin Fido (2001) reveals that the accused had to be stopped from masturbating when he entered the courtroom during his trial, which would seem to indicate that he was both mentally ill and totally oblivious to events surrounding him. Indeed, in July 2009 Erskine had his murder convictions reduced to manslaughter on appeal, after the Lord Chief Justice and two other judges in the Court of Appeal accepted that at the time of the murders Erskine was suffering from an 'abnormality' of the mind that substantially diminished his responsibility for his crimes. Such handicaps severely limit a potential serial killer's capacity to kill repeatedly, as does the fact that Erskine falls into the disorganised category. Nevertheless, by targeting the elderly, he was able to gain access to seven highly vulnerable victims before he could be stopped.

Old age and the serial killer

The fact that Shipman, Mackay, Erskine and Norris all targeted the elderly should make us question the provision of social and economic protection for this sector of society. And, as the case of Shipman proves, something must be done to address the current lack of monitoring and control of the medical profession. Moreover, we need to reach an understanding of the meaning of serial killing at a societal level. The actions of these serial killers allow us to identify where society has broken down, where it has failed. At least some good might come out of these tragic stories if they lead us to rectify the present situation. Serial killers prey on groups who have been rendered vulnerable because of their inability to compete within the structural conditions of capitalism: the people who, for various reasons, are unable to answer back to those who hold the power in society, including those who exploit that power to kill. Shipman and Norris fit this pattern perfectly, while the cases of Mackay and Erskine support it, too. The latter two were caught relatively quickly because they did not have the same intellectual resources to escape detection, nor the same level of social and cultural power, as was possessed by a respected local GP and a male nurse.

Shipman and Norris were eventually caught, but every day thousands of other trusted individuals have access to elderly people and therefore the opportunity to act in awful, murderous ways. Only time will tell if we have to add more names to the list of British serial killers who have targeted the elderly and whether Action on Elder Abuse will succeed in convincing Britain's politicians that legislation is urgently needed to provide 'comprehensive protection' to the nation's elderly population.

Harold Shipman was able to murder for as long as he did because there was inadequate social protection for the elderly. His activities, and those of Mackay, Erskine and Norris, reveal all too graphically that the voices of old people in our community are too rarely heard and too easily ignored. Like Alec Taylor, the elderly more generally are simply relegated to being 'bodies in the attic'.

Final thoughts

> [Serial killers] are not mere freaks: rather, they can only be fully understood as representing the logical extension of many of the central themes in their culture – of worldly ambition, of success and failure, and of manly avenging violence. Although they take several forms ... they can only be accurately and objectively perceived as the prime embodiment of their civilisation, not twisted derangement.
>
> Elliott Leyton, *Hunting Humans* (1986)

More than anyone else, the Canadian social anthropologist Elliott Leyton has championed a social analysis of serial murder, rather than an approach that relentlessly focuses on the individual, psychological motivation of the killer. Leyton does not see serial killers as odd or unusual 'freaks', but rather as the inevitable outcome of the dominant values of our culture. This is an important insight because it helps to explain why Britain had no serial killers between 1915 and 1943, but sixteen such killers between 1979 and the present day, including a serial-killing 'high point' in 1986. In the past thirty years, over three hundred people have fallen victim to serial killers, six times the number who were murdered by such killers over the previous ninety years. I put less store in Leyton's argument that serial killing should also be viewed as a form of 'homicidal protest'. This theory does not work for any of the groups that have typically fallen victim to serial killers in this country: the elderly, gay men, prostitutes, babies and infants, and young people leaving home for one reason or another.

Nevertheless, I wholeheartedly support Leyton's insistence that the phenomenon of serial killing must be viewed from a social rather than a psychological perspective. Having worked as both a prison governor and a criminologist, I have learned to distrust much of what serial offenders offer by way of explanation for their behaviour. And once their first-hand evidence is dismissed, the medico-psychological tradition is left with little more than speculation, guesswork and presumption. Consequently, I have found it much more worthwhile to consider serial killing from the perspective of the victims.

My contact with serial offenders also led me to question the public's fascination with these 'real-life Hannibal Lecters'. Contrary to their popular media portrayal, they are overwhelmingly banal, socially conservative, weedy and needy. The extent to which the public's fascination with them has been created, sustained and shaped by the media is a moot point, especially since serial killing has become a commodity to be bought and sold like any other. To me, Leyton's assertion that public interest in serial killers is generated because they are the 'prime embodiment of their civilisation' is debatable. As we live in a capitalist society, if Leyton's suggestion were true, surely we would be equally spellbound by biographies of hedge-fund managers, yet (thankfully) we are not. Moreover, Morrall's (2006) notion of 'werewolf culture' and the rather more familiar concept of *schadenfreude*, while helpful, provide only partial explanations for the public's enduring fascination with serial killers. But does it matter that this fascination continues to defy explanation?

I feel that it matters a great deal on several levels. On a pragmatic level it is significant because several serial killers have claimed that they started to murder in order to 'become famous'. In other words, they have used the public fascination with and commodification of serial murder for their own ends. Consequently, if we can gain an understanding of the source of that fascination, we might be able to limit the numbers of new serial killers by reshaping the public's conception of who serial killers really are, as opposed to how they have been portrayed. In doing so, we might also begin the complex process of devaluing serial killing as a 'product'.

Public fascination with serial killing also matters on a social and cultural level because surely we should not engage in a process that affords status and celebrity to those who repeatedly kill. Moreover, it matters because our fascination with serial killers tells us something about ourselves. As Leyton implies, what it says about our culture is not only unflattering but downright frightening.

However, because serial killing has proved so intriguing, a wealth of information is available on the topic, and this can be harnessed to reduce the prevalence of serial killing. As this book has shown, serial killers are usually able to kill only in specific social circumstances and at certain times, so analysis of those circumstances and times should help us to limit the number of victims in the future.

Between 1915 and 1943, people mattered in this country. They were seen as having something to offer both to their communities and the state, so their lives were cherished. A little later, at the end of the Second World War, steps were taken to formalise this situation through the development of the Welfare

State. This is not meant to imply that everything was 'better back then', because in many ways it was not. Homosexuality was illegal (which helps to explain why there are no contemporary records relating to deaths of gay men); women were still far from equal in civil society; and communities that looked out for one another could often be stifling and claustrophobic rather than encouraging and welcoming, especially towards newcomers and anyone considered out of the ordinary. However, particularly when compared to Nazi Germany, Britain's inter-war social and economic arrangements reveal that people were highly valued.

Could that be said of Britain in 1986, when four serial killers were active simultaneously? It is surely more than a coincidence that this 'high point' of British serial killing coincided with the 'high point' of Thatcherism. By 'Thatcherism', I mean the 'new-right' ideology that was based on theories developed by Friedrich von Hayek in the 1940s, Milton Friedman in the 1950s and Robert Nozick in the 1970s. After coming to power in 1979, Margaret Thatcher implemented a succession of new-right policies to counter what she saw as the over-involvement of the British state in civil society, and specifically to reduce the amount that was being spent on welfare. She felt that demands on the government were too high, as were business taxes, which limited the private sector's profit-making and wealth-creating potential. The argument was that there should be less government regulation and intervention in the economy as well as far less provision for those who were poor and unemployed, in order to stop the further development of 'welfare dependency'. I do not want to push this analysis too far, not least because much of the Welfare State managed to survive Thatcherism, but it is scarcely controversial to argue that Britain changed significantly after 1979.

The economist Will Hutton (1995) suggests that, as a

consequence of new-right thinking dominating the policy agenda, Britain has become a '40/30/30' society: 40 per cent of the workforce are in full-time, secure employment; 30 per cent are insecurely self-employed or working casually; and the remaining 30 per cent are 'marginalised' by being unemployed or working for 'poverty' wages. Hutton says that since 1979 'capitalism has been left to its own devices', which we can now see has led to the credit crunch and failing banks around the world. The '40/30/30' society saw Britain become a low-cost, deregulated producer, with correspondingly low social overheads and a minimal Welfare State. For example, supplementary benefit for the unemployed as a proportion of full-time earnings dropped from 26 per cent in 1979 to just 19 per cent by 1993; union membership was discouraged and fell dramatically from 13.3 million to 9 million over the same period; and Hutton argues that the state also tried to 'wash its hands of future generations of old people'. Nick Davies (1997) draws attention to the three million people who were unemployed in 1993, but also to the fact that between 1966 and 1977 wages of all men in all social classes grew at the same rate, while from 1979 onwards their incomes started to diverge. Between 1979 and 1992 those on the highest wages saw their salaries grow by 50 per cent; meanwhile, over the same period, those on the lowest wages became worse off than they had been in 1975.

Both Hutton and Davies were writing before New Labour's election victory in 1997, but the end of eighteen years of Tory government did not seem to have significantly altered the course of state policy. In Chapter Nine I mentioned the continuities in youth and criminal justice under New Labour, as well as several changes that Blair's government introduced that would not have been out of place under a Conservative administration. New Labour's social and economic policies have been similarly consistent with those of their predecessors, despite being labelled a 'Third Way' and claiming to bind social justice to a dynamic economy. Tony Blair and Gordon Brown have both drawn directly from neo-liberal discourse in their analysis of the global economy, and 'globalisation' has become a favourite justification for New Labour policies. Just as it was under Thatcher and John Major, the mantra has remained that Britain must make itself as attractive as possible to investors by maintaining a deregulated economic approach and limiting any social interventionist strategies.

All of this is important when looking for an explanation of why serial killing in Britain rose so dramatically in the 1970s–1990s, even if there would seem to have been a slowing down of the incidence of serial murder in recent years, and especially after Harold Shipman was arrested. It is also important to acknowledge that by 2010 the Conservatives, initially in coalition with the Liberals, were in power and ushered in an age of 'austerity'. How has this austerity contributed – either positively or negatively – to the levelling off of serial murder in the last decade? I would suggest that the more recent lull in the numbers of murders attributed to serial killers should not make us complacent. I have already drawn attention to the 726 homeless people who died in 2018. I have my suspicions that this suggests that a new vulnerable and marginalised group may be being targeted. My hypothesis would be that there still exists the same numbers of offenders who want to repeatedly kill, but that advances in forensic science, the development of HOLMES, and the establishment of a national DNA database makes it much more difficult to repeatedly kill. In other words, the would-be serial killer is caught much more quickly and has far fewer victims when he is apprehended. Even so I would also suggest that the underlying factors that generated the increase in serial murder towards the end of the last century remain strong. Consequently, most of the vulnerable groups that have been the focus of this book remain in danger of being targeted by a serial killer.

The one exception might be children. The reconstruction of childhood that I mentioned in Chapter Nine has led to far greater intervention in and control of young people's lives. As a result, the opportunities available to someone like Robert Black have probably been reduced. Whether this will significantly reduce the total number of children killed is debatable, though, because the vast majority of murdered children fall victim to members of their immediate family or their carers, rather than serial killers. Meanwhile, I fear that runaways will remain as vulnerable as ever. Ongoing research by the Children's Society indicates that large numbers of young people continue to run away from home, stay away from home or are thrown out of their homes every year in this country. This group remains resolutely on the fringes of society, but it is tempting to view another of our vulnerable categories as less marginalised. Gay men and women are more visible than ever before in British society, and the recognition of their relationships in the form of civil partnerships is certainly a step in the right direction towards full integration and acceptance. However, the recent case of Stephen Port suggests that this does not mean that they will be attacked less often by serial killers.

The two groups most at risk of being targeted by serial killers have always been and remain women working in the sex industry and the elderly. Nothing in recent public policy has significantly extended state protection to either of these groups. Sex workers' calls for safe zones in which to operate have consistently been ignored, while the poverty, isolation and powerlessness that make elderly people so vulnerable have not been alleviated despite governments of different colours holding power. So, as the case of Peter Farquhar suggests, they remain targets for those individuals – including serial killers – who seek to exploit that isolation and powerlessness for their own ends.

As we saw in Chapter One – in terms of my strict definition of what constitutes a serial killer – at least forty-one serial killers killed at least 409 people (both of these figures are likely to be underestimates) between 1888 and 2019. That means, on average, that three people have been victimised by a serial killer each year over the past 130 years. However, since 1979, at least twenty-six serial killers have killed over 350 people. In the same four decades at least two serial killers were usually active during any given year. Of course, Harold Shipman's uniquely long period of killing (over two decades) and the unprecedented number of people he murdered skew these statistics somewhat. Nevertheless, I believe that the recent trend is still significant.

These figures suggest that, as I write, two serial killers are currently active in this country. One day we might learn that they killed as many as seven people between them each year they were active. We might never know the identities of these killers – especially if they are 'organised' and mobile – but we will probably discover what they did and whom they murdered. However, we do not simply have to stand by and accept that this trend is destined to continue. We have it in our power to change the future of serial killing in this country by acknowledging who is vulnerable to attack and what causes that vulnerability. Nor do we need to continue to give celebrity status to those who repeatedly murder their fellow human beings, which is one reason why this book has been written from the perspective of the killed rather than the killers.

Above all, Britain needs to learn that serial killers exploit fractured communities, where some lives are viewed as more valuable than others and where people increasingly have to struggle simply to survive. Serial killers exploit police incompetence but also public indifference to runaways, vulnerable women who sell sexual services, and gay men whose lifestyles are seen as challenging the status quo. They exploit the isolation, loneliness and powerlessness of the elderly. And they exploit the policies of governments that no longer value the young or the old, and prioritise the rich over the poor.

Appallingly, serial killing tells us something about our culture, our values and our civic society. Our public policy has created a culture of 'them' and 'us' and a society where the gap between the 'haves' and the 'have-nots' continues to widen. In such societies, some people stop being viewed as assets and so are cast adrift in order to lessen the 'burden' on the state's resources. In these circumstances, groups that are characterised in this way become targets for serial killers and are of interest to the rest of society only when they turn into victims. It is surely no surprise that no heart surgeons, TV producers, journalists, bankers, accountants, lawyers or academics appear as victims in this book. Instead, the young and the old, those who are gay, the homeless and women forced to sell their bodies feature time and again. Now that we know that these groups have been targeted repeatedly for 130 years, isn't it time we started to do something to help them?

A Guide to Further Reading

Introduction: my academic work related to serial killing can be found most readily in the *Journal of Forensic Psychiatry and Psychology*, the *Journal of Investigative Psychology and Offender Profiling* and *Crime Media Culture*. For those who are interested in this academic work see in particular: K. Soothill and D. Wilson (2005) 'Theorising the Puzzle that is Harold Shipman', *Journal of Forensic Psychiatry and Psychology*, Vol. 16, No. 4, pp. 658–98; and, S. Hall and D. Wilson (2014) 'New Foundations: Pseudo-pacification and special liberty as potential cornerstones for a multi-level theory of homicide and serial murder', *European Journal of Criminology*, 11 (5): 635–655. The former article deals with the background to the Shipman case and attempts to apply Elliott Leyton's 'homicidal protest' thesis to the murders that Shipman committed. I broadened the argument at the heart of this article in an academic and theoretical book in 2006 called *Serial Killers: Hunting Britons and Their Victims, 1960–2006* (Winchester: Waterside Press), and many of the later examples provided in that work are recounted here. A more popular approach to my work can be found in (2008) *Hunting Evil: Inside the Ipswich Serial Murders* (London: Sphere), which I co-authored with the Sky broadcast journalist Paul Harrison and which attempts to view these murders from the perspective of those who were killed as opposed to that of Steve Wright. The thesis that serial killing should be viewed as a form of 'homicidal protest' is contained within Elliott Leyton (1986) *Hunting Humans: The Rise of the Modern Multiple Murderer* (Toronto: McClelland and Stewart). The development of my theoretical approach to serial murder has been done in conjunction with Professor Steve Hall – the 'founding father' of Ultra Realist criminology. I also wrote about Mary Ann Cotton in (2013) *Mary Ann Cotton: Britain's First Female Serial Killer* (Winchester: Waterside Press) and with my colleagues Adam Lynes and Elizabeth Yardley (2015) *Serial Killers and the Phenomenon of Serial Murder: A Student Textbook* (Winchester: Waterside Press). This latter book is now used in several universities as an introductory text.

Chapter One: I first became aware of the disparity between the incidence of serial killing in England/Wales and Germany in the inter-war period through reading Phillip Jenkins (1988) 'Serial Murder in England, 1940–1985', *Journal of Criminal Justice*, Vol. 16, pp. 1–15. It is also interesting to note the way in which Jenkins defines 'serial killing' and to compare his list of serial killers to that produced here. A number of American academic books deal with defining 'serial killing' and I draw specific attention to the work of Ronald Holmes and James DeBurger (1988) *Serial Murder* (Newbury Park, Ca.: Sage) and Ronald Holmes and Stephen Holmes (1994) *Profiling Violent Crimes* (Thousand Oaks, Ca.: Sage). Also of use is James Fox and Jack Levin (2005) *Extreme Killing: Understanding Serial and Mass Murder* (Thousand Oaks, Ca.: Sage). More are listed in the bibliography of my *Serial Killers: Hunting Britons and Their Victims, 1960–2006*. A much smaller number of true crime overviews of British serial killing exist. Of these, Martin Fido's (2001) *A History of British Serial Killing* (London: Carlton Books) is of interest (and the list of serial killers that he produces is worth consulting). However, Fido writes from within the individual discourse about specific serial killers so includes those who are merely suspected of having killed three or more victims but have never been convicted. Danny Dorling's work on murder is found in (2005) 'Prime Suspect: Murder in Britain', in P. Hillyard, C. Pantazis, S. Tombs, D. Gordon and D. Dorling (eds) *Criminal Obsessions: Why Harm Matters More than Crime* (London: Crime and Society Foundation). Peter Morrall's (2006) *Murder and Society* (London: John Wiley & Sons) is a very sensitive account of the social, economic and cultural circumstances that produce murder, but it has not generated the same level of interest as Dorling's work. A more general introduction to murder is Fiona Brookman (2005) *Understanding Homicide* (London: Sage), which has quickly established itself as the standard student introduction to this subject. Also worth consulting is S. D'Cruze, S. Walklate and S. Pegg (2006) *Murder* (Cullompton: Willan). I use and draw on a number of true crime books in this and other chapters, including Brian Masters (1986) *Killing for Company: The Case of Dennis Nilsen* (London: Coronet Books) – for me, still the classic British example from within this genre because of the access that Masters gained to Nilsen and his writings; Brian Masters (1996) *'She Must Have Known': The Trial of Rosemary West* (London: Doubleday) – which is more polemical; Gordon Burn (1998) *Happy Like Murderers: The True Story of Fred and Rosemary West* (London: Faber and Faber); and Howard Sounes (1995) *Fred and Rose: The Full Story of Fred and Rosemary West and the Gloucester House of Horrors* (London: Time Warner). It is interesting to note how many of these true crime books use a picture of the serial killer on their front covers to advertise what will be found inside. Until *Hunting Evil: Inside the Ipswich Serial Murders*, no victim's picture appeared on a front cover, which suggests the hold that the individual discourse of the medico-psychological tradition has on the public's imagination. Indeed, Fido's *A History of British Serial Killing* features the Wests, Haigh, Christie, Brady and Hindley, and Nilsen on his front cover. I also mention in this chapter John Bennett and Graham Gardner (2005) *The Cromwell Street Murders: The Detective's Story* (Thrupp: Sutton), and the work of the forensic psychologist David Canter. The latter's work is widely available and includes (2003) *Mapping Murder: Walking in Killers' Footsteps* (London: Virgin). This is of particular interest as Canter adopts a historical approach to 'geographic profiling' and includes a discussion of the case of Jack the Ripper. Nicci Gerrard writes about Holly Wells and Jessica Chapman in (2004) *Soham: A Study of Our Times* (London: Short Books). Finally, I argue that Peter Tobin is Bible John in *The Last British Serial Killer: Closing the Case on Peter Tobin and Bible John* (London: Sphere).

Chapter Two: given that this chapter identifies my sources within the text, I will not dwell on the various books that I have consulted about Jack the Ripper. However, I have thought about these murders again since the publication of the first edition, especially through reading Hallie Rubenhold (2019) *The Five: The Untold Lives of the Women Killed by Jack the Ripper* (London: Doubleday). 'Jack the Ripper: The Case Reopened', first shown on BBC1 in April 2019, can still be viewed on BBC iPlayer. For those who are new to the subject, Stewart Evans and Keith Skinner (2000) *The Ultimate Jack the Ripper Sourcebook* (London: Robinson) remains the best introduction, given that readers can consult primary sources for themselves, including the Macnaghten memorandum. Within the chapter I introduce the concept of offender profiling, and note that this was originally employed by the Federal Bureau of Investigation

(FBI), who suggested that offenders could be described as 'organised' or 'disorganised'. Readers might like to consult the FBI's own crime classification manual, edited by J.E. Douglas, A.W. Burgess, A.G. Burgess and R.K. Ressler (1997) *Crime Classification Manual: A Standard System for Investigating and Classifying Violent Crimes* (New York: Simon & Schuster). A good introduction to the subject of offender profiling remains Peter Ainsworth (2001) *Offender Profiling and Crime Analysis* (Cullompton: Willan), while a critical examination of the validity of this premise can be found in Laurence Alison (ed.) (2005) *The Forensic Psychologist's Casebook: Psychological Profiling and Criminal Investigation* (Cullompton: Willan), which also has the advantage of introducing the reader to a more psychological approach to profiling and suggests the variety of ways in which psychologists help with police investigations. Of note, one of the chapters included in the *Forensic Psychologist's Casebook* – J. Ogan and L. Alison, 'Jack the Ripper and the Whitechapel Murders: A Very Victorian Critical Incident', pp. 23–46 – is an examination of Jack the Ripper and the Whitechapel murders from the perspective of this being a 'critical incident'. Materials related to the trial of George Chapman – who was at one time believed to have been Jack the Ripper – can be found in H.L. Adam (1930) *The Trial of George Chapman* (Edinburgh: William Hodge & Company).

Chapter Three: a good starting point to build up a picture of 'coverture' and the legal position of women in Victorian culture more generally is Mary L. Shanley (1989) *Feminism, Marriage and the Law in Victorian England, 1850–1895* (Princeton, NJ: Princeton University Press). I have relied on her conclusions throughout this chapter. Cream's trial papers have been edited and collected by W.T. Shore in (1923) *The Trial of Thomas Neill Cream* (London: William Hodge & Company); Smith's edited and collected by E.R. Watson in (1922) *The Trial of George Joseph Smith* (London: William Hodge & Company); and Chapman's edited and collected by H. L. Adam, as mentioned above. The various poisonous effects of tartar emetic – the common name for antimony potassium tartrate – are well described in John Emsley (2005) *The Elements of Murder: A History of Poison* (Oxford: Oxford University Press). Those who wish to follow the experiments conducted by Sir Bernard Spilsbury in the 'brides in the bath' case should consult Colin Evans (2007) *The Father of Forensics: The Groundbreaking Cases of Sir Bernard Spilsbury, and the Beginnings of Modern CSI* (Cambridge: Icon Books).

Chapter Four: in trying to build a picture of the social, economic and cultural life of the 1920s and 1930s I used a variety of books and articles. Chief among these were Stephen Constantine (1983) *Social Conditions in Britain, 1918–1939* (London: Methuen), which is now a little dated but contains a wealth of detail that is hard to resist; and Andrew Thorpe (1992) *Britain in the 1930s: The Deceptive Decade* (Oxford: Blackwell). I also found Roy Hattersley (2007) *Borrowed Time: The Story of Britain between the Wars* (London: Little, Brown) of interest, as it drew my attention to myriad developments during the period in education, suffrage, car-ownership and the impact of sport and the BBC. The background to the Hadow Reports is well presented by Derek Gillard at www.infed.org/schooling/hadow_reports.htm.

It was Howard Taylor's article (1998) 'Rationing Crime: The Political Economy of Criminal Statistics since the 1850s', *Economic History Review*, Vol. 51, No. 3, pp. 569–90, that first drew my attention to the fact that most murders during this period went uninvestigated and that there was, in effect, a 'quota' for the number of murder trials. I have previously mentioned Phillip Jenkins (1988), 'Serial Murder in England, 1940–1985', *Journal of Criminal Justice*, Vol. 16, pp. 1–15, which compares serial murder in Britain with the phenomenon in Germany. I also used two autobiographies by senior police officers to try to see behind the crime statistics: Robert Mark (1978) *In the Office of Constable* (London: Collins) and Keith Hellawell (2003) *The Outsider: The Autobiography of One of Britain's Most Controversial Policemen* (London: HarperCollins). I consulted Home Office statistics found in compendiums at the Institute of Criminology, Cambridge University: (1926 and 1937) *Criminal Statistics* (London: The Home Office). There is a wide range of books related to the history of the police. I found Clive Elmsley (1991) *The English Police: A Political and Social History* (London: Longman) and Phillip Rawlings (2002) *Policing: A Short History* (Cullompton: Willan) particularly useful in placing the autobiographies of Mark and Hellawell in context. Issues related to the development of forensic science during this period can be gleaned from the biography of Bernard Spilsbury written by Colin Evans, mentioned above. I also quote from Keith Simpson (1978) *Forty Years of Murder* (London: Grafton Books, 1980 edn) – who is regularly critical of Spilsbury – and Molly Lefebure (1955) *Evidence for the Crown: Experiences of a Pathologist's Secretary* (London: Heinemann). Lefebure was Simpson's secretary during the war, and her recollections of the period are worthy of further study. Indeed, she was sufficiently intrigued by her work with Simpson that she wrote a number of other books, including (1958) *Murder with a Difference – Studies of Haigh and Christie* (London: Heinemann), which are also of great interest.

Chapter Five: Molly Lefebure's book on Haigh and Christie, mentioned above, provides some rich colour and detail that later books about these cases would do well to emulate. However, a basic overview about their lives and crimes can be found in Martin Fido (2001) *A History of British Serial Killing* (London: Carlton Books), pp. 56–114. Also of use is David Briffett (1990) *The Sussex Murders* (Southampton: Ensign). Haigh's collected letters to his parents can be accessed at the Institute of Criminology, Cambridge University, and I have previously written about what these letters contained in a *Guardian* article entitled 'A Very English Serial Killer', 19 November 2007. The controversy surrounding Christie – specifically whether he was also responsible for the murders of Beryl and Jeraldine Evans (for which Timothy Evans was hanged) – can be found in F. Tennyson Jesse (1957) *Trials of Timothy John Evans and John Reginald Christie* (London: William Hodge) and in Ludovic Kennedy (1961) *Ten Rillington Place* (London: Victor Gollancz). These books have become the 'standard version' of the Evans case, while John Eddowes (1994) *The Two Killers of Rillington Place* (London: Little, Brown) refutes much of what they argue. Each reader will form their own conclusion as to Christie's guilt or innocence in the murders of Beryl and Jeraldine. I relied on contemporary newspapers – particularly the *Scotsman* – to build a picture of the murders committed by Peter Manuel, although a recently published book by A.M. Nicol (2008) *Manuel: Scotland's First Serial Killer* (Edinburgh: Black & White) was of use. I had never heard of Trevor Hardy – who started to kill on New Year's Eve 1974 and murdered his final victim in March 1976 – until I read a rather obscure autobiography: Geoffrey Garrett and Andrew Nott (2001) *Cause of Death: Memoirs of a Home Office Pathologist* (London: Robinson). It was Garrett who conducted the autopsies on Hardy's victims. I did not include Hardy in

Serial Killers: Hunting Britons and Their Victims, 1960–2006; he also seems to have escaped any other academic consideration, and Fido does not mention him in his list of British serial killers. This is surprising as in the mid-1970s Hardy was sufficiently notorious to be dubbed the 'Beast of the Night' by the local Manchester press and he was a serial killer by any criminological definition one might care to use. Perhaps he has been consistently overlooked because his crimes, capture and conviction were never picked up by the national press. With colleagues at BCU I wrote academically about this case in (2010) 'When Serial Killers Go Unseen: The Case of Trevor Joseph Hardy,' *Crime Media Culture* Vol. 6 Issue 2, 153–167. In much the same way, few have heard of the murders of the Welsh serial killer Peter Moore, although he started to become better known as a result of a very interesting Channel 4 documentary called *Dressed to Kill*, broadcast in 2001.

Chapter Six: the exchange that opens this chapter is taken from Peter Sotos (2001), 'Afterword', in Ian Brady, *The Gates of Janus: Serial Killing and Its Analysis by the 'Moors Murderer'* (Los Angeles, Ca.: Feral House). This book is the closest that Brady has come to writing an autobiography, but he almost always generalises from his own experience to discuss other serial killers; and, as can be imagined, the book is a rather self serving affair. It is also difficult to find in Britain. I relied heavily on true crime accounts of Dennis Nilsen throughout the chapter, including the aforementioned *Killing for Company* by Brian Masters, and Brian McConnell and Douglas Bence (1983) *The Nilsen File: Inside Story of the Cricklewood Murders* (London: Futura), which provides some rich detail about London in the late 1970s. I should also acknowledge that a copy of Nilsen's unpublished autobiography was leaked to me from prison by a circuitous route in 2006, but I have not been swayed by its contents to amend the basic picture provided by Masters. More generally, Anna Gekoski (1998) *Murder by Numbers – British Serial Killers since 1950: Their Childhoods, Their Lives, Their Crimes* (London: André Deutsch) provides some biographical detail that is worth considering, especially in relation to Colin Ireland, with whom Gekoski seems to have corresponded after his imprisonment. In relation to Ireland, I mention that he may have been influenced by Robert Ressler's (1992) *Whoever Fights Monsters: My Twenty Years Tracking Serial Killers for the FBI* (New York: Simon & Schuster). Details about David Morley have been constructed from newspaper accounts and from the website www.davidmorley.co.uk. I benefited from acting as a consultant on the Channel 4 documentary about Peter Moore, *Dressed to Kill*, an excellent account of his background and crimes that includes several interviews with Moore's family, friends and neighbours. At a more academic level, readers might wish to consult Byrne Fone (2000) *Homophobia: A History* (New York: Metropolitan Books) for a general and historical overview of the subject; Gail Mason (2002) *The Spectacle of Violence: Homophobia, Gender and Knowledge* (London: Routledge); and J. McManus and I. Rivers (2001) *Without Prejudice: A Guide for Community Safety Partnerships on Responding to the Needs of Lesbians, Gays and Bisexuals* (London: NACRO), which con siders homophobia within a recent British context. The background to the 'Spanner Case' can be found in Terry Thomas (2000) *Sex Crime: Sex Offending and Society* (Cullompton: Willan). Those interested in 'cop culture' should consult Robert Reiner (1992) *The Politics of the Police* (Hemel Hempstead: Harvester Wheatsheaf), and compare his thesis with a more 'appreciative' understanding of this culture in P.A.J. Waddington (1999) *Policing Citizens* (London:

UCL Press). A general introduction to this debate can be found in D. Wilson, J. Ashton and D. Sharp (2001) *What Everyone in Britain Should Know about the Police* (Oxford: Oxford University Press). Details about Steven Grieveson – the 'Sunderland Strangler' – are few and far between, partly because his three murders were not linked until after his arrest.

Chapter Seven: the opening quote from Ian Brady is taken from the aforementioned *The Gates of Janus*. All other quotes in this chapter relating to the Ipswich murders are taken from interviews that I either conducted or was privy to at the time, or from interviews conducted by Paul Harrison of Sky News, which we subsequently published in the aforementioned *Hunting Evil*. The official attitude to sex work is best explained in two Home Office reports: (2004) *Paying the Price: A Consultation Paper on Prostitution* and (2006) *A Coordinated Prostitution Strategy and a Summary of Responses to Paying the Price* (both London: The Home Office). Natalie Pearman's story is recounted by Nick Davies in (1997) *Dark Heart: The Shocking Truth about Hidden Britain* (London: Chatto & Windus), while the murders of sex workers attributed to 'Jack the Stripper' have been described by David Seabrook in (2006) *Jack of Jumps* (London: Granta) and most recently Robin Jarossi (2017) *The Hunt for the 60s Ripper* (London: Mirror Books). For background to the Peter Sutcliffe case, see Michael Bilton (2003) *Wicked beyond Belief: The Hunt for the Yorkshire Ripper* (London: HarperCollins) and Gordon Burn (1984) *Somebody's Husband, Somebody's Son: The Story of Peter Sutcliffe* (London: Heinemann; rev. edn London: Faber and Faber, 2004). Lawrence Byford (1981) *The Yorkshire Ripper Case: Review of the Police Investigation of the Case – Report to the Secretary of State for the Home Office* (London: The Home Office) was made public under a Freedom of Information request in June 2006 (and therefore after Bilton and Burn had published their accounts of the case). It can be downloaded from the Home Office website at www.homeoffice.gov.uk. I also make use of Sir William Macpherson (1999) *The Stephen Lawrence Inquiry: Report of an Inquiry by Sir William Macpherson of Cluny*, cm 4262 (London: HMSO), and the aforementioned autobiography of Keith Hellawell, given that Hellawell interviewed Sutcliffe in prison.

Chapter Eight: excellent accounts of the murders committed by Fred and Rosemary West can be found in the previously mentioned true crime books on the topic by Howard Sounes and Gordon Burn. Detective Superintendent John Bennett's aforementioned account of the investigation describes how clinical psychologist Paul Britton assisted the police. David Canter uses West's prison autobiography to good effect in *Mapping Murder*. I am less convinced by the arguments in Brian Masters's '*She Must Have Known*', but the book is of value in that it challenges assumptions about what happened in Cromwell Street. Martin Amis writes about his cousin Lucy Partington in (2001) *Experience* (London: Vintage). This remarkably moving book is almost unique in exploring the life and times of a victim of a serial killer in depth. Two of the Wests' own children eventually wrote about their lives: Stephen West and Mae West (1995) *Inside 25 Cromwell Street: The Terrifying True Story of Life with Fred and Rose West* (Monmouth: Peter Grose). Issues relating to children running – or being 'thrown' – away from home can be found in the published research of the Children's Society. See, in particular: C. Newman (1989) *Young Runaways: Findings from Britain's First Safe House*; The Children's Society (1999) *Still*

Running: Children on the Streets in the UK; G. Rees (2001), *Working with Young Runaways: Learning from Practice*; and G. Rees and J. Lee (2005), *Still Running II: Findings from the Second National Survey of Young Runaways* (all London: The Children's Society).

The life and times of Stuart Shorter and the various difficulties of the homeless in Cambridge can be found in Alexander Masters (2005) *Stuart: A Life Backwards* (London: Harper Perennial). I also again make use of the stories told by children to Nick Davies and published in *Dark Heart.*

Chapter Nine: there are a variety of popular and academic books related to children and childhood. I relied on Libby Brooks (2006) *The Story of Childhood: Growing up in Modern Britain* (London: Bloomsbury); Chris Jenks (1996) *Childhood* (London: Routledge); Jenny Kitzinger (1997) 'Who Are You Kidding? Children, Power and the Struggle against Sexual Abuse', in A. James and A. Prout (eds) *Constructing and Reconstructing Childhood* (London: Falmer); Frank Furedi (2001) *Paranoid Parenting: Abandon Your Anxieties and Become a Good Parent* (Harmondsworth: Penguin Press); and Philippe Ariès (1962) *Centuries of Childhood* (London: Jonathan Cape). Good starting points for the growing criminalisation of children are John Muncie (1999) *Youth Crime: A Critical Introduction* (London: Sage), and John Muncie and Gordon Hughes (2002) 'Modes of Youth Governance: Political Rationales, Criminalization and Resistance', in J. Muncie, G. Hughes and E. McLaughlin (eds) *Youth Justice: Critical Readings* (London: Sage). Comparatively little has been written thus far about ASBOs, but Neil Wain and Elizabeth Burney (2007) *The ASBO:Wrong Turning, Dead End* (London: The Howard League for Penal Reform) is an excellent introduction, especially as Wain is a Manchester-based police officer. For background on the Allitt case I used Nick Davies (1993) *Murder on Ward Four: The Story of Bev Allitt, and the Most Terrifying Crime since the Moors Murders* (London: Chatto & Windus), and C. Clothier (1994) *Allitt Inquiry: Independent Inquiry Relating to Deaths and Injuries on the Children's Ward at Grantham and Kesteven General Hospital during the Period February to April 1991* (London: The Stationery Office Books). I wrote more academically about health care professionals who kill with Elizabeth Yardley in 'In Search of the "Angels of Death": Conceptualizing the Contemporary Nurse Health Care Serial Killer,' *Journal of Investigative Psychology and Offender Profiling,* 13: 39–51 (2016). Gekoski's *Murder by Numbers* offers good background information on the Moors Murders while Colin Wilson's 'Introduction: The Moors Murders' in Brady's *The Gates of Janus* was also helpful. (It should be noted that Brady makes no comment about the Moors Murders in this book.) R. Wyre and T. Tate (1995) *The Murder of Childhood: Inside the Mind of One of Britain's Most Notorious Child Murderers* (Harmondsworth: Penguin) provides a wealth of background information and detail about the murders committed by Robert Black.

Chapter Ten: the website of Dame Janet Smith's inquiry into Shipman's crimes, www.the-shipman-inquiry.org.uk, was of use, as was www.elderabuse.org.uk. Carole Peters (2005) *Harold Shipman: Mind Set on Murder* (London: Carlton Books) is one of the better true crime accounts of the Shipman case. Meanwhile, I wrote about his crimes from a more academic perspective in the aforementioned article co-authored with Professor Keith Soothill, who had previously written persuasively about serial killers in C. Grover and K. Soothill (1999) 'British Serial Killing: Towards a Structural Explanation', *The British Criminology*

Conferences: Selected Proceedings, Vol. 2, available at: www.lboro.ac.uk/departments/ss/bccsp/vol02/08GROVEHTM.

Sir Liam Donaldson tries to explain the 'Shipman phenomenon' in (2001) *Harold Shipman's Clinical Practice, 1974–1998* (London: Department of Health). Keith Simpson – whom we encountered in earlier chapters – discusses murderous medics in *Forty Years of Murder.* Eliot Freidson adopts a more sociological approach to analysing the work of doctors in (1970) *Profession of Medicine: A Study of the Sociology of Applied Knowledge* (New York: Harper and Row). Patrick Mackay's case is less well known than Shipman's, but it is reasonably described in T. Clark and J. Penycate (1976) *Psychopath: The Case of Patrick Mackay* (London: Routledge & Kegan Paul). I know of no reliable true crime account of Kenneth Erskine, so what is recounted here is culled from contemporary newspaper accounts. Colin Norris – the 'Angel of Death' – who was found guilty of murdering his four elderly victims while working as a male nurse in Leeds, was convicted of these killings only in March 2008, even though the murders occurred in 2002. Consequently, I have relied on newspaper summaries of the case, particularly from the *Guardian.* My research with Professor Elizabeth Yardley about so-called 'Angels of Death' suggests difficulties with this conviction.

Final Thoughts: the aforementioned *Hunting Humans* by Elliott Leyton has been republished several times by a variety of publishing houses, often with a different subtitle. The origins of the 'new-right' ideology are in Friedrich von Hayek (1944) *The Road to Serfdom* (London: Routledge & Sons); Milton Friedman (1953) *The Methodology of Positive Economics* (Chicago, Ill.: University of Chicago Press); and Robert Nozick (1974) *Anarchy, State and Utopia* (Oxford: Blackwell). A more general overview can be found in Stuart McAnulla (2006) *British Politics: A Critical Introduction* (London: Continuum). Will Hutton's (1995) *The*

State We're in (London: Jonathan Cape) was useful. Finally, yet again, Nick Davies's *Dark Heart* proved invaluable. Although it was one of the first accounts of how Britain changed as a result of Thatcherism, it remains a passionate and troubling book that deserves to be more widely read. I relied on newspaper accounts to build up a picture of the murder of Peter Farquhar in 2015 and then subsequently interviewed the SIO on the case at the HQ of Thames Valley Police.

Acknowledgements

Acknowledgements 2009

A variety of people helped in many ways to ensure that I had the space, time and ability to complete this book. First, I am grateful to colleagues at the Centre for Criminal Justice Policy and Research at Birmingham City University, who encouraged me at every stage of writing, including Professor Chris Painter, Dr Neil Staunton, and Dr Edward Johnson, who kindly read a draft of Chapter Four. I am also grateful to the staff and librarians of Birmingham City University, Cambridge University Library, and the Radzinowicz Library, Institute of Criminology, Cambridge for permission to quote from John Haigh's letters and, in particular, I would like to thank Mary Gower and Stuart Stone.

Barbara McCalla, Judith Timms, Naomi Faulkner and Runjit Banger at Birmingham City University made life easy for me in a number of ways: from printing endless drafts of the book, to ensuring that I remembered when I was supposed to be teaching or attending meetings. My undergraduate and postgraduate students at the university continue to stimulate my thinking and have helped to shape a number of the ideas that are presented in this book.

At Little, Brown I would like to thank Antonia Hodgson, Vivien Redman, Linda Silverman and Kirsteen Astor for their continued dedication to the book, and I benefited enormously from the skilful editing of Humphrey Price and Philip Parr. At Curtis Brown, Gordon Wise was ever patient and is aptly named, and it would simply not do to forget Jacquie Drewe, Adam Banham and Renay Richardson.

Outside of the academy I would like to thank a variety of friends who listened patiently as I went over innumerable aspects of the book, and would demand – as only friends can – that I 'stop talking nonsense' (or words to that effect) and start making sense. When writing about some very dark places, they reminded me that there is always light to illuminate the gloom. The Thursday night group at the Bull and Butcher in Akeley was particularly important, including Paul Carr, Ross Collins, Julian Cook, David Cotterill, Ian Dreyer, Tim Graham, James Hole, Stuart Holton and Paul Wildman. Here, too, I would like to thank Paul Harrison and Harriet Tolputt of Sky News.

A number of other individuals and friends helped me, including Judi Martin, Neil and Sue Foster, Andy and Sarah Setterfield, Brian and Trish Taylor, Peter Harness, Libby Brooks, Matt Seaton, John Logan and, especially, Matt Logan.

Last, but never least, Anne, Hugo and Fleur continue to make life worth living.

Acknowledgements 2020

I look back at the acknowledgements from the 2009 edition with a smile, but also some sadness: Dr Neil Staunton and Judith Timms have died, and most of the other colleagues that I mention at BCU have since moved on, or retired. There have also been changes in personnel at Little, Brown and at Curtis Brown and, amongst my friends, a divorce and a marriage. As such, it is the right and proper to update the acknowledgements for this second edition. At Little, Brown I would especially like to thank Rhiannon Smith, my trusty Editor who encouraged me to consider a second edition; at Curtis Brown I need to thank Luke Speed, Emma Power and Madeleine Newman-Suttle; and among my friends thank you Sarah and Mark Bucknill, Emilia Fox, Emma Kelley, Claudia Lewis, Simon Winlow and Liz Taylor. It would also be remiss of me not to thank a number of new colleagues and friends at BCU: Professors Michael Brookes and Liz Yardley, Liam Brolan, Lukas Danos, Adam Lynes and Dan Rusu.

I am delighted to say that Anne, Hugo and Fleur continue to make my life worth living and it is a joy to also welcome Suzi and Tom to the family.

Index